The Cape Cod Baseball League

Cape Cod Bay

Cape Cod Canal

Wareham

Bourne

Falmouth

Cotuit

Hyannis

Yarmouth-Dennis

Harwich

Brewster

Orleans

Chatham

Nantucket Sound

Western Division
Bourne Braves
Cotuit Kettleers
Falmouth Commodores
Hyannis Harbor Hawks
Wareham Gatemen

Field Locations

Eastern Division
Brewster Whitecaps
Chatham Anglers
Harwich Mariners
Orleans Firebirds
Yarmouth-Dennis Red Sox

CAPE DREAMS: A SEASON WITH THE BREWSTER WHITECAPS WAS ADOPTED INTO THE NATIONAL BASEBALL HALL OF FAME LIBRARY IN COOPERSTOWN, NY, ON FEBRUARY 5th 2025

CAPE DREAMS

Dedication

CAPE DREAMS: A Season with the Brewster Whitecaps is dedicated to every single volunteer who gave up their time to make the Cape Cod Baseball League one of the most cherished amateur athletic organizations of any sport in American sports history.

A short time before this story *CAPE DREAMS* became published the Cape Cod Baseball League lost a giant. Jeff Trundy, the long-time manager of the Falmouth Commodores lost a valiant fight to cancer. This Cape Cod Baseball Hall of Famer represented all that was right about not only Cape Cod Baseball but about our national pastime.

Definition of a Whitecap

A whitecap is the white part on top of the wave in the middle of the ocean. It's a symbol for us that no matter what the ups and downs are and what adversity and obstacles we face, we're always going to stay on top of the waves, whether they are going up or down. That's what Brewster will always mean to me—and the entire team. Regardless of if we won or lost, we were always riding on top of the waves.

—DeAmez Ross, center fielder, Brewster Whitecaps
(University of Central Florida)

Table of Contents

~

Cape Cod Baseball Map	i
Dedication	vii
Definition of a Whitecap	ix
National Anthem—Foreword by Mr. Peter Gammons, Baseball Hall of Fame	xiii
First Pitch—Introduction	1
First Inning—Searching for Paradise	7
Second Inning—The Lineup	23
Third Inning—The 2024 Cape Cod Season Begins	69
Fourth Inning—Falmouth Turns Its Lonely Eyes to Paul Mitchell	85
Fifth Inning—The Gala	117
Sixth Inning—MLB Workout Day, Fenway Park	133
Seventh Inning—Morning Clinics: Sharks and Minnows	159
Seventh-Inning Stretch—"Sweet Caroline"	169
Eighth Inning—2024 Cape Cod Baseball League All-Star Game	201
Ninth Inning—Orleans Firebirds at Whitecaps	213
Bottom of the Ninth—Whitecaps at Harwich: Do or Die, One Moment in Time	223
Extra Innings—Just Like That...	267

Love That Dirty Water—Acknowledgments	275
Major Leaguers from Brewster	281
Whitecaps' Final Hitting and Pitching Statistics	284
CCBL Standings	288
Postgame Announcements—Testimonials	289

National Anthem—Foreword

Mr. Peter Gammons, Baseball Hall of Famer

"One of my biggest thrills while writing this story was interviewing the legendary Peter Gammons at the Cape Cod Baseball League All-Star game for this story."

MR. GAMMONS WAS OFF AND running when the Brewster Whitecaps were mentioned. This is what the American baseball icon and Hall of Famer enshrined in Cooperstown had to say.

"Brewster is a great place. Hopefully Chase Utley (Brewster Whitecaps, 1998) will be going into the Hall of Fame next year. And that Billy Wagner—I've been coming to games on the Cape for a long time, and in my opinion, Billy Wagner (Brewster Whitecaps, 1992) is the best pitcher who I've ever seen pitch in this league. I remember the first time I saw Wagner pitch, and I couldn't believe it. That Chase Utley just outworked everyone. I saw Aaron Judge play for Brewster."

Mr. Gammons continued, "This Cape Cod Baseball League is invaluable. I think MLB has done a disservice to the Cape League. They don't care, though. Look at how many Minor League teams have been eliminated in just the last few years. It used to be you had the same players on a Cape roster all summer. Now each team has about fifty players who come through every year. An SEC coach came to Hyannis last summer and, in the middle of the game, was trying to get a few players to transfer to his school and leave with him the next day. That's terrible when that happens.

"Money in college athletics is ruining our national pastime. Buck Showalter (the longtime MLB manager and Cape Cod Hall of Famer as a player) told me last week that some college players are making almost as much as some of the MLB players are getting paid," Gammons said.

Mr. Gammons was also quick to point out "that the life that these kids live here is a major step in their careers in professional baseball. This league is important."

"Every baseball fan should read this book, *CAPE DREAMS*. This league is so important."

—Peter Gammons, recipient of the J. G. Taylor Spink Award, Baseball Hall of Fame 2004, Cape Cod Baseball League Hall of Fame 2018

First Pitch—Introduction

IN MANY WAYS THIS STORY has been seventy-two years in the making. You must first understand what growing up in the middle of Red Sox country was like for a boy whose family had been closely connected to sports since long before I was even born. It's a rite of passage passed down from generation to generation.

My dad, Charlie Epstein, was one of the most important sports figures in Central Massachusetts history. Dad has a monument erected at Elm Park in Worcester, Massachusetts. Elm Park is the second-oldest public park in America. He only had one sports hero in his life: Ted Williams. For Dad, Ted epitomized all that was great in America. A true American icon, Williams was known as much for his heroics in war as he was known as the greatest hitter who ever lived.

I literally grew up in Fenway Park in Boston, home of the Boston Red Sox. From when I turned seven, Dad would take my brother and my two sisters and every kid in the neighborhood who could fit into his overstocked (and I mean overstocked) van into Fenway several times every year to cheer on our beloved Sox.

As I grew older, a radio was tucked under my pillow at night so I could listen to Curt Gowdy call every Sox game. I just had to know if the Sox won before I closed my eyes. Yes, this was also true for games that started three hours behind on the West Coast. (Maybe this was why I was such a lousy student growing up.) This ritual continued well into my sixties, I'm embarrassed to say.

Our family attended so many games as we grew into our adult years that Dad eventually purchased season tickets for all the games. The seats were located directly behind the Sox first base dugout. From seven rows behind the middle of the dugout, I felt I had a permanent home. From 1976 to 2002, I had every crack on the Massachusetts Turnpike from Worcester to Boston memorized. Unfortunately, I was a witness to just about every heartbreaking loss in franchise history. Games such as the Bucky Dent home run game, when the Sox lost in a one-game playoff in 1978, caused me permanent damage. As did losing game seven in the 1975 World Series to the Cincinnati Reds. I'm not sure why I ever held on to those ticket stubs. I did hold on to the stub from when Hall of Famer Carl Yastrzemski got his three thousandth career hit. Witnessing Ted Williams return to Fenway to throw out the first pitch at the 1999 All-Star game is something I'll also cherish for the rest of my life.

There is also a personal historical backdrop to note that has to do with the team I grew up disliking the most. That, of course, is the New York Yankees. I attended the games where both Mickey Mantle and Derek Jeter had the last at bats of their careers. Both players ended their careers at Fenway Park, forty-six years apart. Mantle played his last game at Fenway in 1968, and Jeter played his last game at Fenway in 2014. The most unique feature of these two milestones is that they both happened on September 28.

What must also be mentioned here is that as much as I was passionate about my second-favorite sport, baseball, basketball was the sport that ruled our family. Not only was I addicted to the Red Sox, but I also attended as many baseball games played in my community as possible. If I wasn't on a basketball court somewhere, I would watch every baseball game my friends played in. Do you notice I keep mentioning the verb "watch"? I was a terrible player. I loved playing, but I was always the last one picked if I even did get picked at all.

A SEASON WITH THE BREWSTER WHITECAPS
First Pitch—Introduction

Our family sporting goods business in Worcester was called Charlie's Surplus. The store that I helped run with Dad gave the entire Epstein family and our many friends access to create friendships with many of the greatest Red Sox players in their storied history. It's important that I mention here, though, that neither my dad nor any of his children ever got to meet the great Ted Williams.

A close friendship was built with the former president and part owner of the Red Sox, Haywood Sullivan, and the Epstein family. It wasn't uncommon to have many of the players travel to Worcester on a weekly basis to say hello to Dad and to purchase whatever it was they needed. Charlie's Surplus was like the unofficial home of the Boston Red Sox in Worcester.

Once I entered my college years, Cape Cod weekends in the summer became a ritual, like they were for almost every college kid in New England.

My basketball buddies and I spent a great many weekends partying and hanging out on Seagull Beach in Yarmouth. It was about this time that I casually drove past a baseball game being played behind Dennis-Yarmouth High School. Out of curiosity, I pulled over in a mostly empty parking lot and watched a few innings through the metal fence. I became a little intrigued, but not enough to keep me away too long from what I might have been missing back on the beach.

The next summer I drove by the high school again, and there was another game being played on the baseball field. I pulled over and stayed for the entire game. Afterward I sped back to the cottage that we rented and started telling all my friends about this baseball team at the D-Y High School that was rather good. No one seemed interested in listening. The next weekend, back I went and became hooked into the Cape Cod Baseball League. I became mesmerized as to the level of play. The crowds back in the seventies consisted of several hundred fans, but the league had yet to explode on the national scene.

So along with all my other sporting interests, Cape Cod Baseball was now clearly ranked near the top.

Cape Cod Baseball became the way of life on weekends in the summers for my two daughters, Brooke and Karli, and myself. The girls were never given much of a choice to attend the games after a day on the beach, dinner, and of course an ice-cream cone at the Sundae School Ice Cream in Dennis Port. There were always playgrounds close to the ballparks that they could play on as their dad stayed engrossed in the games.

When I moved away to South Carolina in the late eighties, summer vacations were planned out on the Cape around both the Red Sox and Cape Cod Baseball schedules. When I remarried in the early nineties to a South Carolina girl (good news—I just celebrated my twenty-eighth wedding anniversary to beautiful Barbara), Barbara became appreciative of the level of play and the entire atmosphere at all the ballparks. Being a University of South Carolina graduate, Barbara would enjoy watching players from her alma mater. There always seemed to be enough Gamecocks players to keep her attention.

Summer after summer we would spend two weeks at Dennis Port or, more recently, Falmouth, and Cape Baseball became a big part of our enjoyment.

Once my daughters graduated college and started their own families, much to the surprise of no one, my grandchildren became regular attendees at the Falmouth Commodore games played at Fuller Field on Main Street in Falmouth.

Over the last forty years, I've probably taken in over two hundred Cape League games. I've also attended at least several hundred Red Sox games. When I moved to Charleston, Barbara and I had season tickets for the Charleston RiverDogs, a Class A Minor League affiliate of the Tampa Bay Rays. Add the annual summer weekends that were spent in Atlanta watching the Braves. That's a lot of baseball. Three years ago, I decided to volunteer as a greeter for several Falmouth games. That was a milestone. I was now more than just a fan.

I'm sure I have seen many of the greatest players who ever played in the Major Leagues play on the Cape. Without saving the lineup sheets that are given out before every game, there is no way to know who you saw. When the college greats play on the Cape, they are still traveling under the radar. It's not until the players establish themselves as household names in the Majors that you even realize they came through the Cape.

During the pandemic months, I became bored, like so many others. I always knew I had a very intriguing background, some parts good and some not so. I decided to write a book about my past failures and, more importantly, about my work as a civil rights leader in the Deep South to improve educational equality. I named the book *They Call Me Pathfinder: Education-Basketball-Equality*. Much to my surprise, the book won two regional citations. I then decided to write a second. *Jack "The Shot" Foley—A Legend for All Time: With Togo Palazzi and Central Mass Basketball* exploded on the national scene. It became the number-one newly released basketball book on Amazon in 2022. The Naismith Memorial Basketball Hall of Fame selected it as their basketball story of the year during National Library Week in 2023.

Recently, I felt just maybe I had a third book in me? Much to my surprise, I had several national sports figures reach out to see if I was interested in writing their story. I was truly honored, but nothing interested me. The more I thought about it over a year's time, the more I kept coming back to one story that I thought I could tell. Talk to anyone who has written a book: It's imperative to write about something you have a feel for. You need that passion to sit for eight to ten hours a day for almost a year. If you don't have that, it won't happen.

This time I wanted to write a national story. It was the Cape Cod Baseball League. I reached out to the league office, and the president directed me to reach out to the individual ten teams. I selected four. My proposal was accepted by two and turned down by two. I figured that if you hit .500 in baseball, you have a great batting average. I chose the Brewster Whitecaps. The decision on which team I selected was extremely difficult.

I had my niece, Dawn, living in Brewster, and I felt a connection to the town. Also, my sister Diane, who I was extremely close to, had lived with Dawn during her last two years before passing in 2022. I spoke to the team president of the Whitecaps, Luke Dillon. Then I spoke to the manager of the Whitecaps, Jamie Shevchik, and our vision for the story and how to go about producing it matched perfectly. Plus, there was something about Brewster's manager and his family values that hit a chord with me.

There is something I must mention here. The last book on the Cape Cod Baseball League was written over twenty years ago, in 2002, by an author named Jim Collins. The story captured the attention of readers everywhere. The book is *The Last Best League*. The story has hundreds of untold human-interest tales. There was just one thing, though. The league now and the league that Collins wrote about are two completely different leagues. Collins and I have had several phone conversations during the writing of this book. He has become a mentor. His willingness to offer his support is greatly appreciated.

With all that in place, the time was right to share the story of one of the greatest amateur athletic organizations in American sports history.

I hope you will enjoy the story of *CAPE DREAMS- A Season with the Brewster Whitecaps*.

Sincerely,
Mark "Pathfinder" Epstein

First Inning—Searching for Paradise

CLOSE YOUR EYES, TAP YOUR heels together three times, and repeat: "There's no place like paradise."

Where is this special paradise, you're asking yourself? Let's look beyond the rainbow. Buckle up and get ready to go on the greatest road trip you've ever been on.

In today's world of cynicism, a few readers may be wondering if paradise even exists. You may even be wondering, "Where we are heading?" Well, this paradise has existed for 101 years, and if you've never been there, you are now well on your way.

If you're from California and have watched a Major League Baseball game, you've heard about it. If you're from New York and follow the Yankees or Mets, you've definitely heard about it. If you're from Ohio and you're a Guardians fan or a Reds fan—same thing, you've heard about it. If you grew up in Texas and follow baseball, most likely you know about it. From Florida, of course. From New England, paradise is close by.

From every state in the union, sports fans have been hearing about it for years.

When Aaron Judge comes to the plate for the Yankees, announcer Michael Kay of the YES Network may have spoken about it. When Billy Wagner was pitching for the Astros, Todd Kalas, the play-by-play announcer for Space City Home Network in Houston, probably mentioned where Wagner was discovered. If you're from Chicago, Ken Harrelson, better known as "The Hawk," said its name live several times on NBC Sports Chicago when Frank Thomas was hitting bombs for the White Sox. That was before "The Big Hurt" was enshrined in Cooperstown. The legendary Hall of Fame beat writer Hal McCoy has written about it a few times in the *Dayton Daily News*, especially when Sean "The Mayor" Casey was playing for the Reds. Wayne Randazzo, the play-by-play guy for the Angels on Bally Sports West, is currently reminding everyone where their shortstop phenom Zach Neto was first scouted. Red Sox fans heard the late, great Jerry Remy talk constantly about it on NESN, especially when Nomar Garciaparra was playing in Beantown a few years back.

Yes, prepare yourself to go on a baseball journey that harkens back to when baseball was our national pastime. When games were played without the new NCAA with its name, image, and likeness (NIL) agreements (can you even imagine?). When the games were still played on sandlot fields. When so-called advisors were not keeping a close eye on their commodities. When players didn't wear oversize mitts on their hands when they ran the bases. When college hitters used wooden bats. When ticket prices were not $2,500 to sit in the front row at Yankee Stadium. Also, let's remember when fans grew up and remained loyal to their hometown team because that's what was handed down.

Once upon a time, baseball was pure. Players were not yet counting their money while still in college. Everything about sports in America has changed. The one thing that has outlasted all the above and has remained true to the values and principles that founded our great nation is the Cape Cod Baseball League, located on the shores of Massachusetts.

First Inning—Searching for Paradise

Every summer the elite of the elite playing college baseball across America pay their own way to play in the last great amateur athletic organization still standing. Originating in 1923 with four franchises—Falmouth, Chatham, Osterville, and Hyannis—the CCBL now has ten teams. The last expansion took place in 1988, when both Bourne and Brewster were admitted. The ten towns that have teams are the following: Bourne, Brewster, Chatham, Cotuit, Falmouth, Harwich, Hyannis, Orleans, Wareham, and Yarmouth-Dennis.

From Wareham on the starting edge of the Cape to the hip-hop town of Chatham seventy miles away, players and fans alike have been coming from all over the world to get a close-up look at this American treasure.

People who have never been to Cape Cod may be skeptical, thinking the legendary stories are nothing but mythical fables passed down by the fanatical sports fans of New England.

The ball fields are parts of public playgrounds. In fact, all ten ballparks are still run by the towns on the Cape. They remain nothing special, but they are tended to by the hundreds of volunteers who donate their time and resources to keep them in tip-top shape.

Wooden bats are used by the players. This contrasts with the aluminum bats that are used at every other level of baseball except at the Minor and Major League levels.

Players are not housed in fancy hotels or resorts. This may come later after they leave the Cape. If they are drafted and are eventually given fortunes by MLB teams, they'll be able to afford a luxurious lifestyle. For all—Cape dreams die hard.

In keeping with the over one-hundred-year tradition, the players are all placed with host families. This tradition sits at the very heart of this special organization. Relationships are built, and friendships become bonded. Many times, the players not only become part of the family while playing and living with their hosts, but they also remain part of the family chemistry for the remainder of their lives.

Taking a family to a sporting event has become very expensive. The looks on the faces of first-time guests attending a Cape game are, many times, ones of shock and elation. When a family is greeted at the gates to a ballpark and allowed to attend free of charge or by giving a small donation, they realize that this entire experience is going to be extraordinary.

There are so many aspects that make playing baseball on the Cape a summer of sheer heaven. Besides showcasing their abilities as possible future Major Leaguers, the players have access to some of the best beaches in America. From Bristol Beach in Falmouth to Nauset Beach in Orleans to the Flats in Brewster, the players have an opportunity to enjoy a little time on the beach and to possibly meet a pretty college coed as they tan themselves.

Families of the players enjoy vacationing on the Cape while watching their sons play ball. All the towns provide a vacation-type atmosphere. The slow pace of the Cape communities is quite different from that which a player is sometimes used to. Many players on the Cape play college baseball at mega-sized campuses of a Southeast Conference university like the University of Florida or the University of South Carolina.

Durning any Cape Cod game, it is not unusual to find as many as fifty MLB scouts evaluating the elite athletes. The theory is that if a player can show he can hit a 95-mph fastball with a wooden bat, then they in fact may become a highly rated MLB prospect.

For the pitchers, they are also being evaluated. The theory is that if they can get the best hitters out, then they will more than likely hear their names called when they are eligible to get drafted.

The CCBL has placed over seventeen hundred former Cape players into the Major Leagues since 1923. Currently there are 380 former Cape Cod players playing in the Major Leagues. This number makes up 35 percent of the total found throughout the rosters of all thirty MLB teams. In 2024, 197 Cape players heard their names called during the three-day MLB draft.

The age of innocence persists.

CAPE DREAMS is being written with three goals in mind. First, to inform readers from all over the country what the Cape Cod Baseball League (CCBL) is all about.

Secondly, you will read an extraordinary story of a group of elite athletes who all came together and represented the 2024 Brewster Whitecaps of the CCBL. This 2024 cast of characters not only had one of the greatest rosters put together in the history of Cape Cod Baseball, but they will also take you on one of the most unique journeys in baseball history.

Lastly, this story is being shared to all those whose imagination wants to be fulfilled and go on a journey unlike any that remains in America.

Hopefully, after reading this amazing story, you will decide that Cape Cod, Massachusetts, is where you want to spend your next summer vacation and experience a paradise where time stands still.

THE ROAD TRIP LEADS TO THE CAPE

The day has come when the SUV is all packed and you're ready to hit the road. The trip will take you on a magical carpet ride. You're driving from South Carolina, Texas, or maybe Arkansas, or maybe even Wyoming. It doesn't matter where the journey originates. All roads lead to the Cape.

If you're bringing the family, the kids are all pumped up. If it's a friend who's sharing the driving, the anticipation is bringing goose bumps. If your partner is keeping you company, the chatter will be nonstop until you arrive.

As you drive along, some skepticism may start to seep into the conversation. The drive is worth taking. Depending on where you're coming from, it's probably a good idea to drive about five hundred miles per day and grab a room overnight.

Maybe you'll decide to fly to Logan Airport in Boston and rent a car for the remainder of the sixty miles to the Cape. Hyannis Regional Airport on Cape Cod is also available and very convenient. Whatever means of transportation you choose to take for the journey, any negative thinking you may have will disappear the moment you arrive.

Cape Cod is in the far east end of Massachusetts. It sits between Cape Cod Bay and Nantucket Sound. Both bodies of water are direct tributaries into the Atlantic Ocean.

Cape Cod is divided into fifteen towns, and each of these has a number of unique villages. Some villages are located near the beach, and others might include a historic or commercial district.

The town of Brewster is a picturesque seaside town on the Cape located ninety miles from Boston, the capital city of Massachusetts. On any summer day, it will take approximately ninety minutes driving by car to make the trip.

The town of Brewster has approximately ten thousand year-round residents. During the summer months, the population grows to almost three times as many. Brewster is broken into four smaller villages and neighborhoods. This quaint town was settled in 1640.

When driving onto the Cape, regardless of what direction you are coming from, the two Cape Bridges will leave you breathless as you approach them. The Bourne and Sagamore Bridges both lead the residents and visitors over the Cape Cod Canal and onto the Cape's mainland. US Highway 6 connects all the towns and villages located on the Cape.

As you drive over the bridges and onto Route 6, which is also called the Mid-Cape Highway, you will probably think that this famous summer retreat is not unlike any other location on the map. The main highway of Route 6 can do that to a first-time visitor.

The highway drive might even take away some of your excitement as you scratch your head and say to yourself, "This isn't what I expected." Just wait a few minutes: Brewster is just up ahead. When you get to the main Brewster exit, everything will change quickly. Exit 85 on Route 6 going east will take you to the long-awaited paradise you have been dreaming about.

The chatter in the SUV is getting louder. The view from the windows has gone from highways to picturesque natural beauty. After you've turned right onto Route 137, follow the road as it will take you through the small villages that make up the town of Brewster.

Now you're getting the idea. Before you drive straight about five miles to Route 6A, which is Main Street in Brewster, and find something to eat, you're probably anxious to get a look at the ball field. So, you drive on 137 for three miles until you get to Underpass Road. When you take a right on Underpass at the bike trail that crosses 137, you come to Stony Brook Elementary School. You take a left and follow the winding driveway for about a quarter of a mile. There it is. The ball field sits directly behind the school.

Welcome to Brewster

Stony Brook Field has come a long way since the Brewster Whitecaps moved from their original home at Cape Cod Tech, located in their neighboring town of Harwich, in 2006.

The ball fields on the Cape are all run by the towns they are located in. The many volunteers of each team take care of the ballparks and invest lots of resources and man-hours maintaining them. You look out at the field, and at first sight it reminds you of the ball field from your own high school you once attended. "Nothing special," you may say to the others in your group. In fact, the longer you look, you wonder if the greats you came to watch even like playing on sandlot fields.

Well, welcome to the charm of the Brewster Whitecaps. Yes, the sandlot fields that are used on the Cape are the first signs that you have landed in a time capsule. "Quaint" may be the perfect description of the ballpark and the entire town of Brewster.

After contemplating if in fact the trip is going to be worth it, you jump back in the car and head over to Main Street for something to eat. Several wonderful restaurants can be found on Route 6A–Main Street.

JT's Restaurant is known for its fresh seafood and yummy ice cream. The Brewster Chowder House is known for its—well, take a good guess. If you look behind the restaurant, you'll find the legendary night spot called The Woodshed. Every now and then, you might find a Whitecaps player dancing the night away if he's twenty-one and has his license with him.

As you drive along, you come to the town's general store. You pull in to peek inside. Two hours later you come out with three bags loaded with everything you didn't want to buy—from candy to soap to T-shirts to jams and jellies to linens and kitchen gadgets. You'll be making this unique store that has a history that goes back to the 1800s your go-to for your entire stay in town. There is no such thing as peeking in the Brewster General Store.

Everywhere you go in town, everyone keeps telling you to check out the beach flats. So, you drive a short way on Route 6A to Linnell Landing. Here's the thing about the Brewster tidal flats. If you're from New Jersey, Florida, the Carolinas, or even California, you've been surrounded by beautiful beaches your whole life. You're probably not expecting the beaches on the Cape to be in that category. Well, as soon as you park your car in the Linnell Landing parking lot, the natural beauty of one of the most beautiful beaches in the world grabs your attention.

First Inning—Searching for Paradise

The Brewster tidal flats measure approximately twelve thousand acres and extend some 9.7 miles along the shore from Brewster to North Eastham. Stay around for the sunsets and the views are spectacular. Wait for the low tides and you can walk along the flats for miles. Parents have been bringing their families to Brewster for decades to experience the beauty and the safe tidal pools that shape the landscape.

Once you get back in your car and explore the area further, you realize that Brewster is unique for another reason. For a town of over ten thousand year-round residents, an oddity for this day and age makes you smile. The town of Brewster does not have a red light anywhere in town. The word "quaint" comes back into the conversation.

The time is getting closer to the start of the Whitecaps game. The games start earlier in Brewster than in the rest of the Cape. Stony Brook doesn't have lights. They must start the games by 5:00 p.m. If they begin later, they won't be able to get nine innings in before dark.

You drive back to Stony Brook Field. The college interns who are working as the greeters at the main entrance hand you the game roster sheet with a big cheerful welcome. The roster sheets have the names, colleges, and statistics of both teams.

You notice the crowd of over fifteen hundred fans sitting all around the field. Most are sitting on the sides of both baselines in the metal bleachers. The others congregate on the large hill overlooking first base.

In 1988, a group of longtime Brewster residents and baseball fans petitioned the Cape League to expand by adding Brewster and Bourne. The main objective was to eventually get the town to build a ballfield. Brewster had never had a ballpark for its residents.

The Brewster expansion efforts were spearheaded by Barry Souder and Claire and Mike Gradone. They were determined to build a much-needed place for the schoolchildren in town to play ball. Bourne's expansion efforts were led by John Aylmer.

Mike Gradone was the school superintendent at the time for the Nauset Regional School District that serves Brewster. With the political clout that comes with the job, the group recruited the help of Robert Drummond, Dennis Hanson, Alan Harrison, Jim Hartwig, Bob Heckler, Bob Riedl, Linda Riedl, and Paul Saint. Together they were relentless in pursuit of their dream.

Once the CCBL approved the admission of the Brewster Whitecaps, Claire Gradone served as the team's first president. After almost forty years, you will still find the Gradones on the board of directors for the team. Mike currently works as the team's treasurer, and Claire volunteers on game-day operations. This type of lifetime dedication is commonplace throughout the entire league.

As the game is about to start, the voice of Chris Lynch, a proud Brewster fan, is heard over the public address speakers. Lynch has been volunteering at Brewster games in several capacities, including helping as a host to the players, since 2012. Lynch has a perfect voice and delivery.

The game begins, and the size and skills of all the players put you on notice. The pitchers are throwing in the mid-nineties on the radar gun. Some of the college hitters look like bodybuilders. The speed and grace the players use to field their positions are of high Minor League caliber.

A hitter turns on a fastball and tattoos one well over four hundred feet. You turn to your partner, and with a slight nod, you are both thinking the same. Welcome to Brewster for a Cape Cod League Baseball game.

The Brewster Whitecaps have a proud history. Many of the greatest Major League players have filtered through the Whitecaps' rosters since 1988. Some of the greats are household names in the baseball world. Add the name of Aaron Judge, who has brought back the glory days to the New York Yankees. Also, the young and current phenom shortstop Zach Neto, who played for the Whitecaps in 2021, has exploded on the Major League scene with the Los Angeles Angels.

Other former Caps' legends include former National League MVP Ryan Braun, pitching great Billy Wagner, Sean "The Mayor" Casey, former Red Sox favorite David Ross, Tony Gwynn Jr., Todd Walker, Mike Avilés, Jason Grilli, Yasmani Grandal, Mike Myers, Kyle Hendricks, Dave Staton, Geoff Blum, Aaron Rowand, Chase Utley, Andy Sheets, Luke Weaver, and Reid Detmers. (See the back of this book for the complete list of MLB players from Brewster.)

The list goes on and on. Over 160 Brewster Whitecaps alumni have at one time or another suited up to play in the Major Leagues. Consider that Brewster was an expansion team that was only admitted into the Cape Cod Baseball league in 1988, and you have an idea as to the strong pride that runs through the veins of Whitecaps Nation.

In a just a short time, there will be several more added to this illustrious list, as the recent Whitecaps' rosters have been loaded with topflight Major League prospects.

The rest of the league also has been contributing many great MLB players for over one hundred years. The rest of the CCBL has sent so many players into MLB that its own Hall of Fame is a who's who of the greats of yesteryear.

The legends who have also played on the Cape fields include:

Paul Mitchell—Falmouth
Pie Traynor—Falmouth
Red Rolfe—Orleans
Thurman Munson—Chatham
Carlton Fisk—Orleans

Frank Thomas—Orleans
Todd Helton—Orleans
Mitch Moreland—Bourne
Ron Darling—Cotuit
Mike Flanagan—Falmouth
Chis Sale—Yarmouth-Dennis
Lance Berkman—Wareham
Nomar Garciaparra—Orleans
Chuck Knoblauch—Wareham
Will Clark—Cotuit
Mike Lowell—Chatham
Joey Cora—Chatham
Andrew Miller—Chatham
Darin Erstad—Falmouth
Carlos Peña—Wareham
Steve Balboni—Falmouth
Jeff Reardon—Cotuit
Buck Showalter—Hyannis
Glenn Davis—Chatham
Jeff Kent—Chatham
Whit Merrifield—Chatham
Steve Pearce—Cotuit
Daniel Bard—Wareham
Jackie Bradley Jr.—Hyannis
Bill Mueller—Bourne
Craig Biggio—Yarmouth-Dennis
Tim Lincecum—Harwich
John Tudor—Falmouth
Jeff Bagwell—Chatham
Kevin Millar—Harwich
Kevin Youkilis—Bourne
Jason Varitek—Hyannis

John Valentin—Hyannis
Aaron Boone—Orleans
Bobby Witt Sr.—Chatham
Brian Roberts—Chatham
Buster Posey—Yarmouth-Dennis

Of course, the list goes on and on. These superstars are only a few of the hundreds who were discovered on baseball fields across Cape Cod who went on to become MLB legends.

At different times Brewster can be a bit on the sleepy side. It's not the typical tourist town you'll find elsewhere on the Cape. You won't find any fast-food chains or motels and hotels.

Bed-and-breakfasts and Airbnb's are the places of lodging. The hotels and motels that are part of the Cape culture are in the surrounding towns and villages.

Brewster plays host to the world-famous, luxurious Ocean Edge Resort and Golf Club. The golf club is the only Jack Nicklaus-designed course on Cape Cod. It covers 429 pristine acres. People come to Ocean Edge from every corner of the globe to enjoy its many splendid amenities. There are other golf courses located around Brewster that are for public use.

Nickerson State Park, located on Main Street, is one of the most popular family campgrounds on the Cape.

There are several museums to visit, namely the Cape Cod Museum of Natural History, the Crosby Mansion, Stony Brook Grist Mill and Museum, and the Cobb House Museum. There are also several arts and crafts fairs that are held throughout the year.

During the summer months, there are outdoor band concerts and plays to enjoy in the evenings at Drummer Boy Park. The Brewster Ladies' Library is extremely active. Two of the most popular outdoor activities are riding bikes and walking on the many trails and bike paths that travel through town.

For the shoppers, Brewster offers several antique stores that attract many out-of-town guests.

Towns around Brewster that attract visitors who enjoy a little more of a faster pace include Chatham, Harwich, Eastham, Orleans, and Dennis.

Brewster has provided the ideal family Cape Cod vacation for generations in a serene setting.

WOODEN BAT LEAGUE

For many generations, baseball was only played with wooden bats. The original wooden bats that dated back to the early origins of baseball were made of hickory and ash. Hickory was found to be a strong, durable, and flexible wood. The traditional bats had hammer and ax handles and were extremely heavy. Northern white ash, the driest wood, had similar properties but was much lighter. Ash became the choice of batters at every level early on.

Despite the lighter wood available, many of the greats from the dead ball era used heavy, long bats. Babe Ruth swung a forty-seven-ounce bat in 1927 when he hit sixty home runs. Lou Gehrig, Jimmie Foxx, and others, many times, used bats that weighed over forty ounces. By the time Roger Maris broke Babe's home run record in 1961, hitters had begun to understand the importance of bat speed. The thin-handled thirty-two- and thirty-three-ounce bats of the next great generation of great hitters such as Ted Williams and Hank Aaron became standard. No longer would you find bats that were longer than thirty-five inches or weighed more than thirty-six ounces.

In 1968 a brand-new revolution of bats was brought forward. No longer would players have to replace hundreds of broken bats every season. An older wooden bat might cost a hitter twenty-five dollars to replace. After a full season, this became quite a financial burden on the players. The baseball manufacturer Worth produced the first aluminum bat. Soon Worth became part of Rawlings Company. A short time later, Easton Bats joined in. Once Louisville Slugger, the popular wooden bat company, started manufacturing aluminum bats in the late 1970s, the revolution exploded on the national scene at all levels.

The problem with aluminum bats is how the ball explodes off the bat. Yes, the bat lasts longer, and they save the players quite a bit of money. With aluminum, balls coming off the bats has impacted the way the game is being played—and not in a good way. The balls are exploding at such dangerous speeds that pitchers and position players are in danger if they can't get out of the way of a batted ball hit by aluminum.

Today, with the light weight of an aluminum bat, the hitters can swing at much higher bat speeds. Balls are now going farther. Hitters have inflated batting averages and home run totals. Games are getting out of hand with what the latest technology has brought into play. College level and below are the levels of play using aluminum bats.

Barnstable Bat Company in Centerville, MA, located just outside of Hyannis, has been making wooden bats since 1992. Tom Bednark, the founder and owner of Barnstable Bat, has produced wooden bats for over 250 former Major Leaguers. A woodworker by trade, his life's passion has been baseball. The friendly owner loves to tell all the visitors that visit his shop (located in the back of his home) how he has been able to combine his trade with his life's passion.

"I got into this business one evening when I was attending a Cape game with my son. I told him, 'I'm going to start making wooden bats for all levels.' What started off as a hobby became a booming business. At one time I employed five workers and shipped bats all over America. Some of the MLB players that have used our bats are Nomar Garciaparra, Manny Ramirez, Mo

Vaughn, José Canseco, Chase Utley, and others. The three most popular types of wood we use are ash, birch, and maple. The business has changed in recent years. I can no longer afford Major League license fees. The ash wood is currently in danger. The emerald ash borer is destroying so many trees. It remains the most popular wood, though, but the price of an ash bat now costs $170."

Metal bats continue to be banned in Major and Minor League Baseball for safety and competitive reasons. For players making the transition from using metal bats in high school and college ball, struggles frequently abound. The sweet spots on aluminum bats are much larger, and the physics of using a metal bat are noticeably different.

Players at the Cape or entering Minor League Baseball must relearn their swing and learn a new muscle memory if they hope to become successful at the Major League level. Many purists argue in favor of the classical wooden bat at all levels, but one can see that aluminum bats have many appealing qualities for a ballplayer.

The Cape Baseball League used aluminum bats from 1974 to 1985. In 1986 they switched to wooden bats, and that is when some lifetime followers feel the CCBL exploded.

MLB scouts were now able to accurately evaluate the elite college talent that came to the Cape to perform. The players would put their aluminum bats away when their college season ended and start working on the transition to the bats used in professional baseball.

Second Inning—The Lineup

ZACH NETO—THE PHENOM FROM BREWSTER

EVERYONE LOVES AN UNDERDOG. EVERYONE loves an underdog who has never been given one thing. Everyone loves an underdog who grew up without an ounce of entitlement. Finally, everyone pulls for the ultimate underdog who becomes a superstar through hard work alone. Welcome to the world of the current shortstop phenom of the Los Angeles Angels. If you haven't heard about him yet, write his name down. There is little doubt that this record setter is well on his way to becoming a household name all over America. The name is Zach Neto, and he was discovered playing baseball for the Brewster Whitecaps in the Cape Cod Baseball League.

Zach Neto recalls it all clearly. This is how Neto describes his Cape Cod Baseball journey: "Oh man, there are so many memories. If I had to pick just one, I'd have to say it was the home run I hit when the Whitecaps were losing 5–0 in the Cape Cod Baseball League Championship game. It was the first inning, and we got down early. Everyone was shocked when they came off the field and into the dugout. The game started with a gut punch. The dugout was dead. When I came up in the bottom of the first, there was a runner on base. I got ahold of one and the energy in our dugout exploded. We were back in the game. The lead was narrowed to 5–2. We went on to win the 2021 Cape Cod Baseball

League Championship. Stony Brook Field went into a frenzy. It brings me chills to talk about it still. It remains one of the greatest thrills in my life. Hitting my first home run for the Angels with my parents in attendance is number one. Getting drafted in 2022 by the Angels in the first round is number two. Winning the Cape Championship in Brewster will always remain one of the greatest thrills in my life."

Neto continues, "No matter how long I play on the biggest stage of the sport, I'll never forget the moment of the championship we won. The Cape is so special, and the tradition of the league is so important. Brewster is a part of my heart now. It was a very special time for me because of my journey and how I even ended up in Brewster in the first place. I was released from Cotuit early in the season, and Brewster gave me a home. That's pretty special. Manager Jamie Shevchik gave me the opportunity to come in and establish myself. I took it and ran with it."

Neto is fired up to talk about his love affair for all things Brewster. "When I went back to school at Campbell University for my MLB draft season in 2022, my time in Brewster had put me on the map. I used my success with the Whitecaps to propel me into a first-round draft choice and an MLB career with the Los Angeles Angels. No matter how long I play in the Majors, when I look back after I retire, most of my favorite stories will be about playing for the Brewster Whitecaps."

"I still remember my host family. The Wilkinson family of Brewster took me in. I reported to Brewster after the season had already started. They didn't have to do that for me. Seth and Alison have two of the nicest children. Able and Nyssa treated me like I was their big brother. I still stay in touch with the entire family. My time in Brewster remains the most fun time I ever had in my life. Just being on the Cape was pretty special, and being able to win the championship is such a blessing," says Neto.

Second Inning—The Lineup

Neto laughs as he remembers a couple of his favorite people. "That Jane Sullivan—she was just awesome from the first day I arrived until my last day. She has so much energy. She is such a special lady. Jamie Shevchik is an awesome guy. I love him to death. He's a great leader, a great role model, and a great friend. I was very fortunate to have the opportunity to play for him."

This past season of 2024 was a breakout year for this under-publicized star. Neto broke the Angels sixty-three-year-old record for home runs hit by a shortstop with twenty-three. Along with knocking in seventy-seven RBIs and stealing thirty bases, Neto's second season as the Angels' everyday starting shortstop has given the organization a solid foundation to build their future around. Neto says about his future in the Majors, "I still need to improve my mental approach to the game. I think that's very important. Mike Trout, the three-time American League MVP [who is a teammate of Neto's on the Angels], has taken me under his wings. It's very important when you get to the Majors to have a short-term memory when going from inning to inning on the field or from at-bat to at-bat. I need to be able to flush things from my memory during each game. Trout has really helped me with that."

Neto isn't done sharing his excitement about Cape Cod, though. "Guys who have played on the Cape that play in the Majors all share stories about their experiences and memories. It's like a big brotherhood. We talk about the Cape all the time. The stories keep going and going. I think the stories will always keep going because the Cape hits home for a lot of the guys."

"When I'm on the road and I see someone wearing a Brewster logo at Fenway or Yankee Stadium, I always make sure I stop and say hello or give them an autograph. I always make time for the Brewster faithful. The Cape humbled me. Playing on sandlot fields against the best of the best was a wakeup call. Overcoming failure in baseball is one of the biggest challenges to have a successful MLB career," says Neto.

"I grew up in Miami and attended Campbell University in North Carolina. They gave me an opportunity just like Brewster. I took advantage of it. They were loyal to me first, and once they showed that to me and my family, we returned the loyalty. I never had any thoughts of transferring to a bigger school to play in a power conference. My family has always been the type that wants to give back. Brewster was special for me. I believe I am the right person for this interview. I've been so blessed. Thank you, Pathfinder, for including me in this story," said Neto.

Brewster Manager Jamie Shevchik shares his personal insight into his former star: "Neto is the unicorn. He's a once-in-a-lifetime, generational-type player. He's the underdog that everyone roots for.

"There are great players and there are great people. Zach Neto is both."

AARON JUDGE—HOST FAMILY, THE ROMES

In 2012 the most powerful slugger in the game today would sit on the couch in the basement of the Rome family home in Brewster, Massachusetts, and eat Cheez-Its and drink a gallon of milk while watching *Family Guy*.

Aaron Judge was dropped off at the front door of David and Laurie Rome's home by an uber in June 2012. He was met on the sidewalk by their son Ben, a giddy and excited recent high school graduate. Judge got out and towered over Ben and the entire Rome family. Right away the connection with the future Baseball Hall of Famer was powerful. The Rome family resided in a very comfortable neighborhood of Brewster. David and Laurie Rome have two sons, Sam and Ben.

David is formerly from Worcester, MA, and has been in business on the Cape for decades. Laurie is a ball of energy with a personality that any college athlete would be thrilled to spend their summer with. She enjoyed a career working with special education students.

The Rome family are all baseball fans and love their Red Sox (sorry, Aaron). For many years the Rome family hosted Whitecaps players during the Cape Baseball season.

2012 was going to be different. Ben was getting a little disappointed with the caliber of players that they had been hosting in prior summers. As Ben puts it, "The players we had prior to Judge weren't Major League caliber. They were all great guys, but once they finished their college careers, none of them made it very far in professional baseball. I wanted to have a future star living with us. I followed college baseball closely, and I had been hearing about Judge while he was in his sophomore season at Fresno State University. When the housing director for the Whitecaps contacted our family before the season started, she allowed me to choose any player on the roster to live with us. That's how Aaron Judge became part of the Rome family throughout the entire summer of 2012."

David Rome remembers clearly, "Aaron was just a great guy. A real gentleman. He was soft-spoken and very kind. He was a home body. He liked to sit on our couch in the basement and watch movies and eat Cheez-Its when he wasn't at Stony Brook Field. He went through more milk than anyone I've ever seen. He was very close to his parents. He was a loving son. In fact, his parents flew out to Brewster to watch him play, and we all went to dinner together. I remember when he first moved in, I took him to a seafood restaurant where he ate fried clams. Another time he ate his first lobster dinner. I wanted him to experience life on the Cape away from the ballpark."

Laurie Rome, who served as his summer mom, can't say enough

nice things about the legendary athlete she used to cook for. "Oh my, that boy could eat. But what a sweetheart. He hasn't changed a bit. I listen to his interviews, and he conducts himself with everyone the exact same way he did when he lived with us. He was just a big kid back then. He was very humble. I remember when I would go to the refrigerator for something, and he would stand behind me and reach over and grab a gallon of milk. I'm not even five feet tall. I used to laugh at the way he towered over me. He was just a nice guy. His bed he slept in was a little small, so he had to sleep corner to corner. He never complained about anything. He was very content in our home. He wasn't into the Cape nightlife or going out with his teammates after games. He liked coming home to the comforts of his summer surroundings. I remember his favorite show was *Family Guy*. I've always been proud of him. Not just because of what he became, but more importantly *who* he has become and how he represents himself and his family. His mom was an educator. What a great job both his mom and dad did raising both Aaron and his older brother."

Ben himself was an outstanding baseball player growing up in Brewster. In fact, he once attended Stony Brook Elementary as a young boy. Ben also was an outstanding high school baseball player. He looks back with fond memories. "To think Aaron was my friend and family member one summer is surreal. I still can't get over what a tremendous career he is having. I definitely didn't see this coming. He actually didn't have that good a season for the Whitecaps. He was very average at best and struck out a lot. I remember one of his home runs. To this day I have never seen anything like it. It went high above the trees in left field and disappeared into the clouds. Everyone knew he had potential, though. If anyone tells you that they saw this coming, they're not telling the truth. To think he hit sixty-two home runs a couple of years ago and won the American League MVP is crazy. He's going to win a second MVP for what he did in 2024. Sometimes it's like a dream to me."

Cape Cod Baseball is known for building relationships. Some last and some fade. The ones that last make for great stories to share as years go by. Players remember their summer hosts, but they become caught up in their lives and the demands put upon them while playing in the MLB. This is true for Aaron Judge. Maybe after his career is over, he will reconnect with his special family hosts. Ben explains, "For a couple of years we stayed in touch with him. We know how much we meant to him during the summer of 2012. For a couple of years, we would text back and forth. We haven't heard from him in several years. There are no hard feelings. He has moved on with his life. He has become one of the greatest players in MLB history. There are times when I close my eyes and can't believe it really happened. He was just this giant that had potential. Before the Yankees drafted him in 2013, every team passed on him. I still can't believe it. He developed into an American legend."

DAN CUVET—INFIELDER, UNIVERSITY OF MIAMI

Daniel Cuvet came to Brewster with the hopes of improving his position in the 2026 MLB draft. Part of the lore and mystique that surrounds playing in the Cape League are the host families. Sitting on the front porch of Jeff and Joan Cassidy's home on a beautiful Cape morning in Brewster, Cuvet displays maturity well beyond his nineteen years.

Cuvet grew up in Fort Lauderdale, Florida. He spent his first two years in high school attending St. Thomas Aquinas High. His final two years, he attended Elite Squad Baseball Academy. Cuvet grew up in a very close-knit family. His dad, Patrick, played jai alai for twelve years professionally in Miami. Now he works as a nurse at the University of Miami. Jessika, his mom, has lived her whole life in Southern Florida. She currently works as a schoolteacher. His older brother, Mikel, also played baseball as a pitcher, and in fact the Cuvet brothers were high school teammates during Dan's first year at St. Thomas. Sophie, his eighteen-year-old sister, is a freshman in college.

It's important to understand the family background of this young baseball phenom. Cuvet committed to the University of Miami as a high school freshman. It was always important for Cuvet to have the support of his family in the stands for as many of his college games as possible.

If you watch this third baseman play, you will notice all the natural ability that he possesses. Just how fluidly Cuvet swings the bat will capture your attention. The grace and confidence he displays at his position is pretty rare for someone who is still just nineteen years old.

As a high school senior, Cuvet was rated as the number-one third baseman in America for his graduating class. When the 2023 MLB draft came along, he was selected by the Pittsburgh Pirates in the seventeenth round. It was clear then that he would be attending college and would not be entering professional baseball out of high school.

Cuvet's freshman year at Miami became an introduction to baseball fans throughout America. Cuvet's power is literally out of this world. After his freshman year, Cuvet was named a first-team Division 1 Freshman All-American. When it was all said and done, Cuvet's numbers matched his natural abilities. For the season, Cuvet hit .351 with twenty-four home runs and seventy-five RBIs for the Hurricanes.

With Cuvet it's not only about the numbers. It's the confidence, the swag, the "IT" factor—call it what you will, but some players play way beyond their years. On top of it all, Cuvet is as likeable and down to earth as any player playing on Cape Cod.

J. D. Arteaga, the manager for the Miami Hurricanes, points out that Cuvet is a mature hitter beyond his years. "Dan doesn't put himself first. He works hard to win. What makes him such a great hitter is that he doesn't come to the plate and just swing away. He learns from at-bat to at-bat. He sees what the pitcher is throwing and adjusts. He's beyond his years as a hitter," says Arteaga.

Cuvet says, "I started playing baseball when I was nine. From then on, I played on a travel team every weekend. I traveled two months every summer. We would travel all over. Those were the best times of my life. I was with all my friends. My parents took care of all of us in my family. We never had to worry about anything. Coming to Brewster is amazing. The Cassidys are great hosts. In fact, everyone in Brewster has been awesome. The town and the people go way out of their way to make all the players comfortable."

The Cassidys have been hosts for Whitecaps players for nine years. Joan Cassidy shares some of her experiences: "My husband and myself enjoy getting to know the players. For the most part, it doesn't take too long for the players to feel at home. It's great for us to spend time with the guys. We're both retired now, and we find that the relationships we develop with the boys help to keep us both young."

CARSTEN SABATHIA—FIRST BASEMAN, UNIVERSITY OF HOUSTON

Carsten Sabathia, the son of the great future Hall of Fame pitcher CC Sabathia, might just go down as the one of the most likeable players that ever played on Cape Cod. To say Carsten is a great young man is an understatement. Carsten Sabathia is everything any parent would be proud of.

Carsten was having the summer of his life both on and off the field until a serious hand injury ended his season. Carsten had come to the Whitecaps after finishing his sophomore year at Georgia Tech. It didn't take any time for the first baseman to become one of the most popular players on the Caps. Sabathia was making a solid contribution platooning at first base until he was shut down with a broken bone in his hand.

Even after the injury, Carsten stayed with his hostess, Jane Sullivan, for a few extra days. "I just love being here. I don't want to leave. I'm just so comfortable being with the guys and spending time with everyone. The Whitecaps feel like a family to me. We all get along so well and pull for each other. I want to stay and cheer on my teammates," says Carsten.

"I've been dreaming about playing here for several years. You hear about all the great players that have come through the Cape. It's almost mythical in nature. It's fun for me to be around these guys and pick their brains about how they go about their business. I play this game to develop different relationships with different people. These are the friends I'll want to have at my wedding someday. I'll cherish these memories forever," says Carsten.

Carsten was placed with Sullivan as his host family. He couldn't stop his praise for Sullivan. "I just love Jane. She's awesome. I feel like she's my mom away from home."

Then the conversation changed to his famous dad. When I mentioned that CC said he was living his dream watching his son play against great competition on the Cape, Carsten was taken aback. "That's amazing that he said that. I spent my whole life watching him. I've always been so proud of him. For him to be in the stands watching is so special. That's enough for me. He never put any pressure on me to play. I gravitated to the game naturally from the time I was little. Dad was always just Dad to me. I was a baseball geek. So having the opportunity to be around the game has always been a great opportunity that I've never taken for granted. I grew up in a very grounded home. It was never about the material stuff with either my mom or dad. My brothers and sister, we didn't grow up that way. I feel I have the best two parents around."

The next part of our interview had Carsten falling out of his chair laughing. The famous Red Sox vs. CC Sabathia and the New York Yankees rivalry was brought up. "I loved it when dad pitched at Fenway Park and everyone was all over him. That's what competition is. That's what you live for. That's what you crave. I loved it. He loved it. He lived for those situations. The fans in Boston were hysterical. They never said anything to me. He absolutely loved all of it," Carsten said as he laughed hysterically. "Those days were awesome. He thrived on the craziness of it all. It was like a dream come true for him. This is the best interview I've ever had. This is a blast, sitting here talking about this. I've had many interviews, but no one has ever asked me about those days. They were the absolute best of times for our family. This is awesome—this is just awesome. I can't wait to call Dad tonight and tell him about this interview. He's going to love it. This whole thing has been great. What a cool interview this is."

As the interview ended with one of the nicest young men I have ever met, we sat and laughed together for another ten minutes. Carsten Sabathia then got up with the biggest smile and walked into the dugout so he could cheer on his lifetime friends.

RYDER HELFRICK—CATCHER, UNIVERSITY OF ARKANSAS

Ryder Helfrick could go down as one of the most humble and quiet players in the history of the Cape Cod Baseball League. Helfrick grew up riding dirt bikes. That was his hobby of choice. Helfrick explains, "Dirt bike racing was my first love. My dad was into it pretty heavily, and I just loved it. Even my mom would ride. I'm the middle son. There are no girls in the family. My brothers and I grew up in a little town called Discover Bay, California. It's just a small town sixty miles east of San Francisco. The high school I was supposed to go to didn't have much of a baseball program, so for four years my brother and myself would travel close to an hour away to attend Clayton Valley Charter High School in Concord, California. I got a lot out of where I ended up going. I received a good education, and the coaching staff was excellent. My mom was amazing in how she supported my baseball playing. She drove me everywhere for years. What's funny about her is that as many games as she watched, she still wouldn't be able to tell me where the shortstop position is."

Now here's the thing about Helfrick. When asked about the all-conference and all-state awards he received in high school, he can't answer. Helfrick says, "I really don't know. They were never important. I never paid attention to that stuff. I think if you looked them up online you might be able to find some. There were two high school all-star events that I wanted to be selected for that I was able to compete in. I was happy about that." One was the Perfect Game USA Select Showcasing, in which he was named the MVP for the entire tournament. The other was the High School All-Star All American Classic hosted by MLB. Indeed, there are lots of Helfrick's awards available online to read about.

When you're ranked as the thirty-third high school prospect in America, you receive lots of honors and awards. When you're Ryder Helfrick, you stay grounded and stay focused on your continued improvement. "I thought about staying on the West Coast for college, but I wanted to play in the best conference, which is the SEC. I decided on Arkansas. I love it; we have beautiful facilities and a huge fan base. We had a great season. For a couple of weeks, we were rated number one in the nation. We lost in the NCAA Regionals to Kansas State. I started about half the games. We had a catcher, Hudson White, who was selected in the ninth round by the Red Sox. I shared the catching position with him, and we became great friends."

Helfrick is eager to share his feelings about the Brewster Whitecaps. "I love my teammates and coaches on the Cape—they're awesome. The fans, especially the kids, have all been terrific. Right now, I'm working on hitting to all fields. I don't worry about performing for the scouts. I just play my game, and I don't worry about what others think."

As you continue to read this story and learn more about Helfrick, you will come to realize if you haven't already that Ryder Helfrick's baseball ceiling is through the roof.

ANDREW FISCHER—INFIELDER, UNIVERSITY OF TENNESSEE

Andrew Fischer was one of the elite baseball talents playing on Cape Cod during the 2024 season. "Cape Cod is the premier summer league in America. It's an honor to be here. I always continue to work on my craft. Growing up I wrestled along with playing baseball. I love wrestling. My dad, who I'm close to, is the wrestling coach at Wall High in New Jersey. That's where I went. Everything I learned from wrestling has helped me with my work ethic for baseball. I wasn't a highly ranked baseball player coming out of high school. I had to work my way up from the bottom. I went to Duke in my freshman year and transferred to Ole Miss for my sophomore year. Dad, through wrestling, taught me how to be mentally tough. Wrestling has prepared me for not just baseball but for the rest of my life."

Fischer continues explaining his approach to baseball. "One of the big things about baseball is that every day is a new day. You can bat zero for five or five for five in a game, and after the game you must turn the page and prepare for the next one. If I have a bad game, there are still things I feel I can do to contribute. Whether it be to help a slumping teammate or to pump up a pitcher coming into a game. There are ways I can still contribute. If I'm in the dumps and being selfish, that's not going to help the team win."

"I wanted to play in the SEC and win a National Championship, so I transferred to Mississippi. I want to play in front of big crowds where everyone's eyes are on me. Forget about the hype or rankings. All I want to do is show up every day and play. I love baseball. It's such a blessing to put on my spikes every day. Baseball is the greatest sport in the world. The sun is shining. What more could I possibly ask for?" says Fischer.

The conversation changes to the Brewster Whitecaps. Fischer has this to say: "I'm with other players who have some serious talent and who come from all over the country. I love listening to everyone's stories and the journeys they take to get to where they are. Brewster is a great town. The fans are here every day. The people are amazing. The coaches do a great job of player development. I look forward to coming to the field every day. I couldn't have chosen a better place to continue my baseball journey."

Toward the end of the summer, Fischer transferred once again for his junior year to the University of Tennessee. The Volunteers had just won the NCAA 2024 College Baseball World Series. Fisher is the twenty-fifth-ranked MLB prospect in the 2025 draft. "Tennessee gives me the best opportunity to win a College World Series. Winning is my ultimate goal," says Fischer.

As this story unfolds, so does the personality and talent of one of MLB's future stars. Hold on to your hats—there is nothing boring about Andrew Fischer.

JACOB MARLOWE—THE MIRACLE OF BREWSTER

There will always be athletes who persevere and find ways to make miraculous comebacks. Their stories resonate. There has never been a story in Cape Cod Baseball history like that of the kid who grew up in Naples, Florida, and attends Florida State. Jacob Marlowe didn't just make a miraculous baseball comeback. He pulled himself out of a life-and-death situation to pitch for the Brewster Whitecaps after undergoing not one but two open heart surgeries seven months before he reported to Brewster.

This is his story. As a young boy, Marlowe grew up playing all sports. As he got a little older, he switched to baseball full-time. All throughout his adolescent years and his teenage years, Marlowe experienced nothing but success on the mound as a pitcher. While attending Barron Collier High, he pitched his team deep into the Florida State High School Championships. In fact, as a senior, he received the 2021 Southwest Florida High School Sports Player of the Year.

Marlowe was born with a heart defect called aortic valve regurgitation. His mom, Janet, explains, "Jacob has always been through heart examinations before every season he would play. The doctors every year approved his medical condition. He had just transferred to Florida State after two great seasons at Central Florida University. In fact, during his sophomore season in 2023, he led his team in innings pitched with over sixty innings. It was as he was preparing for his first season at Florida State that we received a call from their coach. His condition that we thought would eventually need surgery when he was in his thirties had worsened. They shut him down and advised us to visit a cardiologist immediately. We flew up to Massachusetts General Hospital in Boston in October 2023. They agreed that corrective surgery needed to be performed immediately. Within days Jacob had open-heart surgery."

Janet Marlowe continues, "We all hoped and expected that the surgery would correct the problem and he would be able to resume his baseball career in a few months. Well, his heart didn't accept the surgery. In fact, while he was in recovery at the hospital, his heart rate dropped to a low of twenty-three beats per minute. The normal heart rate for an individual is sixty beats per minute. A second open-heart surgery was performed five days after the first one. No longer were we concerned with baseball. This became life-and-death for Jacob. Even his high school coach, Charlie Maurer, who has been by his side every step of the way since he first met Jacob, flew into Boston to be with him."

After the second surgery, Jacob Marlowe was finally told what everyone had been praying for. The second surgery was a success. Marlowe looks back at his ordeal as he eats breakfast at Café Alfresco in Brewster with his mom and grandmother, Eileen, before a Whitecaps game: "After the second surgery, I started to feel better immediately. That's when I started thinking about playing again. In fact, when I woke up from my second surgery, there was a baseball in my hand. My high school coach, who had been waiting in the waiting room with my family, placed it there for me. I was told I needed to wait a few months before I could start with light exercises. It felt great to continue with my conditioning. I couldn't wait to get started. Of course, this past season Florida State gave me a medical redshirt season."

"Here I am in Brewster pitching for the Whitecaps this summer. I love the town, the coaches, and my teammates. Everyone has been cheering for me during my comeback. I couldn't be more excited about how everything turned out," says Marlowe.

Remember the name Jacob Marlowe. As you follow along with this story, everyone will learn that the journey of this talented left-handed hurler is the story of *The Miracle of Brewster*.

JANE SULLIVAN—HOST FAMILIES AND MS. WHITECAP

One of the most unique aspects of the CCBL is that all the players live with volunteer host families. Brewster follows this same special tradition. What sets Brewster apart is that one of the most special people to ever volunteer in any capacity of any team on the Cape resides in Brewster.

Every team has an abundance of hardworking volunteers. Volunteers are at the very heart and soul of what makes the Cape League so special. In fact, it is quite known in baseball circles around America that without the volunteers, the CCBL would not exist. The most popular and one of the hardest-working volunteers is the assistant general manager of the Brewster Whitecaps, Jane Sullivan. Sullivan wears so many different hats that she is at the forefront of every decision that is made by her Whitecaps.

This diminutive ball of energy works twenty-four hours per day, seven days per week, fifty-two weeks out of the year. Every waking moment Sullivan gives of herself to make sure the tradition of the Brewster Whitecaps will always remain intact.

Sullivan, who has lived in Brewster for fifty-three years, wears the pride of her town on both arms like two full-sleeve tattoos. Ms. Sullivan spent over forty years in public education, and most of them were spent working on the Cape. Between Cape Cod Tech and Barnstable High, all her students became very close to her. Even today she still treats them like they are her children.

A colleague at Cape Tech in the 1980s encouraged her to volunteer to help bring about an expansion team, which is now the Brewster Whitecaps. Even her three children became Cape Cod Baseball fans. In fact, her middle daughter, Katie, even volunteered as a host for many years as well.

Sullivan represents everything good about not only her Brewster Whitecaps but also the Cape Cod Baseball League. She even finds time to serve on the Cape's executive board. When she first started her volunteering with the Caps, her main function was as the housing director. Today she serves as the assistant general manager to her close buddy, General Manager Jon Mecca, and as the housing director. Together they form the perfect team. Neither of them ever stops smiling.

Sullivan's biggest undertaking is finding housing for all the Brewster players. Not only does she find the perfect host and hostess for each player, she also takes one or two players into her own home. Finding the right housing situation can be a monstrous task. Throughout the course of a summer, as many as fifty to sixty-five players are filtered through the organization. Jane works tirelessly with each player, most times becoming their mother figure while "her" boys are spending their summer months playing for the Brewster Whitecaps.

Overseeing transportation details as the players come and go also falls under the Sullivan job description. Sullivan loves to tell everyone she comes in contact with that she plays no favorites. "I love each one like my own son," she is proud to say. The feeling is quite mutual for not only the players but also the coaches, college interns, Manager Jamie Shevchik, and me (the author). Loyalty runs deep for this special lady. She passes out her love unconditionally, and in return every single person who becomes part of Whitecaps Nation returns it tenfold.

Brewster Whitecaps Manager Jamie Shevchik with
author Mark Pathfinder Epstein

Second Inning—The Lineup

If finding housing is no easy task, add to that the responsibility of making sure every player is fitted with three sets of the team's baseball game uniforms and all their practice gear. It's also her job to make sure each player returns all their uniforms if they leave early so she can resize them and give them to the next replacement player.

If you think this isn't enough, she is also part of the group that feeds the players and interns after every game that is played. Jane Sullivan bleeds Whitecaps teal. If you ask Jane to name her favorite player, you may think her readymade answer is maybe her way of staying politically correct. If you repeat the question again later in the season, expect to hear the same answer. Finally, if you repeat it toward the end of the season, like this author did, she may even get annoyed. When asked again months later, by phone, she reminds the author, "How many times you have asked me this same question?" Sullivan's answer is 100 percent genuine. "I have loved every player that has ever played for the Brewster Whitecaps the same. I love them all like my own sons."

When it comes to some of her favorite memories, she's quick to point out the time that a player came to her a little homesick after being in Brewster for a few weeks. Like so many players who travel to the Cape from all over America and spend ten weeks away from their families and girlfriends, players can start to get a little homesick. Well, when this happens Sullivan has a ready answer that gives the players a shot of reality. Sullivan tells each one, "Maybe playing MLB isn't for you. Have you given any thought about another career where you're not going to someday be playing 162 games per year?" This is the number of games in a full MLB season. Within seconds the player usually becomes motivated again. Sullivan really does wear many hats.

Another of her favorite memories is about James Tibbs, who played for Brewster in 2023. Tibbs was playing in the outfield for Florida State when the Seminoles came to Boston to play at Boston College. Like every other player who has played for the Caps over the years, Tibbs adores Sullivan. A group of Brewster Whitecaps volunteers traveled ninety miles together to BC to support Tibbs. Tibbs was in a little slump before he got to Boston. During the game Tibbs summoned Ms. Whitecap to where he was standing in the on-deck circle. Without saying a single word, Tibbs held out his bat, which was a tradition started in Brewster between the player and Sullivan. Sullivan touched the barrel for good luck. Well, what do you know—when Tibbs came to the plate, he lined a double into the gap to bring in two Florida State runners—slump over. But this is not the end of the story. Tibbs came to bat two innings later with the same scenario. Two Florida State runners were on base. Once again Tibbs held his bat out for the Sullivan magic. Yup, another line shot up against the BC outfield fence for another two-RBI double.

Pure Jane Sullivan at her very best.

Fast-forward to July 14, 2024, the day of the first round of the MLB draft. James Tibbs was with his family, nervously waiting to possibly hear if his name would be called.

During the anxious moments before the draft, Tibbs sent a photo to Sullivan of both of them together from the summer before as he sat watching ESPN.

"With the thirteenth pick of the first round, the San Francisco Giants select James Tibbs—outfielder from Florida State by way of the Brewster Whitecaps!"

And just like that, tears of joy flowed from James Tibbs's favorite Brewster Whitecaps mom.

JAMIE SHEVCHIK—THE SKIPPER AND HIS FAMILY

Baseball manager Jamie Shevchik is a baseball lifer. But baseball manager Jamie Shevchik is not your typical baseball lifer. Shevchik is a family man first and a people's person second.

Shevchik was interviewed many times for this story. The first was one month before the 2024 CCBL season started in mid-May, and the last was one week after the season ended in mid-August. Through it all, the manager of the Keystone College Giants and the Brewster Whitecaps has remained the same easygoing, down-to-earth, grounded gentleman. There was never one day when Shevchik let the roller-coaster topsy-turvy 2024 Cape Cod Baseball season change his demeaner or his outlook. He masked it well. Looking back, there sure were many opportunities for that to happen.

Another word that has been synonymous with the word manager in baseball is "skipper." In today's world of college athletics and winning at all costs, the skipper of the Whitecaps is a breath of fresh air. Shevchik was quick to point out early on what his baseball philosophy has always been: "I've been involved in baseball my entire life. I decided from the very beginning that I'm not going to win at all costs. I'm going to do things with the same good morals and character that I was raised by my parents with. My goal is to develop great human beings. I'm going to treat everybody with respect and dignity. I'm not going to win at the expense of my players. If I lose, I'm going to be OK with that as long as I don't change who I am as a person."

Shevchik also shared the theory that he uses when he manages Brewster: "I don't like to cut players. I have heard some horror stories of players and the way some of them have been treated by other managers on the Cape. I put myself out there and make myself vulnerable by treating people the way I want to be treated. If someone takes advantage of me, it hurts even more. If a player comes to Brewster on a temporary contract, I want them to at least get into a couple of games and leave here with a shirt and hat. I want each player that plays for the Whitecaps to experience the thrill of playing baseball on Cape Cod."

Shevchik also has plenty to say about his three greatest loves and how he has been able to combine all three into his life.

Family, Baseball, and Brewster—in that order—are what fulfills Shevchik's life the most. "When I first got to the Cape, Brewster was looked at as a small market team. We were looked at as the Milwaukee Brewers of the Cape. We were the ultimate underdogs. Our fan base was very loyal, but it was one of the smallest on the Cape. Our annual revenue was behind other organizations like Chatham, Cotuit, Orleans, and Falmouth. The Whitecaps were still looked on as an expansion team. They had only one league championship. The year was 2000. I'm going into my tenth season, and we have all worked very hard together to bring the franchise lots of respectability. We have won two championships since we arrived. The first was in 2017 and again in 2021. We've come a long way since we started. I don't think we're a small market team anymore."

Shevchik changes the conversation toward his family. "I have three daughters and a loving wife. My family is very important to me. Baseball can be hard on a family. In the beginning I sacrificed my family more than I probably should have to build a college baseball program. I spent more time recruiting when I started off, and I wasn't around as much as I should have been. Now all three of my kids are involved with the Brewster organization helping as student interns. My oldest daughter, Brielle, is a student at Keystone College and works in sports media for the team. My middle girl, Giana, is a high school student and works with the game day staff. The youngest, Raina, is ten years old, and she is one of the team's bat kids. I've been married to my wife Maria for twenty years now. Our entire family looks at Brewster as their home away from home. The entire community has become like a second family to all of us. It's become our happy place. When my daughters get older and they sit around the kitchen table, their conversations are going to be about their summers on Cape Cod. That's very important to me."

Sitting down with the entire Shevchik family at their Cape cottage, where they all live together for ten weeks every summer, brought about a lot of hearty laughs. Brielle explained, "I've been around baseball my entire life. I remember when I was a baby, I'd go to practice with my dad at Keystone, and the girls from the field hockey team would babysit me while my dad was at practice. I even remember the long bus trips during the summers we spent in Danbury, Connecticut. I would go on all the bus trips with Daddy. I love baseball. I also love being at the beach in Brewster. Jane Sullivan has become my best friend at the Cape—I just love her. It doesn't matter that she's in her seventies; age has no boundaries. It's so cool that I get to watch my dad's players he coached play in the Major Leagues. I feel as if Brewster is my second home. I also work as a nanny for a Brewster family. At the end of July, I will work for the Brewster Recreation Department. It's a camp held at Eddy Elementary School." It was easy to see the love that the friendly, soft-spoken rising junior has for her dad.

The Shevchik girls all have different but fun personalities. Giana brought everyone to laughter when she spoke about her dad. "I'm the rebellious one. When I was younger, I enjoyed being with my mom at home when my dad coached. I tried as hard as I could to hate Brewster and baseball. No matter how hard I tried, I just couldn't do it. Now I enjoy playing softball and count the days when I can come back to Brewster for another summer. Now I just love it."

Raina has a little spark to her that radiates in any setting she finds herself in.

"I'm a beach girl, and I'm so proud of my dad. He's gone so far in baseball. He coaches the Brewster Whitecaps. I get to be a bat kid. I have so much fun talking with the other girls who do it with me. I like playing softball too."

Maria Shevchik, the wife of the skipper, summed up the entire family's sentiments. "I wish away ten months a year just to be in Brewster for two months every summer. I love watching Jamie coach in Brewster. He radiates happiness on the Cape."

Jamie Shevchik changes the conversation back to Keystone College. "Growing up, we are all taught to work hard, and the rewards will be there for you. This part is true in many ways; I never would have had the chance to manage in the Cape League if my coaching career was a bust. When I took the Keystone job at twenty-seven years old, it was a blessing and a curse. The blessing was that very few people are offered a full-time college coaching job at the age of twenty-seven. I couldn't pass that up. The curse is it never allowed me to get into the coaching world at the higher levels of college baseball and get into that fraternity of being a NCAA Division 1 coach. I've been the head coach at Keystone College in Pennsylvania for the past twenty years. It's a small, private, NCAA Division III college located in the northeast part of Pennsylvania. It's about fifteen miles from Scranton. Our student population is a little over one thousand students. We're the ultimate underdogs in college baseball. It's where I graduated from and received my first coaching job. We have less resources than almost everyone we play. We have continued to thrive. We have won nineteen straight conference championships in a row. Along the way, we played in three different conferences. Thirty different schools over those nineteen years have had the chance to take us out, and nobody has been able to do it. We've gone to the NCAA Division III World Series twice. We actually lost in the NCAA Division III National Championship game in 2016."

Shevchik finally was getting off his mind what he had been wrestling with for years. "So, no matter how much success I have, I will always be labeled as a Division III NCAA college coach. I know I can be successful at the highest levels of college baseball because my entire life has been based on doing more with less. Imagine what I can do with more? I watch coaches in college baseball making more than a million dollars a year knowing I can do that job, if not better. My struggle that I wrestle with all the time is that my success doesn't match my position. I am not supposed to be a division III coach. I am supposed to be the millionaire. I never thought I'd be the coach who struggles to pay the bills. Not that I need the big house or the fancy cars, but I expected to have financial security based on the success I've had in coaching. This is the struggle I deal with from September to May. From June through August, I am the wealthiest person in the world. This inner struggle has been going on for a while."

The skipper is happy to share his life story. "I grew up the oldest of five children to William and Debbie Shevchik. My sister, Heather, and my brothers, Jeff, Corey, and Kyle, have all done well for themselves. My parents worked really hard to provide for all of us. It was important that we all had a solid foundation based on good moral values and education. My dad coached me on my youth teams when I was growing up. To this day my mom, Debbie, spends a week with us every summer in Brewster. It has become her happy place as well."

"When I was growing up my goal was to become a big-time NCAA Division I college coach. I loved playing, but I was just average throughout high school and college. I played for Keystone while it was still a junior college. I continued with my education at Keystone later, after it became a four-year college. That's where I also received my bachelor's degree. I was working as their part-time pitching coach while finishing my degree. I never had an opportunity to advance my coaching career beyond Keystone. I was given $1,500 to become the part-time pitching coach when I first started out at the age of twenty-three. I was still a kid," said Shevchik.

This baseball legend has always been involved in summer amateur baseball. When he was still a student at Keystone, he organized a summer league for high school and college players in Scranton. The team that Shevchik managed won a total of nine league championships during those summers. As he moved on from Scranton, he took over the managing responsibilities for Dansbury, Connecticut, in the New England Collegiate Baseball Summer League. There he spent eight summers. His last summer, in 2014, was spent living with a host family while his wife was pregnant.

Shevchik also opened up about the 2023–2024 school year at Keystone College. "The past year was my most stressful ever working at Keystone. The school was ready to close, and we were put on 'imminent closure.' Our students didn't know where they were going to school the following year. Our team didn't have our best season, but at the end we clicked and went on to win our nineteenth straight conference championship. Now I'm consumed with trying to win a conference championship for the twentieth straight year. I'm not sure any team sport in NCAA history at any level has ever accomplished that feat. The pressure is all self-inflicted. I ask myself sometimes if it's even that important. I actually think at times it would have been better if we had lost one along the way so I wouldn't put myself under this unnecessary stress."

The Keystone Giants Baseball Hall of Famer is proud of not only what the Brewster Whitecaps have accomplished on the field but also what the organization has done to expand the fan experience. "The entire organization has come a long way. There have been several improvements made that our fans are enjoying. This has helped us increase our attendance and bring in more revenue. We even have a first-class team store that was just completed on time for the 2024 season. Our playing field is in tip-top shape, and we have a brand-new scoreboard that was just donated. In 2017 we had over five thousand fans on hand to watch us win the CCBL Championship. People rushed the field when we clinched the last game. Longtime fans were actually crying."

"Today the Cape League has changed," Shevchik continues. "It's hard to manage the pitchers. We are renting these players. College coaches are making more than a million dollars a year. Our players are their investments. It's a pitchers' league in the beginning of the season. Scouts watch batting practice. It takes until July for the hitters using wooden bats to catch up with a 95-mph fastball. It's usually not until the second week of July that the transition takes place.

Matt Hyde from the New York Yankees is the face of Cape Cod scouting. He was the bat boy for Chatham as a kid," Shevchik adds as he changes the conversation to one of his closest friends.

"On paper at the beginning of the year, every team feels they have the team to beat. Every summer I save the roster and show it to my assistants in the middle of the year. It's going to change a lot. The offense is usually the strongest part of each roster. The pitching is usually questionable. Team USA pulls its team from the Cape rosters. After their summer exhibition season ends, several players don't return to their Cape teams. The NCAA postseason tournament keeps several players from reporting at the beginning of the season. There are just so many moving variables that take place in putting a Cape team on the field. I haven't even mentioned the host families. Jane Sullivan is just incredible. She is so darn lovable. My daughters just adore her," says Shevchik.

The manager of the Whitecaps ends our interview by sharing his most inner thoughts: "My wife doesn't have to work; my girls can experience one of the prettiest places on earth. My family gets to spend ten weeks at the beach. I get to do something that I love to do. There aren't a lot of people in the world that get to experience that every year as a family. For those two months out of the year, every ounce of hard work that I've put in over the past twenty years comes into focus. You can't put a price tag on that. This is why I am invested in the Brewster Whitecaps as an organization and not just the team on the field. The Brewster Whitecaps noticed; the Brewster Whitecaps have invested in me. For ten weeks out of the year, the Brewster Whitecaps have fulfilled a sense of self-worth for me. For two months out of the year, we are millionaires. For that I will always be indebted to the Brewster Whitecaps organization."

Skipper, I believe the feeling is quite mutual, I thought to myself.

LUKE DILLON—THE PRESIDENT

At first impression Luke Dillon will strike you as a quiet, unassuming, successful man who is easy to approach. You don't notice the competitive fire burning within him. It's there all right (trust me), but it's kept hidden.

As a young boy, Dillon grew up in the Central Massachusetts city of Worcester. With a tremendous love of all sports Boston, Dillon gravitated toward basketball. Dillon became one of the finest high school point guards ever produced at St. John's High, a perennial basketball powerhouse. After a stellar career in which he helped lead the Pioneers to back-to-back trips to the Massachusetts state semifinals played at the Boston Garden, he would continue with his education and basketball career at Union College in Schenectady, New York.

After graduating with a Bachelor of Arts degree in English, Dillon received a law degree from Suffolk Law School in Boston. While living just outside of Boston, in Hanover, with his lovely wife, Karen, and his son, Chris, Dillon enjoyed a long, successful career working as a legal expert in the life insurance industry.

Dillon is quick to point out that "Karen is a huge fan, and Chris played baseball competitively while he was growing up."

During his entire working career in Boston, Dillon found the time to support all of Boston's professional teams. The Celtics and particularly the Red Sox he would remain loyal to. In fact, Dillon shared Red Sox season tickets with a friend for over thirty years.

Throughout his adult life, the Dillon family would travel often to their family home in Brewster. As his career started to wind down in Boston, he and his wife frequented their summer retreat more often. During this time Karen encouraged her husband to get involved on the board of directors of the Whitecaps.

This became a match made in heaven. Dillon had an outlet for his deep love affair with baseball and New England sports. As a few years went by working on the Whitecaps' board, Dillon officially retired from his law practice. This opened the opportunity for Dillon to give more time combining his leadership abilities with his passion for the Brewster Whitecaps.

Working as a president for a Cape Cod baseball team is a twelve-month-a-year responsibility. There are no days off. Some of the many tasks include fundraising, finding new business partners, working with the town of Brewster, maintaining Stony Brook Field, and helping support the other board members like Jane Sullivan, Whitecaps Manager Jamie Shevchik, and the caretakers of the field, Alton and Kathy Cole.

The 2024 season had mixed results for the team on the field. Off the field it was a completely different story. There were noticeable improvements to Stony Brook Field. A beautiful scoreboard and souvenir store were added to the facilities just in time for the season. Both improvements brought more fans to the ballpark and in turn created more revenue for the entire organization.

Dillon took time out of his hectic schedule to voice a concern that every team in the league deals with: "The big issue we face now is the number of players that come through Brewster every summer. It used to be that players stayed for the entire summer. During the 2023 season, sixty-two players suited up for the Whitecaps at one time or another. This past season (2024), we had fifty-two players. That was the fewest in the entire league."

At the end of the season, for the first time ever, the Brewster Whitecaps were the recipient of the highly prestigious Paul Galop Commissioner's Cup for the 2024 season. The award is presented annually to the team demonstrating the highest level of integrity and professionalism on and off the field in the Cape Cod Baseball League.

JON MECCA—GENERAL MANAGER

Jon Mecca is another leader for the Brewster Whitecaps that comes from a proud basketball background. Mecca grew up in Waterbury, Connecticut, where he attended Holy Cross High. During his high school days, Mecca spent four seasons contributing to the great basketball tradition at his school. During his time at Holy Cross, the basketball team made great runs in the state tournament.

From there Mecca attended Central Connecticut University and received a bachelor's degree. For several years after Mecca graduated from Central, he worked on Wall Street in New York. Mecca said, "After several years commuting to New York from Waterbury with my brother, I got burned out. I moved to Sandy Hook, Connecticut, and started working for Pitney Bowes. After several years of living there and helping to raise our family with my wife, Casey, we decided to move full-time to our happy summer home. Every summer, when we would vacation in Brewster, we never wanted to leave when summer ended. So we decided to move here full-time. Casey and myself and my three kids love it. I get to work from home, and my wife is a schoolteacher in Hyannis."

Mecca continued, "My involvement with the Whitecaps has been a progression. My two oldest children, George and Grace, started helping with the Caps as bat kids right after we moved here. That's how I got involved. After a couple of years, I got voted onto the board of directors. When Ned Monthie, our longtime general manager, stepped aside to concentrate on just his role on the board, it opened an opportunity for me to take over as the GM. It's been a lot of fun for my whole family. My daughter Violet is only five, and in a few years, she'll probably help out as a bat kid also."

Mecca looked back at his first year in a leadership role with the organization. "We accomplished a great deal this year. Receiving the Paul Galop Commissioner's Cup was a tremendous honor for the entire organization. It's awarded annually to the team that best exemplifies the values of the Cape Cod Baseball League both on and off the field. It's the first time the Brewster Whitecaps have ever received it. It's important for the Whitecaps to continue to make an impact on the entire community."

One of the most important jobs that all Cape Cod general managers have as a responsibility is to handle all the player contracts. Contracts have to be sent out to the colleges for both the players and coaches to sign and return in a timely manner.

The Whitecaps are led, off the field, by Luke Dillon and Jon Mecca. These two former outstanding high school basketball players probably make up the finest backcourt combination you can find in charge of a Cape Cod Baseball League organization. Outside of their love for sports, you couldn't find two better people.

The future is shining brightly for the Brewster Whitecaps.

BRIAN DEL ROSSO—PITCHING COACH

For the pitching coach of the Brewster Whitecaps, Brian Del Rosso, it's baseball, baseball, baseball, twelve months a year. "During the year I'm the pitching coach for Jamie at Keystone College. I'm here in Brewster for my second summer, and I love coaching in the premier summer baseball league in the country."

Del Rosso sat down to chat after a couple of games at Pico's Taco Shack while eating a delicious shrimp burrito. "I think we're heading in the right direction as far as getting the guys to mesh and playing as a cohesive unit. Every team is still trying to figure things out. We're in a good spot right now and have the potential to be one of the most talented teams in the league."

For Del Rosso, trying to juggle his pitchers' needs isn't as hard as some may think. "I try to get to know each and every one of them as best as I possibly can in a short amount of time. Some guys come in knowing how many outings they want to make, and others may be here for a bit longer. If they want to showcase their talents to the scouts in short stints, we try to accommodate those requests the best we can. If they want to display themselves as starters, we try and line those up for them as well. My goal is to work with them and help them the best that I can. I try and cater to their needs with the understanding that this is a showcase league. To me, the most important thing is communication. I try to check in as much as possible with all my pitchers daily to see how they're feeling," Del Rosso said.

The Whitecaps started the season with thirty players. Eighteen of them were pitchers. Del Rosso says, "I'm very comfortable having that many. At Keystone we sometimes have a fifty-to-sixty-man roster, and thirty of them are pitchers. If you're consistent with how you approach things every day, you can control things. I give everyone the same attention every day. Each player has their own recovery time after each appearance. I want everyone to be at their best when it's their turn to pitch, but I also want to give us the best chance to win."

The question for Del Rosso is that of course players always want to win, but does it bother them if they don't win in the CCBL in the same way it bothers them during the college season? Del Rosso's answer: "The best players always want to be at their very best when they compete. Pitchers compete individually even though they are part of the team. If a guy goes out and performs well for the scouts but loses, for most that stinks. The guys who have the best character care about the result, not just how they performed."

"Winning is all I care about. I'm extremely competitive. Winning, to me, is what I think about from the time I wake up each morning until it's time for bed. I think the world treats winners a lot differently than they do losers. No one likes a loser," Del Rosso says, laughing.

"In high school in Phillipsburg, New Jersey, I was the ace of my staff, but I also played center field and was the leadoff hitter. In college I was the everyday starting center fielder playing for Jamie at Keystone College. Later on, when I went on to play professionally in independent baseball, I went back to pitching," Del Rosso says.

At this time the pitching coach turns the conversation toward his family. "My sister has won three National Championships as a cheerleading coach. My dad played baseball seriously, and my mom wasn't much of an athlete but always supported my dreams within the game of baseball. My wife, Nancy, allows me to put my best foot forward every day when it comes to my profession. Without having that strong support system at home with my family, I wouldn't be able to perform my daily duties at as high of a level as I do.

"Pitching has evolved in the last ten years. The velocity that pitchers throw at has skyrocketed into the mid to high nineties. You can attribute this to the players' conditioning programs, weight strength training, arm care, the overall health an athlete keeps themselves in, and the information that's available online for the pitchers to study. There is a downside to the era of added velocity, though. Arm injuries all the way down into youth baseball are more frequent. As much as some things have changed in baseball, some things have stayed the same. I still think a well-located fastball is the most important pitch. There is a message behind a hard fastball, and it isn't an invitation to have dinner with me after the game," Del Rosso says.

Data and sabermetrics as they relate to baseball have changed the modern-day approach to all sports but especially to baseball. Del Rosso shares his views on the way they are both used today. "Using analytics can be a huge advantage if used properly. In my opinion, it's important to not get entirely consumed by it. I believe it is important to have a feel for the game and understand the metrics while using your instincts when making decisions. I don't think it's a good idea to base every decision on just analytics alone. You need to keep a happy balance."

Technology in baseball has arrived. Del Rosso enjoys talking about the latest new gadgets that are worn by the pitchers and the catchers. Coaches like Del Rosso and all pitchers and catchers can now use special watches during games to send and receive signs from the bench. "Calling a game with the watches has certainly come with a bit of an adjustment. All in all, this technology has definitely changed the game for sure. Relaying signs to the catcher, the catcher relaying signs to the pitcher, that process has been ingrained into the game of baseball forever. Having this technology where I can give signs to the entire defense on a watch is pretty remarkable. Most guys coming from their schools are used to throwing whatever pitch their coach calls. In the Cape Cod League, it's important for me to encourage them to use their instincts out there. Have a game plan for each hitter, read swings, pick up on little things that you see throughout the game. If that means shaking off to a different pitch than I call and it leads to a strike or an out, I'm all good with that," says Del Rosso.

Scott Grimes—Hitting Coach

Scott Grimes exemplifies everything that is great about our national pastime. Grimes's work ethic, his tremendous playing career, his dedication toward his family and student-athletes, his leadership ability, and his ability to teach all make this man a giant in baseball and in the Cape Cod Baseball League.

Grimes's winding road in baseball has paved his way to Brewster and to work with his long-time baseball mentor and former manager at Keystone College. From the day Shevchik entered the life of Grimes, these two baseball lifers developed an unbreakable bond.

As a young guy growing up in Pennsylvania, Grimes was motivated toward both basketball and baseball. Grimes's schoolwork wasn't high on his list of priorities. Grimes showed tremendous potential in sports, but because of his lack of academic motivation, there were no NCAA Division I scholarships waiting for him. Enter Shevchik and Keystone College. Grimes held a no-holds-barred interview with me where he didn't pull any punches.

The Brewster hitting coach was straightforward and never once minced his words about his life. "Until I met Jamie and came to Keystone, I was facing some serious consequences because I had a poor academic record in high school. He was the only one who was willing to give me a chance. I'm not even sure he realizes how much I feel I owe him. I spent four years at Keystone. The time there was so valuable—not just because of my four-year baseball career but because I grew up to become a man there."

The Keystone Hall of Famer graduated in 2005 with some of the greatest hitting records established in NCAA history at any level. Some of the records he graduated with have not been broken and probably never will be. His record-breaking batting average of .573 during the 2004 season, his junior year, is almost unimaginable. His .506 average his senior year brought MLB scouts to Keystone from all over America. During several conversations with the scouts, Grimes held high hopes of hearing his name called in the 2005 MLB draft. After being misled with unfulfilled promises, Grimes set off on an eight-year odyssey in professional baseball. His career in Independent League Baseball, a division of professional baseball that is not affiliated with MLB, is legendary.

During the 2008 season, while playing for the Worcester Tornadoes in the Canadian American Association of Professional Baseball, Grimes was named the MVP of the league. Looking back, Grimes has fond memories of his time in Worcester. The Brewster hitting coach said, "My memories of 2008 in Worcester are special. My manager that year, Red Sox legend Rich Gedman, is one of the two most important men I have met during my years in baseball—the other one being Jamie Shevchik."

After the 2008 season, Grimes was signed to a Minor League contract by the New York Mets. In an unfortunate turn of events, Grimes's playing opportunity with the Mets never really got off the ground due to injuries.

In 2010 Grimes's journey found him playing for the York Revolution in the Atlantic Independent League. Just like in 2008, Grimes tore the league apart. He was named as one of the two best players in the entire league. His last season playing professional baseball was the 2012 season in York, Pennsylvania.

Over the past twelve seasons, Grimes has built a tremendous reputation in the college coaching ranks. Both LaSalle University in Philadelphia and the University of Delaware have provided Grimes with a solid coaching foundation. Both universities have given Grimes the opportunity to coach hitters at the highest level of college baseball.

In 2019, Neumann University, an NCAA Division III program located in Delaware named Scott Grimes as their head baseball coach.

A SEASON WITH THE BREWSTER WHITECAPS
Second Inning—The Lineup

Grimes is in heaven coaching in Brewster with his close friend Shevchik. Best of all for this baseball lifer is that his wife, Ashley, and his two children, Alexa and Onyx, are always close by.

Make sure you get to the Whitecaps games early. The nine-year-old son of Grimes has a personality that will bring all of Brewster to their knees. Onyx does a phenomenal job of singing the National Anthem before games.

MATT HYDE—SCOUT, NEW YORK YANKEES

One of the most overused words in sports today is "legend." Today everyone is called a legend. Just by showing up at a game, even to watch—if you show up enough, you're a legend. It doesn't matter if a player lost every game when they were young. They'll still probably be called a legend at least once during their lifetime.

The real hall of famers and legends will never say a word about themselves. They have self-confidence and carry themselves in such a way that other people, most times, know that they are to be respected. They don't have to sit around reminding everyone and brag about themselves.

Matt Hyde is a Cape Cod baseball legend. Hyde is the legend of legends around Cape Cod baseball. He might not yet be in any hall of fame, but the day will eventually come when the halls of the Cape Cod Baseball League will call out Matt Hyde's name. Hyde is ranked by the *New England Baseball Journal* as one of the most influential men in baseball.

Upon reading this, Hyde will be embarrassed. Every other person who knows this unassuming baseball giant will nod with a smile of respect.

Hyde's job for the last twenty years has been that of a New York Yankees scout for the Northeast. Cape Cod is part of his territory. Cape Cod is Hyde's home. It always was, and it always will be. Hyde's first introduction to baseball came as a little boy of ten years old, when he became a bat kid for the Chatham A's (now Anglers) in the Cape League. Matt's family had just moved from Connecticut. Chatham is where Hyde grew up and started his lifelong love affair with baseball.

In high school Hyde became the bullpen catcher for Orleans. Hyde sums up his life around the Cape in these words: "I've spent so much time around the Cape Cod League; it's a huge part of my life. It was my summer. Every summer, the entire summer—not just a part of the summer months. It was my first exposure to what Major League Baseball was all about. Night games, being in the dugout, the smell of pine tar. All the little things have become lasting memories. I can still taste it all; it's so special. I coached Brewster in 1998 while I was coaching at Michigan, and then I started coaching at Harvard. I also spent the fall of 1996 at Boston College. I've also coached Chatham and Falmouth in the Cape. I played four years at the University of Michigan as a catcher."

The conversation gets around to the hot topic of pitching on Cape Cod. Pitching limits that are set by college coaches, agents, and so-called advisors have become controversial. "In today's world there are a lot of factors influencing pitchers. Many people are fearful that if someone throws too many pitches and innings, they are overdoing it. We see that all the way up to the big leagues. It's like when Roger Bannister ran the four-minute mile. Before that no one had done it. But after he broke it, everyone started doing it. It's going to be the same way with pitchers in baseball. If pitchers start to throw deeper into games, the whole cycle will start to turn around. The Yankees have started to do this. The pitchers are being rewarded by staying in the games longer. Pitchers tend to develop into a role as they progress up the ladder. Velocity is part of the puzzle. But so is pitch ability. There are certain statistics that we pay attention to along with what we see with our eyes. Pitching twenty innings total on the Cape is just a snapshot of moments. Metrics are useful and help the scouts, but so is what we watch at the ballpark as we try to tell the whole story. Kids coming to the Cape haven't experienced a lot of diversity. I think with the exit velocity and launch angle that are being measured from the hitters, we have more tools to use. There is something about throwing. Long toss is very important. 'Feeding the arm' is something we're starting to go back to," Hyde says.

The legend is just warming up. He continues with his discussion of today's pitchers. "I think with exit velocity and launch angles that are being measured from the hitters, you're seeing even more sabermetrics being used. It would be great to see catchers set up more in the middle of the plate facing the wood bats. Get ahead of the hitters and throw strikes. Throwing to the corners is what they teach in college because aluminum bats are so explosive."

Hyde continues, "It used to be that players stayed for the entire summer. Now there is a bigger turnover because of the MLB draft being moved to mid-July. Cape teams now have two different teams: before the season starts and at the end of the season. Players that will be remembered five to ten years from now have a sense of maturity and are willing to stick it out. Players have a lot of distractions today. The essence of the Cape Cod League is all about earning it between the lines. That's not good for the game. It's easy to get worked up about the guys who leave early and are restricted to twenty innings. It's the guys who get challenged and stick it out that are remembered. Peter Gammons, the Hall of Fame baseball writer, always says the game is about the players."

"The kids coming up today are locked into getting information. They can study how the greats do it. The kids watch the highlights. Today's game is evolving back. Moving runners over, pitchers logging more innings—I think we're starting to see the trends evolving back in time," says Hyde.

The conversation moves to the current-day Yankees. "We're all proud of what the Yankees are doing this season. We have a lot of great scouts that make big contributions. We are constantly traveling all over, looking for good players to help the Yankees win.

"I saw Aaron Judge play for Brewster in Falmouth. He was the biggest player I ever saw on the baseball field. There was something that stood out in the way he conducted himself. His year in Brewster, he hit five home runs and batted .270. He hadn't yet developed into the player he is now. In 1993 I caught the home run derby contest in Falmouth between Darin Erstad and George Foster. Foster was hitting home runs into the pond beyond left field. I had not seen it again until Judge did it in 2012. I'll never forget the Cape workout day at Fenway that same year. Judge was different than anyone else. It wasn't just me that scouted Judge. A lot of people in the Yankees organization put a lot into scouting the two-time American league MVP," Hyde explains.

Hyde changes the subject once again, this time to Hyde's buddy, Brewster Manager Shevchik. "Jamie is all about the players. It's unique to find that in today's game. He's not afraid to teach. He lets his kids play without overcoaching them. He's not afraid to ask questions. He understands what makes this league special. He sets high standards. Most of his players want to stay for the entire season. The history of the league is about guys like Jamie. Players come here, and until they get here, they haven't experienced anything but success. They have never had to deal with failure. They haven't been punched in the face by the game. They don't yet know how to get back on their feet. They haven't even been told to do things in a different way. To have guys see it through until the end of the season—those are the ones that hold winning teams together. Jamie has created a special atmosphere in Brewster. Mentors and coaches who hold their players to high standards are worth their weight in gold."

Shevchik also shared his thoughts about his close friend Hyde with me. "When you think of professional scouts and Cape Cod baseball, Matt Hyde is the name that always jumps out. He goes above and beyond what is required of him as a scout. Each year he puts on scouting seminars for our team and other teams. He's always willing to spend time and answer questions from the players. He's a big part of the fabric of the Cape Cod Baseball League. There is no better representative of the New York Yankees than Matt Hyde."

ETHAN KAGNO—DIRECTOR OF BASEBALL OPERATIONS
Ethan Kagno is entering his first season as the Director of Baseball Operations and Analytics for the Brewster Whitecaps. A recent graduate of Western New England University, Kagno brings an incredible amount of baseball savvy that is way beyond his years to his job.

Kagno absolutely thrives around his first love of baseball. Before the Cape season, the young baseball analytics expert spoke about his responsibilities. "During the year I work as the Director of Baseball Operations for Keystone College. I'm with Jamie Shevchik twelve months a year. I handle all the analytics and data for Keystone as well as in Brewster. Jamie trusts my abilities. Jamie has taken me under his wing. We've become very close. He's a player-friendly coach. He's well connected within the nation's coaching fraternity. This entire experience has been unbelievable. This is exactly what I want to do for a career. I also have an online business where I trade and sell baseball cards and other sports-related items. While I was a college student, I spent two summers working in the Cape Cod Baseball League's front office. I helped with the league's analytics. My dad has been with me from day one on my baseball journey."

Kagno changed the conversation to the 2024 prospects for the Brewster Whitecaps. "The roster we have this coming season is loaded with great hitters. Andrew Fischer, an infielder from Ole

Miss, is a legitimate MVP candidate. Another great player is Daniel Cuvet, who just broke the freshman home run record at Miami. Nolan Schubart from Oklahoma State has a chance to be an MLB star. Our offense will be our strength. I'm concerned about our pitching. Our catching position is loaded with great Major League prospects. When Team USA starts at the end of June, they'll be taking away some of our players. I've had to talk with a few player agents. Some have unrealistic views of the players they represent. At times you have to turn down players who think they are good enough to play on the Cape. Building our roster is a twelve-month-a-year job. College coaches trust Jamie when they send their players to play for him. We value players who want to stay all summer. The new name, image, and likeness policy that the NCAA has approved that allows college athletes to get paid has not impacted the Cape yet. I feel half of our roster will get drafted. The hitters that will get drafted in the first two to three rounds have an easier time adjusting to wooden bats than the others."

Remember the name Ethan Kagno. Not only does he have a naturally gifted baseball mind, but his personality will also help him become a well-known MLB executive in the not too far off future.

QUINN MARTIN—BASEBALL OPERATIONS INTERN
Another young baseball analytics specialist is intern Quinn Martin, a recent graduate of the University of South Carolina.

Before the season Martin shared his excitement of working in the Whitecaps analytics department. "I'm super excited to come to Brewster and gain valuable baseball experience on the Cape. I played baseball in high school and made an all-region team after my senior year. Working for the Whitecaps is the biggest break of my life. I'll be constantly looking over reports on players that we can bring to Brewster when roster spots open up. Also, I'll be evaluating and analyzing data from other teams on the Cape, and we'll use that information in our scouting reports when we face them. I'll also be spending a lot of time using the online Synergy Baseball Database used around the country to evaluate players. One of the most important statistics that the database measures is wins above replacement, referred to as WAR. WAR attempts to measure a player's overall value to a team by comparing the player to a replacement-level player. It's a complex system, but it works," said Martin from his home outside of Philadelphia.

NED MONTHIE—BOARD OF DIRECTORS, FORMER GM

It is impossible to find one person that has anything but wonderful words to say about the longtime volunteer of the Brewster Whitecaps, Ned Monthie. Monthie has been with the Brewster Whitecaps organization for over twenty years. He goes all the way back to when he worked as a greeter when the Caps played their home games at Cape Cod Tech in Harwich in 2004.

To say that Monthie has seen it all is an understatement. The retired educator and swimming and diving coach at Shaker High School in Latham, New York, had served the Whitecaps for many years as their general manager. Monthie and his wife, Kathie, would come to Brewster for their summer vacations while he was teaching. That's when they first were introduced to the Whitecaps. Recently he stepped aside from his position as GM after seventeen years but has stayed on the board of directors. Monthie was a fountain of Whitecaps history for this story throughout the 2024 season. The memories for this loyal Brewster supporter are bittersweet. He remembers what it was like to experience the thrill of the championships won by Brewster in 2017 and 2021. He also remembers the agony of unthinkable heartache and tragedy.

Monthie, who fills the role as historian for the Whitecaps, had this to say about his longtime dedication to Brewster. "Back when I started as the GM, we didn't have as much of a turnover of players coming and going during the summer. I still have every signed contract from every player who ever played during my years as GM. The 2017 Cape League championship was unbelievable. It was ecstatic to witness. What a thrill. The place went wild. We were the underdogs and wouldn't quit. The five thousand fans in the crowd that day were all on the field after the game, all hugging each other. I'll never forget it."

The conversation turned to heartbreak when the name John Altobelli was mentioned. It took several minutes for this amazing man with a kind heart to compose himself and speak of his dear friend. "He was my manager for three years. He was a fantastic man. He was a fantastic man. He was a fantastic coach. He was a fantastic person. He was a fantastic baseball coach. It was a gut punch. Even today it's a gut punch. We worked well together. We weren't best buddies, but we respected each other. He was a great family man. I stood still for several minutes when I first heard the news. It was a gut punch that brought me to my knees."

John Altobelli was the manager of the Brewster Whitecaps from 2012 to 2014. Altobelli and his wife, Keri, and their thirteen-year-old daughter, Allyssa, were all killed in the helicopter crash that took the lives of Kobe Bryant and his thirteen-year-old daughter, Gianna. All were onboard, going to a travel team basketball game where the young girls were playing together as teammates. The tragedy shook Brewster and the entire Cape Cod Baseball League. Even today the emotion of the tragedy brings unbearable grief.

Aaron Judge, the American League MVP of the New York Yankees, who had played for Altobelli during his first year as the Whitecaps' manager in 2012, was at a loss for words at the time of his death. In January 2020, after the crash, Judge could only speak three words about it to the national media. They were "This isn't real…"

The conversation changed back to more pleasant memories. "I have so many great memories of all the players and coaches that have come through Brewster during my years. It's hard to just mention one name. I have enjoyed following the success of all the players, not just the ones who made it into the Major Leagues. There are so many changes impacting college athletics today, and I hope the Cape Cod League will survive them," said Monthie.

Mr. Ned Monthie represents everything that is good about the Brewster Whitecaps.

Chuck Hanson—Project Manager
Chuck Hanson has been with the Whitecaps organization for ten years. As the project manager, Hanson has had his hands on many parts of what takes place within the organization throughout that time. When Hanson was given the opportunity to say whatever it was that came to his mind when he heard the words "Brewster Whitecaps," the engineer by trade was off and going. "Great baseball and family entertainment" were the first two things that Hanson said.

The Whitecaps are extremely fortunate to have this brilliant man on their board of directors. Some of his many functions are overseeing the scoreboard, monitoring the parking lot, building the website, helping Alton Cole with the field maintenance, placing the safety netting all the way down the baselines for the safety of the fans, and several other capital improvements that have been tended to. He modestly summed up his work as "being part of a team where everyone pitches in to help out."

When the subject turned to what goes on during the season with the team and what some of Hanson's favorite memories are, the soft-spoken jack of all trades was quick to respond. "Jamie is a very good coach, just excellent. He's a great mentor and has great relationships with his players and coaches. I'll never forget the 2021 season and the way the team came together to win the championship. That's my favorite on-field memory."

When asked to name a few of his favorite all-time players that have performed well during his years of service, the first of the three names he mentioned was the great Zach Neto, the current shortstop phenom for the Los Angeles Angels. Other players high on Hanson's list are Mason Black, a pitcher with the San Francisco Giants by way of Lehigh University. Another name mentioned by Hanson was Spencer Jones, the top prospect in the New York Yankees Minor League system.

The Brewster Whitecaps are very fortunate to have Chuck Hanson on their team.

Third Inning—The 2024 Cape Cod Season Begins

PRESEASON SCRIMMAGE: BREWSTER WHITECAPS AND WAREHAM GATEMEN AT BOURNE BRAVES

WITH THE OPENING DAY OF the 2024 Cape Cod Baseball League season quickly approaching, it was time for the players and coaches to get to the field and introduce themselves. For the players who had already arrived in Brewster from all over America, the chance to put on their brand-new Whitecaps gear gave them the thrill of realizing that their dream of playing baseball on Cape Cod had come true.

It wasn't just the players who were filled with anticipation. It also was the coaches, interns, and the volunteers that had been waiting.

The dawn of a new baseball season brings unmatched excitement to a community like no other event. All winter long, Brewster Whitecaps Nation had been counting down the days until opening day. The New England winters can be bitterly cold. Even though Cape Cod receives less snow in the winter than some of the other New England communities, the temperature can be brutal.

When baseball arrives back every spring in this sport's crazed region of America, there is a feeling of invigoration that brings smiles to everyone's faces.

It doesn't matter if it's the region's favorite professional sports team, the Boston Red Sox, or the Brewster Whitecaps of the Cape Cod Baseball League. Spring arrives with another baseball season filled with both hope and promise.

Call it what you will, but when you think of Cape Cod Baseball, its imagery can bring visions right out of a Norman Rockwell scene. Yup, straight out of a nonstop dream with all the trimmings. Listen closely, and the sound of the ball and a bat connecting sounds like it's coming from wooden bats. Oh my, what a beautiful sound. It's as beautiful as the ospreys that flock overhead to get a bird's-eye view of the action.

Cape Cod baseball will bring goose bumps to every fan, player, coach, scout, umpire, volunteer, host family member, or anyone who understands the magic that a game in the summer on Cape Cod will bring. Call it tradition, call it historic, call it old-school, but there is no denying that the values that made America so great are interwound in the fabric of this 101-year-old tradition.

The music was blaring as the players and the coaches from the Brewster Whitecaps, the Wareham Gatemen, and the Bourne Braves meandered slowly from their yellow school buses in the parking lot at Upper Cape Cod Regional Technical High School. The temperature was a warm seventy-five degrees. There wasn't a cloud in the sky. As the players walked to the baseball field behind the school in Bourne, the sparkle they all had was that of the hopes that this summer might in fact be their steppingstone to an MLB career.

This gathering of the Bourne Braves, Wareham Gatemen, and the Whitecaps just a couple of days before opening day was to be used to let everyone start getting used to their new coaches and teammates. It was also time to start swinging the bats and loosening up their arms.

The three teams were hand-selected by their managers to

participate in this unusual style of scrimmage. Jamie Shevchik of Brewster, Scott Landers of Bourne, and Ryan Smythe of Wareham are the very best of friends. They all coached together in Brewster and at Keystone College in Pennsylvania for many years. For the managers of the three teams, it was a mini-reunion.

The scrimmage was not just for the players; it was also a warm-up for the many student-interns who traveled to the Cape from all over. The college interns came to Cape Cod to gain some valuable career experiences and to finally put to use their major fields of study. Of course, they also came to enjoy what they hoped would become the greatest summer of their young lives.

Sean O'Neil, a recent graduate of Western New England University, grew up in Hartford, Connecticut. O'Neil came to games on the Cape with his family for many summers. Now he would be interning as a videographer for all the Whitecaps' games. O'Neil was "super hyped" to begin his summer work.

Avery Raimondo, a rising junior at the University of North Florida majoring in video and video production, would be using her summer to gain valuable experience in her field and to network and build new relationships. Raimondo's brother had interned for Brewster a few years earlier.

Shevchik was one of the last to come strolling into Doran Park, the name of the home field for the Bourne Braves. For the friendly skipper, the smile hasn't left his face since he became the Brewster Whitecaps' manager ten years earlier.

There is an air of confidence that Shevchik gives off. It's not cocky, and it's certainly not arrogance. It's probably because he has won two Cape Cod League Championships during his Brewster tenure. It also doesn't hurt that he has won a mind-boggling nineteen straight college conference championships managing the Keystone College Giants in Pennsylvania.

Before the scrimmage started, Jarrod Saltalamacchia, the

former Boston Red Sox catching legend who helped lead the Sox to a World Series Championship in 2013, addressed the players from all three teams.

Saltalamacchia has been coaching in Bourne for three summers. He told the players that they were "the elite of the elite." The players all stood at attention listening to the legend's words carefully. They all understood his place in Red Sox lore, and they each had dreams to follow in his footsteps. Saltalamacchia continued, "I loved my years playing for the Boston Red Sox. The fans were tough, but I welcomed that. They expected us to win, and I liked it that way because I expected us to win also."

The former Red Sox catcher was just warming up. "You are here because of your abilities. The money you will possibly earn will come from what you do here on the Cape. This is your job. Most of you play in beautiful, state-of-the-art facilities in college. The Cape is old-school. Some of the fields might remind you of the old sandlot baseball fields. Take advantage of this."

"This is the most important test in your young careers. Scouts are going to evaluate you in everything you do on and off the field. When you think they are not watching you, they still are watching everything you do and even how you interact with your teammates and coaches. Soon you'll be going up against young Dominican players who are sixteen, seventeen, and eighteen years old whose entire lives are baseball. They are competing for the same future jobs you are being showcased for," the retired catcher added.

"When or if you get drafted, don't hold out for more bonus money. Take what they offer; don't try and get $20,000 to $30,000 more. Your bonus money, even a couple of million dollars, will run out quicker than you think. If you're good enough to make it into MLB, you will make your money. Get your career started as soon as possible, and when your career is over, then go back to college and finish your degree, as I'm doing now." The former catcher concluded his remarks as if he wanted to resume his own playing career.

Every player stood stone-cold, listening intently to every spoken word by Saltalamacchia. You could see their minds racing. They were thinking to themselves, "This is my dream."

The scrimmage was going to be quite different. Players from all three teams lined up and took turns swinging at four pitches each. All the pitchers also lined up and each took turns pitching to four batters. The rotation continued until every player from all three teams had their turn.

The first batter for the Brewster Whitecaps to step to the plate was the young freshman phenom from the University of Miami, Dan Cuvet. This rising sophomore third baseman had just been tabbed as a Freshman All-American.

Cuvet stepped into the batter's box, and you could just sense he was something special on a baseball field. His body and the confidence with which he carried himself showed maturity beyond his years. When you looked at him more closely, he had a look in his eyes—they were laser-focused. He had the handsome look of a young Mickey Mantle. You just had a feeling that Cuvet was not only going to attract attention from the MLB scouts assigned to the Cape, but he was also going to attract attention from some pretty college co-eds.

Cuvet displayed an easy stance at the plate while resting his wooden bat on his shoulder. As the pitcher made his stride to the plate with his delivery, Cuvet cocked his bat back and took a short, smooth, and powerful swing. The fences may not be far enough back for this highly rated player.

The first pitcher to take the mound for the Whitecaps was Luke Schmolke. Schmolke is a rising third-year college player who transferred to Wake Forest after pitching his freshman year for Georgia

Tech. In keeping with the NCAA transfer rules, Schmolke had to sit out his sophomore season at Wake Forest this past season of 2024. This will give him an extra year to perform in college should he decide to stay until he graduates. There is always a chance that he will be rated highly by scouts at the Cape and get drafted and sign with an MLB team in the next year or two.

Schmolke is a left-hander with remarkable poise. Each pitch he threw to the four batters was delivered with pinpoint accuracy. After sitting out, he threw with nice velocity that will surely catch the eyes of MLB scouts once the real games begin.

The scrimmage was a huge success. Everything the three managers wanted to accomplish had been checked off. It was time for the Brewster Whitecaps to get back on the yellow school bus that had been waiting for the ride back to their new summer hometown.

This was definitely not the last bus ride they would take during the summer of 2024.

ORIENTATION DAY

The following afternoon the entire Brewster Whitecaps organization assembled at Stony Brook Field, the home of the Brewster Whitecaps. This was another day everyone was anticipating with great enthusiasm.

Formal introductions were the order of the day. Everyone would be introduced, regardless of what role they would have during the summer months.

Almost 150 eager members of Whitecaps Nation sat in the bleachers on the home side of the infield, which at Stony Brook Field is on the third base side.

Team President Luke Dillon, Whitecaps General Manager Jon Mecca, Cape Cod Baseball League Commissioner John Castleberry, and of course Shevchik all took turns welcoming everyone to Brewster Whitecaps Nation.

Each speaker took turns introducing everyone in attendance and explained the jobs they had been assigned. It was goose bumps time in Brewster.

Two members of the team's board of directors, Pat Eggers and Chris Kenney, have been serving the Caps community in many roles for several years. This dedicated husband and wife team bleed Whitecaps teal.

Like so many others involved in the Cape Cod Baseball League, Eggers gives her heart to the Brewster organization. Eggers had this to say at the orientation: "This is just awesome. My husband Chris manages the team store. We've been hosting players since 2008. I've been on the board since 2009 and have been feeding all the players and interns after each game for the last five or six years."

Organizing team meals after all forty games for sixty players and interns is a massive undertaking. It's an undertaking that only special volunteers enjoy. Eggers's contributions to her team and entire community are enormous. "It takes an entire community to support the Whitecaps. Both my husband and I are proud to support this team. It's a huge time commitment, but we find it all very rewarding," Eggers said.

Kenney, like his wife, joined the board of directors in 2009. During the time since, Kenney has held many different roles. During the hectic afternoon of meeting and greeting, Kenney paused for a few minutes to share the different jobs he has filled over the years. "I've been the treasurer, the assistant general manager, and the president. We got started with the organization when we moved from New York to Brewster. We were friends with someone in our ski club who kept encouraging us to become a player host family. Finally, we said, 'What the heck.' We have two empty bedrooms upstairs in our home, and we finally started to host in 2008. We've been involved ever since."

As the afternoon moved on and everyone was enjoying their meal served by Eggers and Sullivan, friendships had already developed. There was only one last item left on the list.

LET'S GOOOO CAPS...

OPENING DAY—WHITECAPS AT YARMOUTH-DENNIS RED SOX

There is nothing in American sports that makes you feel more invigorated and fuller of excitement than celebrating an opening day to a new baseball season. The euphoria can take your breath away.

Baseball was back on Cape Cod. For the 101st year in a row, the two most glorious words attached to the American Pastime were being shouted at all the ball fields on Cape Cod.

"PLAY BALL!"

On a picture-perfect day at Dennis-Yarmouth High School, the baseball field behind the school looked prim and primed. Merrill "Red" Wilson Field was all set for another season.

Over three thousand fans circled the outside of the field with their lawn chairs. The weather was a perfect seventy-six degrees on this late afternoon in mid-June.

Several of the fans were lined up at the souvenir tent with big smiles, anticipating how good it would feel to wear the new Yarmouth-Dennis Red Sox ball caps they were about to purchase.

Two longtime residents of the Yarmouth-Dennis community, Terry Bradshaw (not the retired football player) and Kathy Baxter, were being honored before the game. Bradshaw, a recently retired longtime educator, sang the National Anthem. Baxter threw out the first pitch. Baxter is a two-time cancer survivor.

Patrick Forbes, standing at six feet three, finished his 2024 college campaign at the University of Louisville with a 0–1 record and a 3.72 ERA. Forbes was selected by Brewster Manager Jamie Shevchik to be the opening-day pitcher for the Whitecaps. Forbes had just recovered from an injury and was fired up to show the MLB scouts in attendance that he was healthy again. In 2023 he also hit .258 with three home runs and nineteen RBIs for Louisville. The talented two-way player was selected to the 2023 All-ACC Academic Team. This is Forbes's second year in Brewster. Forbes said before the game, "I came back to give the wonderful people of Brewster a better season than we gave them last year." He has an air about him that leaves no doubt he is focused on why he is pitching on the Cape. Forbes is being counted on to be the ace of the Whitecaps pitching staff for 2024.

Kellan Montgomery, with a 3–4 record and a 3.95 ERA this past college season for Long Beach State, got the nod as the starting pitcher for Yarmouth-Dennis.

The first batter of the game for the Caps, Nick Dumesnil Jr., an outfielder from California Baptist, led off the season for the Brewster Whitecaps by striking out looking. This wasn't going to happen very often to Dumesnil in the summer of 2024. He quickly made his way to the dugout to let his teammates know that Montgomery threw a changeup, fastball, and slider. Andrew Fischer (transferring from Mississippi to Tennessee for the 2024 season) came up next, and the highly touted infielder got on with an error. Nolan Schubart, the future high draft choice out of Oklahoma State, lined the second pitch he saw to right field for the first hit of the season for the Caps.

Batting cleanup, Cuvet grounded out to end the inning. The six-feet-three, 237-pound Cuvet had just finished a stellar freshman campaign at the University of Miami. He put together a terrific season regardless of what year a player is in. Cuvet batted .351 with twenty-four home runs and seventy-five RBIs. With a .736 slugging percentage, the freshman was invited to attend the training camp for Team USA this summer. All eyes were locked on this incredible baseball talent.

Forbes took the mound, and he wasted no time in taking command of his fastball. Pitching out of the stretch and throwing in the mid-nineties, Forbes showed great control, hitting the strike zone consistently.

In the bottom of the second, Yarmouth-Dennis loaded the bases. Forbes dug down deep to get out of the inning behind a couple of great defensive plays made by the Whitecaps for the final two outs. Forbes walked off the mound and gave his teammates a sly grin, knowing he had just gotten out of a possibly costly jam.

The handsome Louisville Cardinal Forbes is a power pitcher with great lower body strength. His push off the mound reminds some of a young Roger Clemens. Forbes had a tremendous first outing, striking out nine and giving up only two hits in four complete innings of work. He too has been invited to try out for Team USA at the end of June. All the Whitecaps fans are hoping he returns later in the season.

The game was moving along quickly. As in other years, the early season pitching was way out ahead of the hitters making the transition from aluminum to wooden bats.

The Caps scored first in the top of the fourth as they pushed across a run when Schubart scored on an error made by the Y-D third baseman.

Schmolke, making his first ever Cape appearance, was the first pitcher out of the bullpen in the summer of 2024 for Brewster. A transfer from Georga Tech, Schmolke left the big city of Atlanta for a more comfortable fit on the Tobacco Road in Winston-Salem, North Carolina. The crafty sophomore left-hander kept the Red Sox off balance and escaped a bases-loaded jam in the sixth, giving up only one run on a sacrifice fly.

Grant Cunningham of Washington University was brought in to take over for Schmolke with two outs in the bottom of the eighth and retired the next four batters to send the game into extra innings. With pitching dominating the game for both teams, the nine innings were played with lightning quickness in two hours and fifteen minutes.

The Cape Cod Baseball League uses the same rule as Major League Baseball when a game goes into extra innings. Each team starts their side of the tenth by putting a runner on second base. The only difference is that if a game is tied after ten innings, the game is halted, and each team is credited with a tie in the standings.

Brewster was shut down to start the tenth by Northeastern University pitcher Aiven Cabral as he struck out both Caps power hitters, Schubart and Cuvet. In the bottom of the tenth, Y-D finally scored off Cunningham when Johnathan Kim drove in Cameron Kim from second base with the winning run. Y-D emptied their dugout and mobbed the Kim brothers while celebrating an opening-game victory.

The game was a typical early-season Cape game, with the Caps pitching giving up only five hits and striking out fifteen batters. The Caps left ten men on base as they had their chances throughout but just couldn't seem to move their runners over. Both teams combined for seven errors as the play, at times, was a little sloppy.

After the game, Brewster manager Jamie Shevchik said, "Pitching dominates this league, so I'm not worried. I like our makeup. We must fight as hard as we can with each at-bat and play fundamentally better. It will all come together. We're back at it tomorrow for our home opener, and I know our guys will be ready."

CC Sabathia, the retired future Hall of Fame pitcher with the Yankees and Indians, attended the game to support his son, Carsten, who is playing for Brewster. After the game Sabathia said, "This is my dream to watch my son play for the Brewster Whitecaps in the Cape Cod League against the best competition in America."

For delicious clam chowder, Oyster Company Raw Bar and Grill in Dennis Port is the perfect place to go for those who attend a game at Yarmouth-Dennis.

BOURNE BRAVES AT WHITECAPS

Stony Brook Field was all dressed up and looking pretty for opening day. The schoolchildren that attend Stony Brook Elementary School adjacent to the field were playing on their playground during recess. You could hear their loud squeals as they knew their heroes were back in town. On a beautiful late-spring day, you could smell the fresh Cape Cod flowers that had just bloomed. The Whitecaps were finally returning home after a long, cold winter.

Sullivan was her usual giddy self. Running all over the field with big hugs and smiles for everyone she could find, she was gushing with pure enthusiasm. Sullivan had been working literally hundreds of hours doing all kinds of volunteer work for her hometown Cape team throughout the calendar year. Sullivan has been dedicated to the Brewster Whitecaps for many years. Now her boys were back in town.

Dillon was going over last-minute details. Mecca, the Whitecaps' newly appointed general manager, was excited about starting in his new role with the team. The Whitecaps' manager, the ever popular and loveable baseball lifer Shevchik, who has been living his dream on the Cape for the past ten summers with his family, was his usual happy-go-lucky self.

As the pregame ceremonies started, several Brewster community members were honored on the field. Six-year-old Cam Ellis and recently retired longtime educator David Rost each took a turn throwing out the ceremonial first pitch. Althea Alling, aged 103 years young, was recognized as the oldest living Whitecap fan. Jim Nosler, the talented singer, sang the National Anthem.

Over two thousand fans came out to welcome their beloved Whitecaps to Brewster for the summer.

The game started once again with the usual early-season pitching dominating the college players transitioning from aluminum to wooden bats for this showcase league.

The game rolled along until the top of the ninth, when shortstop Chase Mora made a spectacular catch that could go down as one of the top web gems of the year when the season ends. With the bases loaded and his team trailing by two runs in the top of the ninth, Bourne Braves center fielder Isaiah Jackson (Arizona State) hit a looping fly ball toward shallow left field, perfectly placed for an RBI single.

Brewster Whitecaps shortstop Chase Mora had other plans. The Texas State product tracked back from the infield, snagging the ball as he dove into the outfield grass. "When it went up, I knew it was going to be an in-between ball, so I just took off, and he [right fielder Nolan Schubart of Oklahoma State] ended up saying, 'Take it, take it,'" Mora said postgame. "At that point I was like, all right, I got to make a play here. Game on the line, got to make a play."

The acrobatic play all but sealed the win for the Whitecaps (1–1, 0–1 East Division), who went on to earn a home-opening 4–3 victory over the Braves (1–1) on Sunday evening at Stony Brook Field. "To see him come up with that play, that's why he's playing where he is," said Brewster Manager Jamie Shevchik.

Nolan Schubart, the big slugger from Oklahoma State, hit a towering home run for his first of the summer. The homer chased away every osprey flying overhead in the midsummer weather at the Cape. It left over two thousand opening-day fans hungry for more of the same.

"He's got some serious juice," Shevchik said of Schubart. "That's why he's here. That's what we've been watching throughout the college season, waiting for that to come up. He's going hit a lot more." During the just completed college season, Schubart had a game for all time. Playing for the Oklahoma State Cowboys, Schubart hit four home runs in one game in early May against Wichita State.

Darien Smith continued the stellar pitching the Caps had received in the heartbreaking loss in their opener. Smith, the first team NAIA All-American from Southeastern University in Jacksonville, Florida, is back for his second summer in Brewster. He went 4⅓ innings, gave up two runs, and struck out eight. Catcher Gio Cueto out of Stetson University played a brilliant game behind the plate and contributed a double for his first Cape hit of the season.

Shevchik has decided to go with his most experienced pitchers early on in this young season. Jacob Marlowe (Florida State), Will Ray (Wake Forest), and Sonny Fauci (Rutgers) all contributed to keeping the bats quiet for the Bourne Braves.

The appearance for Marlowe was a personal milestone. This young man had not pitched in a year. He is returning to the mound after undergoing two open heart surgeries within a two-month period during the past winter holiday season.

The yummy clam chowder at JT's Seafood, located on Main Street in Brewster, was warming and waiting for all the fans to stop by after the game.

Whitecaps at Hyannis Harbor Hawks

Van Morrison summed up the game in his famous song "Days Like This":

"Oh, my mama told me there'll be days like this."

With the Whitecaps trailing 4–1 to the Harbor Hawks in the top of the seventh inning, Jayden Hylton stood on second base while JD Rogers (Vanderbilt) was perched on first. Helfrick ripped the first pitch of the at-bat foul before letting the next two pass for balls. Then Helfrick drove a 2–1 fastball to the left-center gap. Hyannis left fielder Kane Kepley (Liberty) tracked all the way back to the base of the wall, reached up, and caught it, thwarting the threat and preserving the three-run lead.

The Harbor Hawks went on to plate six runs over the next

two innings, ballooning their lead to as much as seven. In the end, Brewster fell, 10–4, to Hyannis at McKeon Park on Monday. "You learn everything from losing and very little from winning," Brewster manager Jamie Shevchik said postgame.

Hyannis is considered the unofficial capital of Cape Cod. Over twelve thousand year-round residents live in Hyannis. It has an active regional airport in the center of town. Hyannis is famous as the longtime residence of the iconic Kennedy family. The famous President John Kennedy and his high-profile brothers and sisters, with their families, would spend their summer months vacationing in the Kennedy compound along the shores of Cape Cod. Recently, Main Street in Hyannis has undergone a much-needed facelift.

As famous as Hyannis is because of the Kennedy family, it may even be more famous for the clam chowder that Spanky's Clam Shack and Seaside Saloon prepares.

In the top of the first, Brewster scored on a bases-loaded walk from Cooper Vest (BYU). Jayden Hylton (Stetson) then grounded out, leaving three runners on base. In the bottom half, the Harbor Hawks reached on multiple soft-contact hits before a line drive from Wallace Clark (Duke) and a sacrifice fly from Michael Dattalo (Dallas Baptist) scored two to take the lead. From there, Hyannis never relinquished its lead.

Whitecaps starter Ashton Crowther (Miami) then went to work, retiring nine of the final ten batters he faced. On the other end, Nic McCay (South Dakota) worked through the Whitecaps offense, blowing away the heart of the Whitecaps order by retiring Fischer (Ole Miss) and Schubart (Oklahoma State) in the third inning.

Cuvet recorded his first hit of the season, driving in both runners with a double to right field. With Cuvet representing the tying run on second, he was doubled up to end the threat. It won't be long before the word will spread all over the Cape and fans flock to watch this handsome teenager who just turned nineteen years of age.

For Shevchik, as he continues to evaluate his team in the early going, the glaring example in style of play rested in the opposing team's dugout. The Harbor Hawks worked tough at-bats, fouling off pitches and not chasing pitches out of the strike zone often. "We made mistakes because Hyannis had pesky at-bats and forced us into making a couple of errors," said the manager after the game.

Shevchik, the patient manager who has won two Cape championships during his first nine years, is the perfect man to bring along this talented team and to keep everyone moving in the right direction. Brewster fell to one win and two losses as the River Hawks remained unbeaten with three wins in the young season.

All wasn't lost on this night, though. All New England had reason to celebrate the Celtics winning their eighteenth NBA Championship.

Fourth Inning—Falmouth Turns Its Lonely Eyes to Paul Mitchell

You can find several Whitecaps players and coaches milling around the popular hangout Café Alfresco most mornings. This popular breakfast-and-lunch stop is located on Main Street in the heart of Brewster. Twelve months a year, the year-round baseball fans who reside in Brewster use this café as their hot-stove meeting place. Café Alfresco is proud of their relationship with the Whitecaps as they have remained a strong sponsor of the organization. Customers can't help but notice the enlarged photo of the Whitecaps celebrating their Cape championship in 2017 on the wall over the counter.

The day started no differently than any other early-season game day on the Cape. The fans and players alike were still beaming with enthusiasm for the start of a new season. The players on the Whitecaps understood they were being touted as one of the early season favorites to capture another banner.

Coaches were coming in and out of the restaurant, grabbing coffee on the fly as the families of the players were eating Café Alfresco's famous avocado toast in the cozy restaurant.

Jacob Lenau is a nineteen-year-old college student who works part time at Café Alfresco. Like the rest of the community, he was fired up for the start of a new season. "I'm so excited for the

Whitecaps. I can't wait to make it to a couple of games. Let's go Whitecaps!" Joanie Guffin, age twenty-two, also works in the restaurant. "I'm from Brewster. I love meeting the players when they come in. I can't wait to get to some games this season—go Caps!" Kiley Mawn, another summer employee, is sixteen years old. She said, "I'm excited for the season and to make it to a couple of games." Whitecaps pride runs deep in this popular hangout.

The game versus Falmouth gave the Whitecaps an opportunity to steady the ship against some of the tough sailing they were experiencing early in the season.

The players were all in a festive mood on the hour-long bus ride to Falmouth. The team was developing great team chemistry. They were all excited, knowing they were the elite of the elite in America and were handpicked to play in the top summer wooden-bat showcase league in the country. They didn't have to be reminded of some of the greats who came before them in Brewster, like current Yankee great Aaron Judge, the record setting shortstop phenom for the Los Angeles Angels, Zach Neto, possible future Hall of Famer Billy Wagner, former National League MVP Ryan Braun, three-time National League All-Star and Cincinnati Reds Hall of Famer Sean Casey, six-time All-Star Chase Utley, and countless others. This was their turn to open the eyes of the more than one hundred MLB scouts who they would be performing for throughout the season.

Jimmy Buffett was blaring along with some modern rap music. You could hear the players keeping in rhythm. Afternoon rush hour traffic on Route 6, which starts from one end of the Cape and ends at the most eastern part of the Cape in Provincetown, was quite busy on this warm June afternoon.

The laughter was lighting up the yellow school bus as it rocked along through Cotuit on the way to Falmouth. The bus driver, Kayla Ellis, was enjoying the banter with the players sitting up

Fourth Inning—Falmouth Turns Its Lonely Eyes to Paul Mitchell

front. A group of players sitting in the back were enjoying getting to know their new teammates.

You could see the lights of Guv Fuller Field, the home of the Falmouth Commodores, from a mile away on Route 28. Route 28 can be a traffic nightmare when the seasonal summer vacationers start showing up at the end of June.

The Dairy Queen directly across the street from the field had its steady nonstop stream of customers backed up to the curb. Falmouth's Main Street was already prepared for the onslaught of a new summer season. Falmouth Harbor Marina already was filling its boat slips. The beachgoers were already showing up on Falmouth's beautiful beaches. Jim's Clam Shack was preparing its delicious clam chowder for the dinner hour.

Mid-August is also a special time of year when thousands of runners pilgrimage to Falmouth for the world-famous Falmouth Road Race.

Falmouth has had a team in the Cape League going all the way back to when the league first formed in 1923. In 1964 the team moved from Falmouth Heights and began using Fuller Field on Main Street, right behind the town's police station. Guv Fuller Field has been their home ever since.

The Commodores have a rather large band of followers and volunteers, like Ms. Emerald, who cheerfully works in the concession stand.

Their tradition gets mixed reviews. In the past fifty-three seasons, the franchise has only one championship to show. About 35 percent of the Commodores have made it to the Majors, and about 80 percent have been drafted by MLB teams. But they have only hoisted the championship trophy once in the last fifty-three years. Their long-time manager Jeff Trundy is one of the most renowned baseball managers in America.

Commodore fans have been entertained by many of baseball's

greats. Former AL Cy Young Award winner the late Mike Flanagan, Darin Erstad, Travis Bazzana, Bill Almon, the late Stan Saleski, and Tino Martinez, to name only a few, have come through Falmouth.

Another thing fans enjoy throughout the games played in Falmouth are the many ospreys that are perched high above the light towers and continually circle the ballpark.

On this beautiful evening in June, many of the longtime fans were sitting around reminiscing about the good-old-days. They have been patiently waiting for a return of the glory years gone by. In the far-off distance, you could almost hear the lyrics of Simon and Garfunkel and their famous song, "Mrs. Robinson." While listening, I noticed there was a slight change of the names in the song.

Where have you gone, Paul Mitchell?
Falmouth turns its lonely eyes to you,
What's that you say, Manager Livesey?
"Mitch the Pitch" has left and gone away..."
Hey...hey...hey...

Paul Mitchell, the Cape Cod Baseball Hall of Fame legend, had the greatest three-year career of any pitcher who has ever pitched in the Cape Cod Baseball League. For three seasons from 1969 through 1971, Mitchell led the Commodores to three straight CCBL championships. The Worcester Academy graduate who grew up in the heart of Red Sox country set the Cape ablaze. His career totals have never come close to being duplicated, and they never will.

During his three seasons, Mitchell won twenty-five games and lost only five. He pitched in a total of 259 career innings. He struck out a total of 315 batters (an astonishing 126 came in one season), still a Cape record. His career ERA (earned run average) on the Cape is a staggering 1.52 runs per game.

Fourth Inning—Falmouth Turns Its Lonely Eyes to Paul Mitchell

Besides pitching in three all-star games and being the winning pitcher in two, Paul Mitchell did something that today's pitchers can't even comprehend. Mitchell completed nineteen straight complete nine-inning games during his final two seasons pitching for the Commodores.

Today Mitchell fondly remembers his glory days in Falmouth. Paul talks candidly even today about today's pitching limits. "Today, when someone is taken out after five innings and eighty pitches, it's a joke. If I didn't go at least seven innings, I would consider it a bad start. I could throw hard, but pitching in Falmouth taught me how to control the plate and become a complete pitcher. That is the most valuable lesson I learned on the Cape. That became invaluable throughout my six-year Major League career.

"Bill Livesey, who coached at Worcester Academy, was my manager in Falmouth. Before my first season there, he took me aside and told me he wasn't taking me out of a game because he had no one better to put in than me," Mitchell explains.

"Strikeouts are high today because everyone is trying to hit home runs. The Sosa-McGwire era of the nineties changed the way kids hit today. When I pitched for Earl Weaver, the Manager of the Baltimore Orioles, he used the philosophy 'If you're pitching well, I'm not taking you out.' How are you going to get better if they send you home after completing twenty innings in one season on the Cape?" Mitchell says. (Many times, that is the inning limit the colleges set for their pitchers when they send them to the Cape.)

"I hear college coaches won't let their better pitchers play at the Cape because of selfish reasons. That makes zero sense to me. How are they ever going to get better? If a kid goes into a game thinking he's going to pitch only five innings, he's going to develop a bad mindset, and that's not good. I had the mindset that I was going to finish what I started," the record setter points out.

"It was the best of times for me. As a college student at Old

Dominion University, pitching in Falmouth was invaluable. Back when I played, we were hated. Falmouth was like the Yankees of our era on the Cape. I didn't go there with the intention of setting records. Teach good mechanics and let the kids pitch," Mitchell concludes.

Mitchell became a first-round MLB draft pick by the Baltimore Orioles in 1971. He enjoyed a six-year Major League career pitching for the Orioles, Oakland A's, Seattle Mariners, and Milwaukee Brewers.

Shevchik knows his team is talented enough to thrive in the Cape Cod Baseball League. For Shevchik and the Whitecaps, that understanding made their loss to Falmouth even more frustrating. "We're just not meeting the expectations of what the talent is supposed to be," the manager said postgame.

In Cuvet, Brewster boasts one of the nation's top rising sophomores. In Schubart, it has an All-American. In Fischer, it possesses a top 2025 MLB draft prospect.

Each has shown their potential through the first few games of the season, but the Whitecaps have yet to put the pieces together. That was evident in the 13–5 road defeat to the Falmouth Commodores at Guv Fuller Field. "Games are decided, in many cases, early," Shevchik said. "The score might have been 13–5, but it could have been totally different when you take a two-run lead that could have been a four-run lead."

Blake Cavill (Western Kentucky) and Luke Gaffney (Clemson) reached base for Falmouth to begin the bottom of the fourth. Brewster escaped the jam in rare fashion. Right fielder Dumesnil caught a broken-bat fly ball and tossed it to Vest at first, who tagged out a retreating Gaffney for the second out. Then, Vest threw to Mora (Texas State) for the out at second, since Cavill had also misjudged the fly ball.

It was only the eighth triple play in Cape League history,

according to league historian Mike Richard, and the first since the Orleans Firebirds completed the feat in 2022.

Cuvet was a bright spot, reaching base in all four of his at-bats with two walks and two singles. After a slow start, he had reached five straight times, including a two-run RBI double in the eighth inning of the previous day's game at Hyannis. "The more pitches that he sees, the more comfortable he gets," Shevchik said. "He's getting better swings."

Still, the loss was marked by Brewster's lack of timely hitting and an inability for the pitchers to limit the damage with runners on base. "When we get into next week, there's things that obviously need to change," Shevchik said. "We're starting 1–3, so we've got our work cut out for us. For the next week, we have to roll with what we got. We won't be adding anyone until after the College World Series.

WAREHAM GATEMEN AT WHITECAPS
When Brewster Coach Dylan Cooper arrived at Stony Brook Field for the Wareham game, he was thinking ahead, hoping like the rest of the Whitecaps coaching staff. They were all waiting for the potentially lethal lineup that had existed on paper to finally show up and start doing some damage. What Dylan didn't realize was that his hitters were waiting for Cooper's wife to arrive from West Virginia with their newborn son. When Tarin Cooper and baby Colten arrived by car from West Virginia at the field, the players greeted the two-week-old with a celebration heard all over the Cape. Instead of champagne and cigars, the Whitecaps' bats finally exploded.

Cooper couldn't stop gushing after the game. "This is one of the most special days of my life. Colten was here for his first baseball game. My wife Tarin drove with him from our home in West Virginia where I coach at West Virginia Wesleyan College.

I'll remember this night for a very long time," Cooper exclaimed while standing on the field.

The Whitecaps had just lost two games in a row by a combined margin of fourteen runs. A lineup full of high-profile prospects was performing well below expectations, resulting in a 1–3 start to the Cape Cod Baseball League season. As Whitecaps Manager Shevchik indulged in a day at the beach with his family the day before the big win (like many involved in the league do during an off day), the roster, as well as future lineup constructions, circulated through his head. "I've been looking at this roster for the past eight months," Shevchik said. "I'm thinking to myself, 'Did I really get this wrong?'" Shevchik didn't get it wrong. It just took a little longer than expected.

Following the first off day of the season, Brewster (2–3, 0–1 Eastern Division) exploded for fifteen runs. Brewster's bats finally came around, winning by the ten-run mercy rule 15–4 in seven innings. A great outing by pitcher Michael Salina (St. Bonaventure) and thirteen runs across the first three innings put the game away early and helped the Whitecaps cruise to their second win in 2024.

"You're not going to have days like this every day," Shevchik said postgame. "But now you have a chance to see what could be. It's a little progress at a time. If we can get half the production that we got today more often, we're going to have a great summer."

The hit parade began in the second inning. Cuvet, who entered the game having reached base in his past five at bats, beat out an infield hit to get the rally started. The ensuing throw went past the Gatemen's first baseman, allowing two runners to score. Fischer and Hylton then knocked back-to-back doubles to right field. Then Mora singled home Hylton, scoring the sixth run of the frame for the Whitecaps.

Following another quick inning of work by Salina, the Brewster bats continued to berate Wareham's pitching in the second

Fourth Inning—Falmouth Turns Its Lonely Eyes to Paul Mitchell

inning. Rogers walked, stole second base, then scored on a single by Helfrick. Schubart and Cuvet both walked, loading the bases for Fischer.

The Ole Miss product had already plated two runs an inning before. This time, riding high into his at-bat, Fischer called his shot. As Cuvet reached a 3–0 count, Fischer sauntered over to the dugout from the on-deck circle and leaned over to Hylton, who was in the hole. "Before I round the bases, I need you to figure out what the home run celebration is going to be," he told Hylton. "I'm about to hit a grand slam." As the dugout laughed at Fischer's boisterous yet confident claim, Cuvet worked a walk. Fischer fouled off a pitch, then saw a ball. On the third pitch of the at-bat, he followed up on his bold claim, hammering a grand slam over the right field wall, tallying his third through sixth RBIs in two innings, and extending the Whitecaps' lead to eleven. After parading around the bases, Fischer, Helfrick, Schubart, Cuvet, and Hylton promptly celebrated in a five-person huddle at home plate.

Despite his big day, Fischer was quick to acknowledge his success wouldn't have been possible without his teammates reaching base in front of him. "You get up there and there's a ton of protection all over the order," Fischer said postgame. "I batted sixth today, and every time I came up, there's people on base. There's nowhere for them to put me, and they have to throw strikes to me. I was able to get my swings off and was lucky that worked out for me today."

Salina finished the day in his CCBL debut allowing five hits and two runs through five innings of work.

Brewster added three more runs in the bottom half of the third inning as Helfrick and Schubart blasted back-to-back home runs.

An offensive outburst resulted in a much-needed win but also an explosive stat line across the board. Rogers finished with three runs and two hits, while Helfrick had three runs, two hits, and three RBIs. Schubart also had a big night, scoring four runs while reaching base four times. Cuvet reached four times as well with three hits. With the biggest hit of the game, Fischer broke out for two runs and six RBIs.

"Nobody expected this, to come out and do what we did," Shevchik said. "Now it shows, and now the expectation level rises."

Well, maybe there was one person who was expecting it. While baby Colten was in the car being driven by his mom to Brewster, Colten knew his proud papa had a giant-sized surprise waiting for him. Now the Whitecaps finally understand why Shevchik is always preaching about family.

Wareham Manager Ryan Smythe is a direct disciple of Shevchik from their time coaching together at Keystone College and in Brewster. Smith got thrown out of the game in the fourth for arguing a reversed call on a ball hit by Schubart that was initially ruled foul and then overturned and ruled a home run.

After the game, Smythe with the same friendly personality that his mentor Shevchik has, shook off the lopsided loss. His return to Brewster always brings back very special memories. Smith said on the field after the game, "It's always special coming back to Brewster; we won two championships together during my six years on the Brewster coaching staff. Jamie and I are extremely close. We have coached together for fifteen straight years. Our entire families are very close. I enjoy coaching against Jamie. It's a fun game. I enjoy it. It's not a rivalry unless we're playing against each other for a championship at the end of the year. I still get goose bumps every time I think about the years I spent with the Whitecaps organization."

WHITECAPS AT CHATHAM ANGLERS

A Friday night Cape Cod game in Chatham is equivalent to a Saturday night New York Knicks game at Madison Square Garden.

A SEASON WITH THE BREWSTER WHITECAPS
Fourth Inning—Falmouth Turns Its Lonely Eyes to Paul Mitchell

The Chatham Anglers and their historic home park, Veterans Field, make up the mecca of Cape Cod baseball. Veterans Field opened in 1927. Chatham was one of the original four franchises of the Cape Cod Baseball League dating back to 1923. The movie *Summer Catch* was partly filmed in Chatham, and the book *The Last Best League*, a popular story about Cape Cod Baseball, was written about the Chatham A's. The ballpark displays a panoramic view from any location a fan wants to enjoy the game from.

Chatham's downtown is the equivalent of New York's Madison Avenue. Visitors to the Cape flock to Chatham's Main Street shopping district. Many of the homes and restaurants are upscale. Shoppers can be seen all summer long gleefully holding on to their shopping bags as they parade up and down Main Street. It's almost like a badge of honor to leave the Cape and return home and boastfully exclaim, "I bought this in Chatham." As for the beaches in Chatham, Lighthouse Beach is a must-visit.

Chatham is the big-market team of the Cape Cod Baseball League. The organization has money, fans, swag, and a tremendous tradition. Mike Lowell, Thurman Munson, Jeff Bagwell, Glenn Davis, and Rich Hill are just a few of the many former major leaguers who performed in Chatham. Cape Cod Hall of Fame Manager John Schiffner was its manager from 1993 to 2018. In 2008 Chatham changed its name from the A's to the Anglers.

It must be mentioned, if you are ever in Chatham, stop by the Red Nun. They have the best clam chowder in town!

The Whitecaps were extremely loose warming up before the game. Star second baseman Fischer was starting to show himself as one of the team's vocal leaders. The second baseman is rated as a high MLB future draft pick in 2025. He also has the confidence and swag (called "rizz" by his Caps teammates) to get his teammates fired up before every game.

Rogers, the muscular and friendly outfielder from Vanderbilt, was telling the coaching staff how he has won three consecutive weightlifting competitions among all his Vanderbilt baseball teammates. There wasn't one person who thought he might be making any of it up. Coach Jordan Art was standing in the dugout munching on a hot dog from the concession stand and chirped out, "Quality dog and an A-plus for the bun." When looking up at the press box, another coach pointed out that "there are over twenty team officials sitting up there," while most other teams usually have a small handful in theirs.

The fog was rolling in early on this Friday afternoon. The affable Shevchik reminded everyone near him that if the fog got to the point where you can't see the center fielder from home plate, the game would get halted. Shortly after he made this announcement, the fog coverage cleared, and the sun came out.

Shevchik was starting to prepare himself for the inevitable roster changes every manager must work through each summer on the Cape. Team USA, an all-star team consisting of top collegiate players throughout the country, was ready to begin its summer workouts. Every summer there is a large turnover of players on every roster. Four players were preparing to leave in a few days. Several new players were due to report now that the College World Series was coming to an end. Others would leave in mid-July due to the change of dates for the MLB draft. Once held the first week of June, the MLB draft has been moved to the middle of July. Players come and go on a regular basis. Some players on the Cape decide to enter the NCAA transfer portal and must report to their new campus. Others get homesick for their girlfriends, while others decide they want a break from baseball and want to enjoy a real summer vacation before they go back to school in August.

For a manager like Shevchik, who has spent his career building a tremendous reputation all around the country, the well never runs dry. Soon Forbes, Cuvet, Schubart, and Gabe Davis

(Oklahoma State) will be attending the training camp for Team USA. As the players leave, Whitecaps Nation will hold their collective breath in hopes they will return when their training ends on July 4. Due to arrive to fill the roster slots are Kellan Oakes, a pitcher from Oregon State, Brody Donay, a catcher from Florida, and Drew Faurot, a shortstop from Florida State.

Once the game started, the Caps jumped out to an early 5–1 lead. But with one swing of the bat, Helfrick had the Whitecaps dugout breathing a sigh of relief. The Arkansas catcher laced a two-run single into left field, scoring first baseman Vest and right fielder Dumesnil for two key insurance runs in the top of the eighth inning. "It was huge," Shevchik said of the play. "It took some pressure off [reliever] Seth Tomczak coming in and not having to deal with two innings of a one-run game. In a one-run game out here, the tables can turn quickly."

The big hit punctuated a 7–4 win for the Whitecaps (3–3, 1–1 Eastern Division).

Another hitting star for Brewster was designated hitter Schubart. He took an inner-half fastball from Chatham starter Evan Chrest (Florida State) in the first inning and blasted it for a towering home run. It was the second long ball in as many days for Schubart, this one coming at 106 mph off the bat and traveling a projected 377 feet to deliver Brewster a 2–0 advantage. "I've just been staying true to my approach up here and resetting after every pitch," Schubart said. "Knowing just to stay on the fastball and adjust to off-speed and go from there."

In the third, Whitecaps third baseman Cuvet joined in on the fun. The University of Miami product tattooed a home run to dead center field, his first big fly of the summer. "I've been watching that all year long on ESPN," Shevchik joked. "So to see it out here with the wood was cool. I've been waiting around for it. He's starting to heat up; he's starting to see the ball a little bit better."

Starter Forbes pitched just 1⅓ innings, striking out one and allowing three hits with one earned run. The shortened outing was planned by Shevchik since Friday marked Forbes's final appearance before departing to Team USA Collegiate National Team Training Camp in Cary, North Carolina.

He was replaced by Davis, who also logged his last action before joining Team USA. The hard-throwing righty hit 99 mph on the radar gun in 1⅔ innings, allowing two hits and a pair of runs. Several scouts in attendance were busy scribbling down the velocity on display by Davis.

The contest marked Brewster's second consecutive multi-homer game, but Shevchik put the emphasis on Helfrick's single, the timeliest hit of the evening. "People don't realize we won by three runs. Schubart hit the home run, but the biggest hit of the game was really Helfrick in the eighth inning, giving us a little breathing room," Shevchik said.

Chase Mora's manager from Texas State, Steve Trout, flew in from Texas to watch his first-team freshman All-American. Trout makes the annual voyage to the Cape every summer to support his players playing on the Cape. "Chase is doing great. He plays second base for us, so it's fun to watch him play shortstop here. He is very athletic and is very steady. Mora is a big fisherman and hunter. I think most of the time he's the best player on the field. He is starting to open a lot of eyes around baseball. I give him a pretty good chance to get drafted, and then we'll see where he goes from there," said Trout.

COTUIT KETTLEERS AT WHITECAPS

As the rain continued to drizzle down onto Stony Brook Field and the sky grew darker, the Whitecaps' two-game winning streak drew closer to getting washed away.

Trailing by five in the bottom of the eighth inning, JD

Fourth Inning—Falmouth Turns Its Lonely Eyes to Paul Mitchell

Rogers reached first on a bunt single toward the third base line. Rogers stole second and third without much competition. The heart of Brewster's order had a chance to flip the game on its head.

The top hitters for Brewster all struck out. After Cuvet swung through the final pitch, home plate umpire JC Fernandez looked toward the Brewster dugout and waved his hands in a crossing motion, signaling the end of the game.

Brewster (3–4, 1–1 East Division) fell in eight innings Saturday evening, 6–1 to Cotuit (4–3, 2–0 West Division), breaking its first winning streak of the summer. After the previous two games in which Brewster hitters combined for twenty-two runs and twenty-four hits, their bats went silent.

After his stellar freshman season at Miami, Cuvet has swung the bat exceptionally well for the Whitecaps recently. He has tallied eight hits and a home run in the past five games. Defensively, though, he had a tough night. This time, when attempting to start a double play, his throw to Fischer at second sailed into right field, scoring the base runner headed toward third.

Parker Detmers (Louisville) is the younger brother of Los Angles Angels pitcher Reid Detmers, who also pitched for Brewster in 2018. Reid threw a no-hitter for the Angels in 2022. Parker Detmers entered for Brewster in the eighth inning. Detmers allowed another run, and that was it.

Shevchik explained after his team's win over Chatham on Friday that games are often won and lost in the first four innings of a game in the Cape Cod Baseball League. After four innings Saturday, the Whitecaps trailed 4–0. Those runs proved decisive, as Brewster ultimately fell 6–1.

Within seconds after the game ended, the Brewster manager walked briskly into the large trailer shed located along the left field line at Stony Brook Field. Without saying a single word, his five assistants all followed. They all knew this was going to be one of the most uncomfortable meetings they had had together.

As they sat down, the fun was over. Playing and coaching baseball for the six coaches for the Brewster Whitecaps is incredibly fun. What was about to take place for Shevchik was going to be agonizing, and each one knew it. No one had to ask what they were meeting about. As the first week of the season had ended, it was time for brutally hard decisions to be made.

There are two different types of contracts that general managers of Cape teams send out to the players and their college coaches during the off season. When a player is recruited and commits to play on a team at the Cape, the contracts must be signed by both and sent back. One type of contract is called a temporary contract, and the other is called a permanent one. When the active roster for the Whitecaps was released for opening day, the roster had eighteen players on it that had signed temporary contracts, and twelve had a permanent one. The coaching staff of each Cape team must decide which players will receive a permanent one and who will be assigned a temporary one.

The likeable and easygoing Jon Mecca is the team official in charge of making sure all contracts are sent out and returned signed by the players and their college coaches. Players with permanent contracts usually play throughout the entire season. Of course, there are circumstances that develop throughout the Cape season. Injuries, loneliness, and players who get tired of the grind of playing every day are examples of this. Almost every player on the Caps roster had just completed their college season before the Cape season began. There are a few situations where a player coming to Brewster might have had to sit out his college season and didn't play. Injuries and being redshirted are the two most common. The Whitecaps started their season with twelve players on permanent contracts and eighteen on temp contracts.

A SEASON WITH THE BREWSTER WHITECAPS
Fourth Inning—Falmouth Turns Its Lonely Eyes to Paul Mitchell

No team can exceed twenty-five temp contracts during a single season.

Temporary contracts are given out to players who had a great college season and are potential MLB draft choices. Players with temp contracts can be released by the team if a player who has a permanent one reports late. Brody Donay (U of Florida), Kellan Oakes (Oregon State), Kaeden Kent (Texas A&M), and Drew Faurot (Florida State) are four players who will be reporting late for the Caps. All four had their seasons extended later than some of the other schools because their teams played in the NCAA postseason Division I Baseball Championship. This happens regularly.

To make room for these players, others must be released. Most players who are released can still be picked up by other Cape Cod teams. Some do get picked if they have performed well and the Cape team who might be interested has a need for that player's position on the field.

A great example of this was in 2021, when a young shortstop named Zach Neto was on a temp contract and playing on the Cape for the Cotuit Kettleers. In the middle of the season, Neto was released by Cotuit and picked up by Brewster. Well, as they say, the rest is history. Brewster picked up Neto, and he ended up leading the Whitecaps to the 2021 Cape Cod League Championship. The next year Neto was drafted by the Angels in the first round of the 2022 MLB draft. To say all Whitecaps Nation is proud when they turn on their TVs during the baseball season and watch their Zach Neto play as the starting shortstop for the Los Angeles Angels is an understatement. In fact, this past season of 2024, Neto broke the Angels long-standing record for home runs hit by a shortstop with twenty-three. Add to that the thirty stolen bases he had and you can see it won't be long before the name Zach Neto will be a household name for all baseball fans everywhere. Another scenario is when a player with a temp contract exceeds the team's expectations and is signed to a permanent contract if an opening becomes available during the summer.

Some released players leave with an appreciation that they have had the greatest baseball experience of their baseball careers. They understand that during the few games they played in, they were showcased in front of dozens of MLB scouts. Not only will they have bragging rights to share with their friends and family members for the rest of their lives, but scouts have evaluated them, and if a scout saw something they liked, it could help them when the MLB draft rolls around. As J. P. Ricciardi, the former Oakland A's executive and Toronto Blue Jays General Manager, is quick to point out, "Any single transaction in a player's career can impact them and their family for the rest of their lives."

The MLB has moved its draft from the first week of June to July 14–16. This has also created some chaos for Cape Cod baseball. To play baseball on the Cape, a player must have some NCAA college eligibility remaining when they report to their Cape team. MLB has an agreement with the NCAA that they will not draft a player until after their third year of attending a four-year college or university. If a third-year college player on the Cape gets drafted in July, they have a choice to make. They can sign their pro contract and start their professional career or go back to school for their fourth year and try to improve their draft position. If they go back, they can possibly hope to get drafted the following year and receive a bigger signing bonus. This is a risky business for players. Injuries or a slip in their play can be very costly.

Another situation that Mecca and Shevchik must deal with occurs when the summer college All-Star team called Team USA begins its training camp. This season, four players from the Whitecaps alone will be leaving at the end of June to report to the team. Of course, everyone affiliated with Cape Baseball is proud of their players when they have been given the opportunity to represent their country. But it still causes quite a bit of confusion for the Cape organization that they are leaving.

Even though these are scenarios that have been playing out for years, the behind-the-scenes situations are even more challenging for each organization. Players' uniforms must be traded out and refitted for the new arriving players. Players' travel itineraries must be reworked. Players are dropped off at airports all over New England for their destinations, and new arriving players are met and brought back to Brewster or another organization they will be joining.

As was mentioned earlier, Jane Sullivan wears so many hats for her beloved Whitecaps that she has run out of room in her basement where she keeps them all. She has a heart of solid 18-carat gold. Each player that has ever played for her Whitecaps becomes like a son to her. The love is mutual.

Sullivan must regroup her list of host families in the middle of the summer and find new hosts that will offer their homes to the new players in Brewster. This scenario never ends. Finding host families for thirty college baseball players takes the popular icon all year long. It's a continuous work in progress. When, in the middle of the season, the team goes through major personnel changes, Sullivan just grinds out another day of hard work. She never complains; the Whitecaps are her family, and she loves every second of her passion.

Shevchik dislikes releasing any of his players. He preaches family twenty-four hours a day. As the manager of the Brewster Whitecaps for the past ten years, he understands all too well his responsibilities. His players understand the business side of playing baseball on Cape Cod also. If they don't know, they sure will find out quickly if they are fortunate enough to ever get drafted and start living their dream in the low minor leagues.

The Kettleers Manager, the legendary Mike Roberts (who once

served as the baseball manager at his alma mater, the University of North Carolina, for ten years and whose son Brian played second base in the majors for fourteen years) is now in his twentieth season in charge of Cotuit. Right after his team's win over the Whitecaps, he spoke about his philosophy of releasing players. Roberts had this to say: "This league is all about the players. The more players that get the opportunity to play on the Cape, the better I feel about my job. I'm thrilled about the way things worked out for Neto. When I released him, we didn't have an opening on our roster because he was signed under a temp contract. On top of that, he was dealing with an ankle injury. I'm not surprised, though, how well he's done. Sometimes you never know how young players are going to grow and improve."

Shevchik echoed the same sentiments as his friend Roberts. "When a player gets released, it offers an opportunity for another player to come to the Cape and experience this rich tradition."

WHITECAPS AT ORLEANS FIREBIRDS

The Whitecaps strolled into Orleans to play the Firebirds next. Named after Louis Winslow Eldredge, who donated the land and was a baseball enthusiast, Eldredge Park opened in 1913 and is the oldest baseball field on the Cape. The ballpark has been described as a Norman Rockwell painting come to life.

The Firebirds, originally called the Cardinals, have the largest fan following out of the ten CCBL franchises. Their fans wake up early and leave their lawn chairs in prime spots on the grass surrounding the field. This way, when they return for the game later in the day, they will have a great vantage place to watch from.

Orleans has had a tremendous number of Major League superstars play for them throughout their history. Add the names of Carlton Fisk, Frank Thomas, Mark Teixeira, Nomar Garciaparra, and Marcus Stroman, along with many others. Orleans is known for its beautiful beaches and an abundance of wonderful restaurants. The natives boast about Sir Cricket's Fish and Chips, which serves up the most delicious clam chowder.

The wind was really howling on this overcast Sunday evening. The crowd was the usual: three thousand fans. Shevchik and pitching coach Brian Del Rosso were chatting about the lineup they'd be facing. Caps first baseman Vest and Fischer were hamming it up. At one point just before the game, Shevchik gave a pep talk in the dugout trying to hype his team. All the players seemed to enjoy the professional baseball concept of playing a game every day.

In a 4–2 loss at Orleans, the Whitecaps got a taste of their own medicine. Trailing 3–2 to the Firebirds in the bottom of the eighth, Brewster reliever Schmolke was on the verge of escaping a one-out, bases-loaded jam. The righty struck out Orleans shortstop Lorenzo Meola (Stetson) on a foul tip and forced the following batter, Ben Zeigler-Namoa (Hawaii), into an 0–2 count.

The Firebirds capitalized, though, after Helfrick made an error on the simplest play in baseball: a catcher's returning throw to the pitcher. Helfrick yanked his toss to Schmolke's right, allowing Orleans center fielder Hudson Shupe (Gonzaga) to hustle home and make it 4–2.

The Firebirds' winning run had already been scored in the fifth, but in a low-scoring game with stellar pitching, the insurance run made all the difference. "It's a totally different mindset when you've got a two-run lead," the Whitecaps manager said postgame. "Anything can happen in a one-run game. When it's two runs, on a day like today, it felt like we were just light-years away. It seemed almost insurmountable."

"They still have to learn how to pitch," Shevchik said. "We threw a curveball to the backstop when we didn't have to. We had two outs, runner on third, challenge a guy, and you throw a bad breaking ball to the backstop and the run scores."

"We'll get right back at it tomorrow," Shevchik said. "We'll sleep on it, keep it fresh, and tomorrow before the game, we'll talk." Tomorrow's game against Yarmouth-Dennis is growing bigger by the minute.

The Whitecaps fell to 3–5 on the season, and Orleans won for only the second time in the young season.

During any baseball season, players can sometimes lose their focus. This can cause distractions to the mental toughness a player needs to make it through the daily grind of a season. When this happens, losing usually isn't too far behind. When playing on the Cape, players need to be self-motivated to play at their peak of performance. Coaches will do their part in motivating their teams, but they only have the players for two months before they go back to school. Playing in a showcase league that has as many as thirty to forty scouts at each game is usually all the motivation a player needs.

Of course, the players are playing as hard as they can to impress the scouts, and winning, most times, will take care of itself. The issue isn't trying to win. The issue on the Cape is becoming complacent with losing. Cape baseball is different. It's set up as a scouting combine. There are ten teams, and the scouts travel around evaluating the talent. If you perform well and the scouts are impressed, the main mission of the player is accomplished. If you lose, you go back to your host family, and there are no fellow classmates, no media, and no boosters to remind you about the loss. Except for your coaches and teammates, no one throughout the day will even mention the game the day before.

All the players playing on the Cape have been big stars since they started playing as young kids. Even though their parents, friends, coaches, and teammates all look up to them and pump up their egos, when they get to the Cape the reality hits like a ton of bricks. For the first time in their baseball lives, they are on an equal playing field with the rest of their teammates.

Fourth Inning—Falmouth Turns Its Lonely Eyes to Paul Mitchell

Philadelphia Phillies scout Casey Fahy, who has spent the last fifteen years on the Cape evaluating players, spoke about the difficulty of his profession. "There are no can't-miss prospects. There are several years between when they play on the Cape and the time they reach the Majors. During that time anything can happen," Fahy explained.

The business side of Cape Cod baseball can be a rude awakening for all the players before they start thinking about the MLB draft.

YARMOUTH-DENNIS RED SOX AT WHITECAPS

The sun was shining brightly on Stony Brook Field before the Caps were to face Yarmouth-Dennis in a rematch of the season opener for both teams. The Caps players were sky-high before the game. They were determined to avenge the heartbreaking extra-inning loss they had suffered in the opener.

Boston Red Sox scout Dante Ricciardi was in attendance as well as several other scouts. Ricciardi comes from the first family of baseball in Central Massachusetts. Dante is the son of the legendary baseball executive and former general manager of the Toronto Blue Jays, J. P. Ricciardi. Dante's brother Mariano just retired after playing nine seasons in the Oakland A's minor league system.

Ricciardi had this to say about his six summers scouting on the Cape: "I always knew I would end up in a career in baseball. The Red Sox have had an opportunity to draft several players because of the opportunity to scout on Cape Cod. Alex Freeman and Jake Smith, two players who no one knew about, were both discovered here."

Ricciardi continued, "This league is better than the competition you will find in the SEC, ACC, Big 12, or any of the other power conferences. This league you have 75 percent of the players that will get drafted. My dad had a huge influence on me. I graduated from Bryant College in communications. Working in scouting is a natural fit for me. Dan Cuvet is a kid we've been following since his high school days in Florida. Growing up in a baseball family, working on the Cape is like a homecoming for me."

In the dugout before the game, center fielder RJ Johnson from Rutgers was telling his teammates about his busy day. "I helped this morning at the baseball clinic the team organizes for the youth of Brewster. I then went to the gym for my workout."

With the College World Series coming to an end in Omaha, Nebraska, new players with permanent contracts started arriving. The first addition, arriving a few minutes before game time, was DeAmez Ross from Florida State. Because Ross had spent the day traveling, he was sitting in the dugout but not in uniform. All the players huddled around and listened to his stories about what it was like to play in the final four of the World Series of College Baseball. Ross exclaimed to all who could hear, "It was an amazing experience. It was a dream come true. We turned everything around from the poor season we had at Florida State the year before." There was very little doubt that Ross was going to fit in with his new teammates very nicely.

It's great that the bat kids who volunteer to help the team are young. They don't pay any attention to the roller coaster of emotions that come with the wins and losses of a long season. Kids are excited to come to the ballpark and hang out with their heroes every game.

For Declan Hart, an eight-year-old, his favorite part of helping as a bat boy is getting to know the players. For Onyx Grimes, a third-grader whose dad, Scott, works as the Whitecaps batting coach, the favorite part of being a bat boy is running out and getting the bats. As he went hopping off picking up baseballs lying on the ground, he turned around and yelled proudly, "I also sing the National Anthem."

A SEASON WITH THE BREWSTER WHITECAPS
Fourth Inning—Falmouth Turns Its Lonely Eyes to Paul Mitchell

On the verge of a three-game losing streak, the Whitecaps were down yet again in the bottom of the ninth. Entering the inning down 5–2, Brewster clawed back when their leadoff hitter got hit by a pitch. After an eight-pitch walk and an RBI single, the winning run came to the plate in Schubart. The big slugger had the chance to be a hero and turn the recent skid around.

Schubart fouled off multiple pitches to stay alive but eventually swung through a high pitch to end the threat. The chance was one that could potentially change the entire season for the Whitecaps. "At the end of the year, you look back at certain games and events and wish you could have a different result. This could be one of those games you want back," said Shevchik after the game.

Brewster (3–6, 1–3 East Division) fell to Yarmouth-Dennis (7–2, 4–1 East Division) 5–3 that Monday evening, dropping its third game in a row. The contest came down to the final pitch but was decided within the first half inning.

Rocco Reid (Clemson) was looking for a bounce back in his second start of his second season in Brewster. His opening start on June 18 didn't go as planned when he allowed seven runs in just 1⅓ innings of work.

His second appearance started looking like it would be much the same. Reid walked the first batter and made an error on a short chopper back to him from the second batter. Both executed a double steal on the bases to get to second and third with no outs. Reid forced two groundouts, but both scored a base runner, putting the Red Sox ahead 2–0 without a base hit. "Games are won and lost, momentum is gained and lost within the first couple innings," Shevchik said. "You start off the game with a walk and an error and those two runs scored without a hit. Everything deflates."

After allowing two runs to open the game, Brewster's offense had little answer for the Red Sox starting pitcher, Ramsey David (Southeastern). The right-hander struck out three hitters while walking one in the first inning, topping out at as high as 97 mph on his fastball while mixing in a devastating slider.

The Whitecaps offense eventually got going in the bottom of the fourth inning. After not recording a base hit through the first three innings, Cuvet got Brewster started by turning a 95-mph fastball to right field. Fischer flew out to left field, but Jayden Hylton hammered a ball up the middle to make it first and third with just one down.

Mora drove in Cuvet with a sacrifice fly to get the Whitecaps on the board, but that's all Brewster would get in the frame. A short time later in the game, Mora was beaned off the helmet by a pitch and had to leave the game. It would be a big blow to the team if he had to miss much time. Four players for the Whitecaps left immediately following the game and reported to Team USA.

Will Ray (Wake Forest) entered in relief of Reid and cruised through his first two innings of work. In the eighth inning, with Y-D leading 3–1, Ray allowed a two-out single and a home run, giving the Red Sox two huge insurance runs.

After the game, Schubart, the ninth-ranked college baseball prospect available for the 2025 MLB draft, was heading to join Team USA, a college All-Star squad made up of the very top MLB prospects in America. Every summer they travel across the country and overseas and perform in exhibition games.

What Schubart told team officials before the game came as a disappointment to the Brewster organization. Schubart shared the news with both Shevchik and Mecca that when the All-Star exhibitions ended on July 4, he would be going home to Michigan and not returning.

Schubart certainly left his mark in Brewster. There was never a question that it was anything personal against anyone or the organization. Remember the name Nolan Schubart. There is little doubt he will be playing baseball for a long time.

A SEASON WITH THE BREWSTER WHITECAPS
Fourth Inning—Falmouth Turns Its Lonely Eyes to Paul Mitchell

Unfortunately, this is becoming a common trend among college players. Of course, there are always going to be injuries and family situations that come up from time to time when a player needs to take a break. When an organization spends ten months building its team around a few players and they go home, it can be disheartening for everyone. Schubart is not alone. Although it's very unfair that a player signs a contract and then leaves, this is becoming business as usual in the Cape Cod Baseball League and other summer leagues around America.

This is what Schubart had to say as he was walking to the parking lot after his last game: "I thought overall my stay here was successful. I wish I had come through on my last at-bat, but it didn't work out." When asked if he knew before he reported to the Caps that he would be leaving after a handful of games, Schubart said, "I knew there was a fifty-fifty chance I'd be leaving early."

Red Sox scout Ricciardi, who was in attendance, commented on the situation. "I see it all the time. These kids make a commitment and think nothing of walking away. It's wrong. I'm old-school. Unless there is an injury or a family situation to attend to, honor your commitment. I know they play a lot of games, but if you're going to come and play, stay for the entire season or just stay home entirely. Don't walk out on your teammates."

Immediately after the game, the charming mother of the Whitecaps manager, Debbie Shevchik, was enjoying walking around the field. She was saying goodbye to the many friends she had made from her trips to Brewster over the past ten years. Debbie had this to say about her successful son: "I love it here. I come every year for a week. I just absolutely love it here. Jamie just loves doing what he's doing. Every boy has dreams of having a career in baseball. I've always been proud of him. Very few people get to do what they love. It's special for me to come here and be a part of the Whitecaps family. I'm just so proud of my son, to see where he is today; I just couldn't be prouder of him."

There's an old expression that is appropriate to add—the apple doesn't fall far from the tree.

Shevchik is always preaching to his players about "grinding it out." Shevchik explains exactly what he means by that saying. "One of the most important things a player can learn on the Cape is how to play through the dog days of summer. All the players here have always been stars. A lot of them have never experienced failure. This league is loaded with future Major League pitchers. These players have never faced that kind of pitching game in and game out. They must learn to fight through their failures. Baseball is a game of failure. If they can't deal with it, they'll never make it to the professional level. Here on the Cape, they play a forty-game schedule. If they find this too tough when they fall into a slump, how are they ever going to make it through Minor League baseball when it's a 144-game schedule? Remember, they play 162 games in the Major Leagues."

After nine games, the overall team batting average for the Brewster Whitecaps is .224. This is a little higher than the overall league average. The hitters who have never played on the Cape before usually go into shock when they realize facing great pitching without their aluminum bats is a huge adjustment. Even though the players have used wooden bats before, they have never faced the challenge of hitting with them when the pitch is coming in at 95–98 mph. Gabe Davis out of Oklahoma State threw three pitches at 99 mph while pitching for the Whitecaps against Chatham.

This team's batting average and learning to deal with failure is exactly what Shevchik is preaching about. Players must learn not to get too down with failure and not too high with success during the season. The Cape is the perfect place to learn how to stay on an even keel.

Fourth Inning—Falmouth Turns Its Lonely Eyes to Paul Mitchell

Coming to the Cape and learning how to play on fields that are used most times for public school use is a huge adjustment. Most of the time, the players that come from major colleges play in facilities that cost almost $100 million and sometimes more. Also, they're used to playing in front of as many as ten thousand fans. On average the attendance for a Cape game is around fifteen hundred to three thousand fans. Players must learn to self-motivate. This is another important lesson that the Cape teaches. Anyone can play in front of large crowds. Evaluating players when they play in front of a few hundred fans is an entirely different story.

On paper the Brewster Whitecaps have a tremendous roster. But great rosters don't win games. Teams playing the Whitecaps will not be lying down when they face the Caps. Brewster found that out in a hurry. Now it's time to find out if the Whitecaps are willing to grind it out throughout the rest of the summer. This valuable lesson will determine the success of the rest of the season. Only time will tell.

WHITECAPS AT BOURNE BRAVES—DUMESNIL BREAKS OUT

Stuck in the depths of a 3-for-27 slump, Nick Dumesnil was searching for answers when he received a pivotal piece of advice from his head coach at California Baptist, Gary Adcock. "Be yourself and destroy the ball," Adcock told him before Tuesday night's game against the Bourne Braves. "Crush it to the pull side."

The advice proved prophetic. With Brewster and Bourne knotted at three in the eighth inning, Dumesnil turned on a fastball and crushed it to left field for a go-ahead solo shot, perhaps the Whitecaps' biggest hit of the season. "I got in a hitter's count, and I was sitting on nothing but a fastball," Dumesnil said. "I was not going to miss my opportunity."

The pivotal moment highlighted Brewster's 6–3 win over the

Braves at Doran Park on Tuesday, a grind-it-out victory that featured contributions from up and down the roster.

Newcomers Drew Faurot and DeAmez Ross, both from Florida State, kicked things off in the second with a pair of strong first impressions.

After right fielder Hylton drew a one-out walk, Faurot cranked a ground-rule double in his first at-bat with the Whitecaps, moving Hylton to third. Ross drove them both home a few batters later, lining a single to center field on the first pitch he saw. "I'm happy for them," Shevchik said. "They came in and solidified themselves on why they're supposed to be here."

Last week, Faurot and Ross were competing with the Seminoles for the College World Series Championship in Omaha, along with a few other new Whitecaps: Boston Flannery (North Carolina) and Brody Donay (Florida).

These fresh faces will help fill the void left by Schubart, Cuvet, Davis, and Forbes, who all departed for Team USA Collegiate National Team Training Camp in Cary, North Carolina.

Luke Guth (Vanderbilt) tossed four innings of two-run ball for the Whitecaps with three strikeouts, all of which came in a dominant bottom of the second. The Braves managed just four hits off the right-hander, who also picked off Bourne center fielder Chris Stanfield (LSU) to end the third.

Jacob Marlowe (Florida State) took over for the fifth and most of the sixth. He dealt a 1-2-3 fifth with two strikeouts but ran into trouble in the sixth, surrendering back-to-back singles and a game-tying sacrifice fly. DJ Primeaux (LSU), who Shevchik called Brewster's "go-to guy," kept the Braves in check from there, pitching $2⅓$ perfect innings with a pair of strikeouts.

Dumesnil stepped to the plate in the eighth. His solo blast made it 4-3 Brewster, a lead the Whitecaps never relinquished. Helfrick followed it up with a solo blast of his own in the top of the ninth, and first baseman Vest added an RBI knock to drive home Faurot later in the frame.

Detmers closed things out in the ninth, working a scoreless frame after walking the first two hitters he faced. With the result, Brewster snapped its three-game losing streak and boosted its record to 4–6 ahead of Wednesdays off day. "You want to get closer and closer to .500," Shevchik said. "Not a lot of teams played tonight in our division, and we gained a little bit of momentum."

The Whitecaps suffered another loss, though. It was determined that when Mora got beaned against Yarmouth-Dennis, he suffered a concussion, and he has been medically shut down. He is currently on his way home to Texas. This is more reason the Caps must continue to fight even harder.

Don't forget Spanky's Clam Shack in Bourne if you need your daily cup of clam chowder.

Fifth Inning—The Gala

ALL THE WHITECAP NATION CAME together during a rare night off. The second annual gala was held at the world-renowned Ocean Edge Resort and Golf Club. The Caps fans and supporters were all dressed and looking chic.

Several players were in attendance as well as all the coaches. Luke Dillon and his lovely wife, Karen, were enjoying themselves mingling with the patrons who all showed up to help out the Whitecaps organization. Jon and Casey Mecca were having a great night out without their three kids. The spirit and camaraderie of this affair was second to none. The Brewster and Cape Cod community are extremely proud of their Whitecaps.

Shevchik and his sweet wife, Maria, were the toast of the evening. Everywhere this couple goes in Brewster, they have the red carpet laid out for them.

Some of the many guests attending were John and Diane King, Dan and Chris Switz, Tom and Clair Meagher, Matt and Nancy Chabot, Janet and Chuck Hanson, Nancy and Bob Wynn, Matt and Amanda Mariani, Paige Ferraguto, Sarah Robinson, Robert and Beth Tobias, Tom and Kathleen Oelschlager, Scott and Kelley St. Couer, Steve Friedman, Diego Salvador, Joe and Ilise Prendergast, Kathy and Ned Monthie, Bill and Lisa Fleming, Mike and Kim DiNapoli, Cindy Wilson, Kristen Weber, Kathleen Flynn, Dan Flatley, Brian Fischer, Bill and Lisa Flaherty, Jane Ypsiilantis,

Barbara D'Agustino. John and Diana King, Scott and Ashley Grimes, Dylan and Taryn Cooper, Stu Forstrum, Jane Sullivan, and Claire Blumenfeld. These and so many others filled the 250-seat ballroom. Event organizer Nancy Chabot, along with her entire organizing committee, did a terrific job.

After dinner the guests enjoyed the chance to bid on the many items that were donated and auctioned off. A happy winner of the auction was Dan Flatley, who outbid Joe Prendergast and walked away with an autographed team photo of the famous 1980 USA Gold Medal Olympic Hockey Team. "The Miracle on Ice" will never be forgotten!

The big winner of the night was the Whitecaps, with the several thousand dollars raised to help offset the cost of having a baseball team playing in the Cape Cod Baseball League.

The entire evening was filled with laughter and with the hopes that this 2024 Brewster Whitecaps team will bring home another championship.

WHITECAPS AT COTUIT KETTLEERS—"KID BRETT" EXPLODES!

Cotuit is a small Cape hamlet located between Hyannis and Falmouth in Barnstable County. You must have an updated navigation system to find it. Even with one, the winding roads can get you lost quickly. With a population of just over three thousand residents, it's the smallest town on the Cape that has a team that plays in the Cape League. Even though Cotuit is a small town, you can still find a great cup of clam chowder at Kettle Ho Restaurant.

Lowell Park, home of the Cotuit Kettleers, is one of the most well-maintained ballparks in the league. The fans that come from the surrounding towns to enjoy their favorite team allow the Kettleers to have a strong fan base.

As the Fourth of July holiday is rapidly approaching, the crowds around the league have started to grow. The unseasonably warm summer weather that usually doesn't arrive until early July has been a rare treat for the fans around the league since opening day.

Both teams have had to retool their rosters quite a bit from the first game, with all the usual transactions that take place. Roberts, the manager of Cotuit, pointed out before the game that seventy different players played for the Kettleers in 2023. Sullivan pointed out that sixty-five players suited up for Brewster in 2023. In all, seven hundred players played in the Cape League during the summer of 2023, the most in the league's history.

It was rather a sleepy day as the fans arrived a little later than usual in the gorgeous New England setting. No one knew what to expect from either team. It was just five days earlier in Brewster that Cotuit beat the Caps 6–1.

Well, this was certainly a night that future Major Leaguer and current Cape superstar Fischer will never forget. After starting the season rather slowly, Fischer brought fireworks to Cotuit a little earlier than anyone expected.

Nicknamed "The Kid" by his Caps teammates (because of his boyish and fun personality), Fischer absolutely exploded right before the eyes of three thousand fans. Enjoying his best offensive night since he started playing baseball as a young boy, Fischer, who plays in the infield, went five for five on the night. His offensive output included two home runs, a double, and two singles, for a total of twelve bases that he accounted for singlehandedly. "That's the reason we signed Fischer in the first place," Shevchik said postgame.

With the nature of the Cape Cod Baseball League, players enter and exit from teams daily. For the Whitecaps, stars like Schubart and Cuvet had recently left to compete for Team USA. Brewster has also seen an influx of fresh talent, including experienced collegiate players like Faurot, Max Kaufer (Texas A&M transferring to South Carolina), and Donay.

Throughout the roster fluctuations, Fischer has been one of the Whitecaps' most consistent pieces. After playing second base for the first set of games, Fischer has moved comfortably back to his regular position at third base.

While the Whitecaps poured it on offensively, Seth Tomczak (Cal State Fullerton) provided fine pitching on the mound. Tomczak has started just six games in his collegiate career but was needed this Thursday following the exit of multiple recent starters. He allowed no runs and two hits while striking out four batters in four innings of work.

Before Tomczak's exit, the Whitecaps continued to pounce on the Kettleers' pitching. Fischer doubled to lead off the inning, his third hit of the day. Behind him in the cleanup spot was Donay, who was playing in his first game for the Whitecaps after an impressive run with the Gators in Omaha. Donay made his presence known in his first game, ripping a line drive over the left field wall for a two-run shot.

"I feel like I've been putting some good at-bats together this whole summer but just not really getting results," Fischer said postgame.

With the final score Brewster 10 and Cotuit 7, The Caps had their biggest win of the summer.

ORLEANS FIREBIRDS AT WHITECAPS
When the Whitecaps took batting practice before the rematch with Orleans, you could hear the crack of the wooden bats all way to Provincetown. The noise was deafening. Every hitter that stepped into the batter's box was absolutely crushing the ball to the deepest parts of Stony Brook Field. The sound was almost as pretty as the songs that Taylor Swift belts out.

It didn't matter if it was outfielder Jayden Hylton, catcher Ryder Helfrick, outfielder JD Rodgers, first baseman Cooper Vest, infielder Tyler Pettorini, outfielder RJ Johnson, or anyone else. The newly acquired additions to the roster were also eager to show off their potential. For Donay and Faurot, it was the perfect way to say a loud hello to their new teammates.

Carsten Sabathia, who wasn't in the lineup because of a sore hand, watched intently and was impressed with the onslaught. Remember, Sabathia has spent most of his life watching his dad, CC Sabathia, pitch in the Major Leagues and has seen a lot of Major Leaguers take batting practice at Yankee Stadium. For the Major League scouts and fans that had arrived early, the Caps put on quite a show.

Rogers was especially fired up. He had been taken out of the lineup the day before in Cotuit. Sitting out is tough for this intense competitor from Vanderbilt. Rogers had been the Caps' best early-season performer. After six games Rogers was hitting .560. After that, Rogers cooled down a little bit. Rogers had this to say before the game: "I'm a competitor, and I just want to play so badly every day. I put a lot of pressure on myself to perform at a high level. I've always been like that. I know I've cooled off. I just have to step it back up again."

Bouncing around chirping at everyone was the still giddy Fischer. Fischer was still coming off his high from the night before when he went 5–5. "Let's play two today, Caps; I'm still feeling it," pronounced Fischer.

In the Cape League, all the hitters are impressive when they take batting practice. It's the future Major League pitchers who a lot of times have the last say.

Just when everything was looking up for the Caps, the hitters except for Helfrick went ice-cold. When it looked like the Caps were going to pull even on the season at six wins and six losses, the opposing pitching had the final say.

Brewster found its first chance to strike in the second. Rogers walked, Johnson was hit by a pitch, and with two outs, the pair advanced to second and third on a balk. But Orleans starter Matthew Dalquist (UC San Diego) struck out second baseman Pettorini to thwart the threat.

The starter, Jake Clemente (Florida), made his Whitecaps debut, tossing four innings of two-run ball with six strikeouts, although he surrendered the Firebirds' early burst. "I think he's going to be really good," Shevchik said of Clemente. "First outing out, though, I think he just has to learn how to pitch away from the aluminum bats that he's used to." Kyle Percival (North Carolina), who entered in the fifth to replace Clemente, tossed scoreless innings in the fifth and sixth.

Helfrick cut into the deficit in the bottom of the seventh, cranking a two-run shot to left for his third homer of the year. "He's just dialed in," Shevchik said of Helfrick. "He's an advanced hitter, beyond his years as a freshman. You're probably looking at a Cape League All-Star. I know it's a bold prediction; it's early still, but you've got to believe he's one of the front-runners at that position."

"There just weren't a lot of hard-hit balls, a lot of soft outs. We made it easy on them," said Shevchik after the 5–2 loss.

The Caps fell back to 5–7 on the season.

Hyannis Harbor Hawks at Whitecaps

Cape Cod has been having perfect baseball weather throughout the first two weeks of the season, which began on June 15. It would be interesting to know if there has ever been another season that started off without any rainouts through the first thirteen games of the season.

Once again Shevchik is grinding his way through another season. After ten seasons at the helm of the Caps, he has become well respected around the baseball world.

A SEASON WITH THE BREWSTER WHITECAPS
Fifth Inning—The Gala

Shevchik knows that building a winning ball club takes time. By nature, Shevchik is a patient manager. The problem on Cape Cod is that you can knock yourself out of contention from challenging for a playoff berth early on if you start dropping in the standings. One of the biggest challenges all coaches face is teaching a sense of urgency to their athletes. The Cape is unique in this way. The Cape in the summer is very laid-back for the vacationers who come from all over the world to enjoy the beautiful surroundings.

Players are not on vacation. They must block out the distractions. This is their job. They have enormous stakes on the line. Any slip-up can cause a drop in their MLB evaluations.

The Whitecaps, on paper (it has been mentioned before), are extremely talented. They are considered by folks around the league to have one of the very best rosters. Here is the tricky part. Every team has an abundance of roster turnover. The wrong additions or subtractions can impact success or failure. Once a team has started to build their chemistry and it's ripped apart, it becomes a little hard to predict what the results are going to be.

The Caps are really having a difficult time right now in this area. They have several players who will probably end up in the Major Leagues. Fischer, Helfrick, Cuvet, Forbes, Kent, Faurot, Donay, Dumesnil, Schubart, and Rogers all have a legitimate shot of someday playing in the "Show."

Shevchik is staying optimistic that very soon he and his coaching staff will be seeing the results that meet everyone's expectations. The players are growing frustrated themselves. There is such a fine line between playing with pressure and letting pressure keep an athlete from performing to their maximum ability.

Dr. Jonathan Katz volunteers as the Whitecaps' sports psychologist. Before the game he met with all the players after they arrived at Stony Brook Field and gave them some inspirational motivation. The message was to help them through the ups and downs of playing in a highly competitive atmosphere.

Before the Hyannis Harbor Hawks game, Katie Meinelt was helping to organize the souvenir store for what she was hoping was going to be a busy Saturday night home game. Hats were being laid out, and hoodies were being restocked. Meinelt is a very friendly lawyer who spends her summers in Brewster and works as an attorney in Boston. She gushes when she talks about her volunteer work with the Whitecaps.

Meinelt couldn't wait to tell everyone what makes the Whitecaps so important to her and for her entire family. Meinelt shared the following stories: "A couple of days ago, my nine-year-old son, Wes, had a big playoff game that he was going to pitch in. Shevchik found out about it, and just before the game he FaceTimed me. Shevchik asked me to put my son on the phone so he could wish him good luck. Suddenly there were fifteen Whitecaps players passing the phone around and inspiring my son. It brings tears to my eyes. That kind gesture meant so much to him.

"Another story that is even sweeter happened two years ago. My son Wes is a bat kid for the team. Wes had a favorite player on the team that year named Kurtis Byrne. I planned a birthday party for my son that year and invited Byrne. We planned to have the party at the ballpark. We were able to get special permission to have the party on the field. We invited Byrne to attend. Suddenly Byrne appeared with ten of his teammates on the Whitecaps and announced to the partygoers, 'Hey, listen up, anyone want to play a little baseball today?' Those stories might not seem important, but it's exactly what every little boy dreams about."

The Brewster Whitecaps are a class act and are led by one of the classiest managers in all of baseball!

Café Alfresco on Main Street in Brewster is the morning-and-noon spot where all things Whitecaps converge to catch a little

A SEASON WITH THE BREWSTER WHITECAPS
Fifth Inning—The Gala

breakfast or lunch. Jimmy Barber is the effervescent owner of the business. Barber also owns another restaurant on the Cape in a town called Sandwich.

Barber has been a major sponsor of the Caps since he started running Café Alfresco in 2012. His son has even become a bat kid for the ball club. Barber is a former baseball player, and he and his family have become huge fans of the team. Café Alfresco sponsors the team with banners and a sign on the outfield fence. They also have gift-card giveaways. Barber appreciates the front office of the Whitecaps and has become close friends with all the folks who run the team. Barber speaks so highly of what the Whitecaps mean to the entire Brewster community. Before the game on this day, Barber and his son were ready to watch their beloved ball club come out victorious.

Just before the game, the Brewster Whitecaps dedicated their brand-new scoreboard that illuminates from left field. Jordan Sprechman and his wife, Barbara Paddock, were honored for their philanthropy and their generous donation. They both enjoy their summers in Brewster and commute regularly from their New York home.

Sprechman and Paddock have been huge fans of the team since 1998. "We're the kind of couple that likes to get involved. When we decide to get involved in something, we go all in," Paddock explained. "Once we met the front office staff and they presented us with a proposal for a new scoreboard, it became an easy decision for us to make. We don't like to take center stage in our involvements with our nonprofit contributions. We tend to stay in the background," Paddock continued.

Both Paddock and Sprechman have enjoyed long careers with J. P. Morgan Chase Financial. They met during their careers with the financial institute. Sprechman has been a renowned official scorer during his adult years with both the New York Mets and the

New York Yankees. He also worked at the Olympics in Atlanta in 1996 as the English language voice for the tennis competitions.

As the game with Hyannis got underway, The Caps jumped out to a quick 5–1 lead after two innings. Fischer, Dumesnil, and Helfrick had hot bats early and led the early charge for the Caps. Then, just like that, the pitchers didn't hold up their end of the bargain.

The Caps are searching for a rhythm right now. When everything starts clicking at the same time, the rest of the Cape Cod Baseball League will be put on notice.

Shevchik and Del Rosso searched for anyone to come in and throw strikes. Much to their dismay, they couldn't find anyone on this night. The Caps pitchers combined to give up eleven walks, and seven of those walks ended up scoring. It wasn't what Shevchik had in mind throughout the winter months while putting together this roster from his home in Pennsylvania.

"It's almost like we didn't have a chance tonight. Our offense kind of did everything they needed to do—granted, there were some stale innings in the middle. But when you get five runs early, you should be able to hold the momentum," Shevchik said.

After the game, Carsten Sabathia, who has been out with an injured hand, was placed on the injured list.

The Caps are now tied for third place with Chatham at 5–8 records in the CCBL East Division. Yarmouth-Dennis leads the division with a 10–3 record. In second place is Harwich at 8–5. Orleans, which has beaten the Caps twice in the early going, is in last with a record of 3–10.

MONEYBALL WITH J. P. RICCIARDI

"If it had been up to me, I would have never done the interview for the movie *Moneyball*," said J. P. Ricciardi. "I received a call from my boss and my best friend, Billy Beane, who was the general manager of the Oakland A's. We go way back together. We were both kids when we were teammates together in 1980 for Little Falls, New York. We were playing for the New York Mets affiliate in the New York Penn League. I had just graduated from Saint Leo's College in Florida, and Billy was drafted by the Mets right out of high school. Since that time Billy has been my closest friend. Billy said, 'J. P., you have to talk to them.' I said, 'Why? They already have enough information from the book.' Then he hit me with a comment that I still laugh about even to this day. Beane said, 'J. P., you're the only one who will tell the truth.'" J. P. Ricciardi shared this memory from his years as a scout, Vice President, Special Assistant to the President, General Manager, Director of Player Personnel, and finally as the special assistant to Billy Beane, the General Manager of the Oakland A's. Ricciardi has recently retired from baseball and is living right outside of his hometown of Worcester, Massachusetts.

Ricciardi continued his recollection of the blockbuster movie *Moneyball*. "I had just gotten settled into my job as the General Manager of the Toronto Blue Jays. The producers called to say they were on their way to Toronto in the next week to interview me. Then I got a call a couple of days later saying they had decided they weren't going through with the movie. In fact, the whole movie idea had been scratched."

Ricciardi said, "Three months later, Beane called to tell me that he had just received a call from Brad Pitt. Beane explained that Pitt had just bought the rights to the movie, and it was back on. He also told me that my part was getting cut out, and they would not be coming to Toronto to do any interviews. So that's why I'm not in the movie *Moneyball*."

J. P. Ricciardi will go down as one of the most influential baseball minds of his generation. After recently retiring from a forty-three-year career in baseball and working during those years in several different roles, Ricciardi will be best remembered for his work with the Oakland A's.

Even though Ricciardi spent nine years (2001–2009) as the general manager of the Toronto Blue Jays and several years as an assistant to the president of both the San Francisco Giants and the New York Mets, he will forever be linked as one of the kingpins of baseball's Moneyball generation.

The Moneyball generation was the Oakland A's brainchild to help small-market MLB franchises compete against the big-money teams like the New York Yankees and the Los Angeles Dodgers. The concept was designed to use sabermetrics, data, and analytics and hire experts to find undervalued players that other teams may have passed over. When this concept works, millions and millions of dollars are saved with players who become bargains.

Ricciardi spent forty years scouting players on the Cape. "In the last twenty years, the Cape League has changed. It used to be the best players came to play on the Cape. The best pitchers don't come to the Cape the way they used to. You can still evaluate the players hitting with a wooden bat, but they're not facing the elite pitchers the way they once did. The evaluation process is a little different. The pitchers are still good, but they're not elite. It's still a great venue to evaluate players using a wooden bat. Scouts are looking to collect as much data as possible. When you put that many outstanding college players together in one place and bring in the scouts to evaluate them, you're going to get more notoriety and exposure. It's an easy league to scout. There are ten teams located close to each other. The scouts are building data. They're getting as many looks at the players as possible. This makes it good for both the players and the scouts. There are a lot of players who fail at the Cape and still get drafted high," said Ricciardi.

The conversation with this former successful high school basketball coach at Holy Name High and tremendous three-sport athlete at St. Peter's High, both in Worcester, changed to the current bonus pool for MLB teams. Ricciardi explained that there is a limit that teams can spend today on their drafted players. In fact, he also pointed out that just because a team finishes with the worst record during the prior season doesn't guarantee that they automatically get the first pick in the draft. "They enter a pool of the six worst teams. The order in which the six teams select in the draft comes out of a pre-draft lottery. This way a team like the Baltimore Orioles, who tanked for several years and have so many great young players now, can't do that anymore.

"If you're going to give a high draft choice millions of dollars as a bonus, you better make sure your evaluations are accurate. I think the 2023 MLB draft is going to go down as one of the best drafts ever because of the guys in the top five to six picks that were taken. The 2024 draft was a good draft, but it's not going to be as impactful as the year before. If a team makes a bad decision in the draft, especially with first-rounders, it can really set your organization back. You have to make absolutely sure your evaluations are accurate. Every team makes mistakes. It's risky, especially with the amount of money the teams give out as bonuses. You can do a lot of damage if a team screws up with their draft picks," said Ricciardi.

"In Toronto it was important that we made good decisions with our choices. We didn't have a lot of money. One year we had the number-six pick in the draft, and we needed pitching. We had a limited budget and couldn't sign a high-priced free agent. We used our pick on Ricky Romero. He was a kid out of Cal State Fullerton. He did very well for us. Over four seasons he won over fifty games. When a team picks in the middle to the end of the first round, there is no slam-dunk sure thing. It's really hard," said the former MLB executive.

"Mike Lewis did a great job writing *Moneyball*. There are so many misnomers about how we did things in Oakland. Beane was a great friend and a tremendous guy to work for. I was in his wedding party. Everything I told him; he trusted me explicitly. If I told him something, he believed me. He didn't have to double-check with anyone. What we actually did was find players that no one else wanted based on scouting. We didn't do it with all this data entry and algorithms. That came later on. We played in three World Series in a row (1988–1990) when I was with Oakland. The Haas family sold the team after that to someone that didn't really want to own it. We didn't have as much money after that. Then it became up to us to find players that we could afford. We went from the penthouse to the outhouse. Now all we had were opportunities for players who wanted to play. We had to dig up players that no one else wanted and surround them with good draft picks. That is the way the Oakland A's recreated themselves," said Ricciardi.

"People want to say we revolutionized the game. Thats not true. We were the first team to scrape a team together that no one else wanted. I did the same thing when I went to Toronto. With very little money, we were able to put competitive teams together because of good scouting and finding guys no one else wanted. That's what we were able to do. We were Moneyball without money. When Theo Epstein went to Boston as their general manager and took over the Red Sox, they were Moneyball *with* money. I tell Epstein that all the time. It's all about good scouting, and the Cape Cod Baseball League is very important in building a good MLB team," said Ricciardi.

J. P. Ricciardi added a personal note. "My career might have been baseball, but when it's all said and done, I want to be remembered as a good husband, father, and son."

The conversation closed with Ricciardi mentioning the pride which he has always had for his hometown. "I'll tell you something that I have always been very proud of. I will never forget my hometown roots. Every chance I had to give a kid from Central Mass. an opportunity to play in the majors, I did. Tim Collins, a kid from Worcester Technical High School, which is the old Worcester Boy's Trade High, I drafted. He was only five feet, four inches when I noticed him. He ended up pitching six years for Kansas City and won a World Series Championship with them. Another was Tanyon Sturtze, who I saw playing shortstop for Quinsigamond Community College. I told my buddy I was with that I was going to draft him and make a pitcher out of him. Sturtze ended up pitching for twelve Major League seasons. Those are some of the things I'm most proud of."

WHITECAPS AT YARMOUTH-DENNIS—FIRST RAIN POSTPONEMENT
When it rains at the Cape, it really pours. The Whitecaps had their first rainout. They were scheduled to play at Yarmouth-Dennis. As the players were loosening up, it started raining buckets. Lightning and thunder had everyone running for cover. The first inning hadn't even been finished and everyone was drenched.

Rogers was ready to play. He is always anxious to look at the lineup card that is placed on the wall of the dugout. When he saw he was batting sixth, he said, "I'm going to push even harder and challenge myself to move up into the top four of the order."

DJ Primeaux has an ERA of 0.00 after four appearances. The Baton Rouge native is going to be a redshirt sophomore in the fall at LSU. Primeaux came to the Cape to show the scouts he could be consistent. Through four games he has proven that and more. At the present time, he remains perfect and has become one of the most reliable relief pitchers on the Cape. "I'm having a blast. I'm getting to meet a lot of people. I want to show myself as a competitor and a winner. Once everyone gets to know each other we'll come together as a team," Primeaux stated.

Dumesnil is an outfielder from California Baptist. "I had a

great year this past season in college. I think I'm showing well. The team here will eventually figure things out. We're actually very competitive. When it comes together, we're going to be very good. I love playing here. The Cape is a cool place to be," Dumesnil said.

Pettorini is a second baseman from Ohio State. He is going into his senior year and is eligible to get drafted in the MLB draft on July 14. He said, "I was all-state every year in high school at Wooster High School in Ohio. This is my second summer playing for Brewster. While I'm here my goal is to win and get better every day. My strength is my consistency. I love it in Brewster and wouldn't want to play anywhere else."

Tomczak is also having a tremendous season so far for Brewster. After three appearances the big right-hander is sitting on a 0.00 ERA. "I think I'm holding my own. I feel like as I've gotten more mature, I understand better how to get hitters out. It's always a work in progress. My best pitches are fastball, changeup, and slider. I can get my fastball up to ninety-six. I'm cautiously optimistic about the upcoming draft. I just want a shot."

Sixth Inning—MLB Workout Day, Fenway Park

THERE ARE ONLY A FEW sports venues in the world that, when they are mentioned, conjure thoughts of legendary greatness. One is the Montreal Forum, former home of the Montreal Canadiens of the NHL for over seventy years. Lambeau Field with its frozen tundra, home of the Green Bay Packers in the NFL, makes people remember Vince Lombardi. Yankee Stadium with its outfield monuments, home of the New York Yankees, is the house that Ruth built and the home of twenty-seven World Series Championships (tough to write that as a Sox fan). Pauley Pavilion, the house that Coach John Wooden built, home to the UCLA men's basketball team, is iconic. The old Boston Garden with its mystical parquet floor, home of the great Celtics teams starring Bob Cousy and Bill Russell, will always be remembered. Let's also remember Wembley Stadium, home to many of England's premier soccer matches.

Add one more to this legendary list: Fenway Park, with its ever-imposing left field wall called the "Green Monstah" by the native Bostonians. Fenway is home to the nine-time World Series Champions. This is the 113-year anniversary of the ballpark that plays home to the iconic Major League franchise the Boston Red Sox.

Walk on this field and you will feel the greatness of those

that once played in this majestic field of green. Feel the spirits of Babe Ruth, Ted Williams, Bobby Doerr, Carl Yastrzemski, Tony Conigliaro, George Scott, Carlton Fisk, Luis Tiant, Jim Rice, Dwight Evans, Fred Lynn, Wade Boggs, Rich Gedman, David Ortiz, Pedro Martinez, Manny Ramirez, Nomar Garciaparra, Mike Lowell, Tim Wakefield, Jackie Bradley Jr., Mookie Betts, plus so many more.

Remember this day! On July 1, 2024, the Brewster Whitecaps invaded Fenway Park and left a lasting impression.

The event was the MLB-sponsored Cape Cod League workout day. Scouts from all thirty teams were represented when Ms. Shannon, the bus driver, dropped off her boys from Brewster at the pearly gates of Fenway. Out jumped the Caps to show the baseball world what they could do. My oh my oh my, what a show it was.

First the scouts put the players through some agility drills to measure their raw athletic abilities. The standing broad jump was used to measure the athletes' leg strength and agility. Then the infielders took to the field for infield skills. The Whitecaps turned heads. Third baseman Fischer, first baseman Vest, and catcher Helfrick showed why they have a chance to be Major Leaguers. They all fielded their positions flawlessly.

Next the players all took turns in the batting cage. With the world-famous left field fence of the legendary "Green Monster" staring them down, all the players took turns hoping that they could muscle one over the thirty-seven-foot wall located 310 feet in front of them.

The overanxious Whitecaps were giddy, hoping that they could join the immortals of yesteryear and pop one over.

The Caps did themselves proud. Outfielders Rogers and Dumesnil both blasted one. Fischer showed why he's one of the best hitters in the Cape League. Helfrick, going into his sophomore year at Arkansas, who might just have become one of the greatest catchers to ever play on the Cape, left the scouts drooling.

Donay, the catcher-first baseman from U of Florida, was also blasting them all over Fenway. Faurot, the highly intense infielder from Florida State, didn't get left out. Max Kaufer also had an extraordinary day, showing why the recent transfer from Texas A&M to South Carolina is one of the top catchers available in the 2025 MLB draft.

The Rogers family had flown in from Indiana to watch their pride and joy. Abbie and Scott Rogers, JD's parents, were gushing with pride at the end of the afternoon. Abbie expressed her love for her middle son by explaining, "JD's character is of the utmost importance. He was having fun out there. I was just overjoyed watching the home run ball he hit. He works so hard."

Scott Rogers added, "He's playing at a high level. God always has a plan, and if it includes baseball that would be wonderful. He put's so much pressure on himself."

JD's younger brother also made the trip from Indiana. Hayden Rogers exclaimed, "Being at Fenway is surreal. Every aspect as an athlete, his character, on and off the field, JD remains the ultimate role model. I look up to him, and he never disappoints me" was how Jayden described the relationship he has with his older brother JD.

JD was all smiles as he hugged his parents in the stands. "I knew I got it all. I turned on it and enjoyed watching it go out. I told the guys as we went out for our last at-bat to go for a big blast. Having my parents here to see it was special."

Fischer was his usual happy-go-lucky self-leaving Fenway. He turned around as he was leaving Fenway and, with his boyish grin, said, "That was really fun." This may not be the last time Fischer plays baseball at Fenway Park. This third baseman plays the game with a boyish personality that hasn't been seen since the great Hall of Famer George Brett retired.

On the way home to Brewster, the mood on the bus was in stark contrast to what it had been driving to Boston. Going to, it had been quiet. You could almost feel the pressure the Caps were feeling to perform at a high level to impress the scouts.

Returning to the Cape, the players were all in a festive mood once again. They were all enjoying the opportunity they had been blessed with to be in college and get the chance to play baseball on Cape Cod.

When in Boston, the Union Oyster House in Fanuel Hall has the best bowl of clam chowder in America. As it was established in 1826, there might be a chance that former President John Quincy Adams ate from the same bowl while he was dining there as president. A special mention here is if you do stop in and the bartender likes you he may let you drink from the same beer mug that Sam Adams used.

The day was a huge success all around and one the Brewster Whitecaps will surely never forget.

Steve DiTrolio—Scout, Milwaukee Brewers

Steve DiTrolio was in his third year as a Milwaukee Brewers scout on the Cape when he sat down to talk about the talent he was assigned to look over. The longtime high school, AAU, and junior college coach has spent his life involved with mentoring young ballplayers around the state of New Jersey.

DiTrolio said, "I've been assigned to follow Y-D and Brewster this summer. Brewster is loaded as usual. They have some really good players. Fischer is definitely a good one. He could be really special. I've seen him play before in New Jersey, where we're both from. Cuvet is another one. I saw him when he was in high school playing down in Miami."

"When I scout the Cape, I'm generally looking at players at every position. After I leave in a week or two, the Brewers will send another couple of scouts here to evaluate the players I saw. That's how it works. There are cross-checkers who follow behind us just to make sure everyone has a chance to evaluate the players we might be interested in," said DiTrolio.

CHATHAM ANGLERS AT WHITECAPS

It was a picture-perfect evening at Stony Brook Field. The Whitecaps were feeling loose in their pregame warm-ups. You could hear the chirping going on between the players. The team's chemistry had really taken off. Shevchik builds his roster on finding the best players available. The other trait he's looking for are players who show great character and will become great teammates.

Before the game it was announced that both second baseman Kaeden Kent and outfielder-first baseman Blake Binderup had joined the team. Both players came from the Texas A&M Aggies. The Aggies had just lost in the championship game of the College World Series to Tennessee. Kent is the son of Major League Baseball legend, second baseman Jeff Kent. Kent the previous year had been a Cape All-Star playing for Chatham.

To make room for the two additions from Texas A&M, both RJ Johnson and Tyler Pettorini were released.

Sitting around in the dugout before the game, the coaches were talking about the 'it' factor. Someone shouted out, "When a player is said to have 'it,' what is 'it' that they really have?"

The debate was on. Pitching coach Brian Del Rosso was quick to point out that 'it' is hard to put into words. "You just know if someone has 'it' right away. Talking doesn't show that someone has 'it.' You must back it up. If someone can't be 'it' every day, they don't have 'it.'"

Jon Mecca had this to say: "Someone who has 'it' has 'rizz' (charisma) also." After debating 'it' and 'rizz' in the dugout for several minutes, it was decided that people with 'rizz' have a special personality about them. The 'it' factor was a little more general. It was agreed upon that you either have 'it' or you don't. If someone does have 'it', you can tell 'it' immediately.

Vest has a bit of 'rizz' to him. The first baseman from Brigham Young has been struggling with his bat. He is going to break out of his slump any day now. Vest has been playing great defense for the Caps, though. Before the game Will Ray was sharing a cute story about an evening he had off the field with Vest.

Ray told the following story: "We were hanging out in Chatham a couple of days ago, and a lady who was celebrating her sixtieth birthday approached Vest on the sidewalk. She was wearing a tiara with the number sixty on the front. That's how we knew it was her sixtieth birthday. Well, wouldn't you know it, the lady became enthralled by our first baseman with 'rizz.' She put a full-court press on him to nab him for the night." At this point in the conversation, this author, standing close by, pointed out to everyone within hearing distance that Vest had a higher hitting average in Chatham than he did playing for Brewster.

The word on the street in Chatham was that the birthday lady struck out in her efforts to make the catch of the summer.

The Chatham Anglers and Brewster Whitecaps came into the game both tied for third place in the East Division standing at 5–8. A win by Brewster against a divisional foe would help the Caps in the standings.

It was a day for the pitchers, make no doubt about that. The Caps put up a run in the fifth to take a 1–0 lead. Pitcher Luke Guth from Vanderbilt was outstanding for Brewster, pitching five shoutout innings. Chatham tied it up in the top of the seventh and scored their winning run in the eighth. Titan Hayes, the flamethrower extraordinaire for Chatham by way of Austin Peay, came on in the ninth and blew away the Caps, throwing 100 mph. Five runners for the Whitecaps were thrown out on the bases, or they would have put this one away early. Hayes showed a personality that went beyond 'rizz'. His personality rubbed the Caps players the wrong way. Hayes definitely has 'it', but he also has a brash cockiness that could be called obnoxious.

The Caps were beside themselves after the game. It's one thing to be a little cocky and play with a bit of 'rizz', but Hayes was strutting around the mound a bit too arrogantly as he took control of the game for Chatham. After the game it was much worse. Smack-talking to the opposition can only fire up the opponent for the next time these two divisional rivals meet. Caps never forget!

After the 2–1 loss to Chatham, Shevchik gave all the credit to the Chatham pitchers. "Sometimes after a loss, you can't make excuses. I tip my cap to the pitchers for Chatham tonight. I like to play aggressively, so even though Chatham made some great plays, we need to keep forcing the action."

For Chatham Anglers first-year manager Jeremy "Sheets" Sheetinger, "The win is just another 'W.'

"We have a long way to go. We need to start getting ready for tomorrow's game," Sheetinger said right after the game. He also said the following about Brewster: "Watch out for the Whitecaps to start making a push. Shevchik has put together another great roster like he does every year. When playoff time comes, Brewster will be right there."

HARWICH MARINERS AT WHITECAPS
Casey Gallant grew up in Brewster. Her family founded Gallant Jewelers in Orleans in 1976. She takes enormous pride in the fact that the Whitecaps are her hometown team. "Brewster doesn't even have a red light, but we have the Whitecaps. The team has put our tiny town on the national map. Words can't describe the pride I have for my beloved Brewster Whitecaps."

Miami Marlins scout Carmen Carcone has been involved in Cape Cod Baseball for most of his adult life. He has been back on the Cape this summer following Brewster. He managed the Orleans Firebirds for three seasons twenty years back. For someone that has been involved with Major League Baseball for almost twenty years, you might think his memories from his Cape years have faded.

Carcone's years on the Cape might be in fact his favorite years in baseball. "Managing on the Cape is one of the ten best managing jobs in America. When I was managing Orleans, we won the Cape championship in my second season. We had players on that team that played ten years in the Majors and still wear their Cape championship rings. In fact, twenty years after the year we won it all, the players got together for a reunion. Cape Baseball is the very best amateur summer baseball league in America. People like Sue Horton, who helps run the Orleans Firebirds, and Jane Sullivan of the Brewster Whitecaps dedicate their lives to keeping this league going. I still get goose bumps when I think back," Carcone explained.

Before the game with the Harwich Mariners, Shevchik brought the entire pitching staff together. He felt he needed to clear the air on several concerns. The Whitecaps, like most teams in baseball, use the latest in technology and data to quantify results and decisions. The biggest concern he had was that the Whitecaps, after fourteen games, were one of the league's leaders in walks and hit batsmen. In all thirty-one of those, players scored after walking or being hit. That is the most of any team in the league.

Shevchik used the meeting to encourage his pitchers to challenge the hitters with fastballs and not throw as many breaking pitches. He explained to his pitchers that when they pitch in college, they are coached to throw a lot of sliders and not to throw fastballs in the strike zone. He explained that the college way of pitching is taught because the hitters are using aluminum bats. With aluminum the ball explodes off the bat. With the wooden bats used at the Cape, the ball doesn't come off the bat with as much explosion. He encouraged his pitchers to change their approach while pitching for the Whitecaps.

Shevchik also spoke with the entire team. He told the players that they were all hand-selected to come to Brewster. He wanted to reassure them that there weren't going to be many more players released. He said that Cuvet and Forbes would be returning to the Caps once Team USA completed their exhibition games. Shevchik concluded the meeting by saying, "I still have enormous confidence that at the end of the season we will be right in the thick of fighting for a championship."

The meeting ended on a positive note.

The game with Harwich, however, did not end on a positive note. It ended with the worst loss of the season for the Caps as they were badly beaten by a score of 13–2.

So much for talking.

WHITECAPS AT HARWICH MARINERS
Independence Day and Cape Cod baseball go together like Santa Claus and Christmas. There is nothing in America that is quite like it. It's magical! The backdrop was a beautiful summer evening with the Caps looking for revenge against the Mariners at Whitehouse Field. The American flags were draped around the fences circling the field. The lopsided 13–2 loss against the same opponent the night before was still stinging.

Before the game Shevchik was still optimistic about the major goal he had set for his ball club. "The whole idea is to be playing your best ball at the end of the year going into the playoffs. I knew there would be growing pains early on. I still like the way this team has been put together. I know we're underachieving right now, but I still feel good about our chances," Shevchik said.

Harwich Manager Steve Englert was glowing before the game.

He was still feeling good about the beating his team put on the Caps the day before. This game day was different for Englert. "This day is unlike any special holiday. We are all so blessed to be able to enjoy the opportunity of being here on this field on this holiday," Englert said, bursting with pride.

Cam Murphy, a scout with the Pittsburgh Pirates for the past seven seasons, spoke about how attending a baseball game on Cape Cod on July 4 was his "favorite day of the year to go to the ballpark."

Luke Schmolke's girlfriend, Kennedy Nemechek, had flown in from her home in North Carolina to join in the festivities. The attractive Nemechek is going into her junior year at Tennessee. "I met Luke at the gym working out in North Carolina. I love Brewster, and I've become a baseball fan. I get nervous when Luke is pitching. I've been to the beach a couple of times. We've gone fishing three times. Today I caught a five-pound bass. We ate dinner one night at the Knack. That's my favorite restaurant so far," said Ms. Nemechek about her stay at the Cape.

As the interview was coming to an end, the University of Tennessee coed proudly announced to everyone around her that her Volunteers had just won the College Baseball World Series the week before. She then sang the University of Tennessee fight song, "Rocky Top," to everyone sitting in her section.

Lynda Linnell of Brewster has been attending Brewster Whitecaps games her entire life. Now in her sixties, Linnell works as a nurse. "I watch the games on live stream when I can't make it in person. I'm not concerned about our slow start. I just love sitting outside and watching the team play. I remember when Carlton Fisk played on the Cape (Orleans, 1966). Now we have Ryder Helfrick, and he's a special player. I just know we're going to win the championship this year," Lynda gushed.

Just before the first pitch, starting shortstop for the Caps Faurot was in an extra-cheerful mood. "Playing on Cape Cod on July 4 is as good as it gets for me," Faurot was heard telling his teammates.

It was only appropriate that the Brewster Whitecaps used this day to explode their wooden bats that had been frozen. The bombs going off on the Cape came from the eighteen hits the Whitecaps were finally able to string together. The biggest blast of the day came from Donay, who lit into a July 4 cherry bomb in the ninth that traveled 441 feet. Afterward Shevchik pointed out, "I've been managing on the Cape for ten years, and that is the farthest home run I have ever seen." Donay had a big smile afterward and proclaimed, "It felt great on contact—I knew I got all of it."

Tomczak gave the Caps what they so desperately needed. He limited the Mariners to five hits and three runs in five innings. "I did what I was supposed to do, and that is throw strikes," Tomczak said after the game.

It certainly was a happy Fourth for the Caps as they traveled back to Brewster with revenge and a 10–5 whupping they put on the Mariners.

It was also a good day at Mad Minnow Bar and Kitchen as they were open and serving up their delicious clam chowder that was voted best chowder in Harwich in 2023.

FALMOUTH COMMODORES AT WHITECAPS

The Whitecaps came back home to Stony Brook Field for a game against Falmouth. Before the game the entire team was given a lecture presentation from former Harvard baseball player Chris McGrory regarding the best sleeping practices for athletes. It was extremely informative but went on a little longer than some of the players would have liked. The presentation worked beautifully as a few of the players were enjoying a comfortable nap before it was over. Once a team warms up and puts on their game faces on, a lecture on sleeping can definitely take away a player's intensity.

It was an exciting afternoon for a couple of players. First, outfielder Rogers was informed that the temporary contract he had been playing on was now a permanent one. Rogers would now be a Whitecap for the entire season. Shevchik emphasized to Rogers that he had played his way into a starting role in the outfield. Rogers was thrilled and stated that he was "proud of myself for proving that I could compete against the best college players in America. My next goal is to make the Cape All-Star team."

Daniel Cuvet returned from his week with Team USA. The entire team was thrilled to have him back. Cuvet would later tell his teammates how much he had missed them. In addition, joining the team for the first time was outfielder Dallas Macias from Oregon State, who never stopped smiling all summer.

With the July weekend in full swing, almost twenty-five hundred fans were on hand on a gloomy, dark day to witness one of the most remarkable comebacks on the Cape during the 2024 season.

During each game played on Cape Cod, teams sell raffle tickets. Several donated prizes are given to the lucky winners. The grand prize is always a fifty-fifty split of the cash proceeds taken in.

Maeve Myles, a summer intern from Holy Cross, handles the raffle duties for the Caps. Every second and fourth inning, a player walks with Myles through the crowd, selling tickets. Myles was handpicked for this responsibility. With her charming spirit and personality, fans are eager to purchase their tickets from her. Maeve enjoyed sharing her experiences. "We bring in the most money when the player I'm paired with has an outgoing personality."

The Caps played their first four innings as if they hadn't woken up from their naps. After falling behind 6–0 in the fourth, it seemed it was going to be another loss for the Caps. But not on this day. In the fifth, Helfrick, the kid wonder at nineteen years old, hit a monster grand slam to bring Brewster withing striking distance.

Sixth Inning—MLB Workout Day, Fenway Park

In the bottom of the seventh, Cuvet, who had barely arrived back in Brewster in time to be in the lineup, came through in a huge way. A booming two-run homer let Cuvet's teammates know how much he had missed everyone.

Then the real drama began. With the skies darkening as each precious second went by, the Caps loaded the bases with one out. Catcher Max Kaufer came to bat. At this point in the game, Brett Antolick, a former teammate of Kaufer's at A&M, was pitching for Falmouth. All Kaufer had to do was make contact and hope it was enough to score the winning run.

The greatest Texas showdown in Cape Cod history was on. Antolick stared in from the mound at his new archenemy Kaufer. Kaufer stared right back. They both snarled. Here they were, fifteen hundred miles from their college campus in Brewster, and they wanted in the worst way to show each other who was going to come out on top. Kaufer dug in with his cleats scraping against the dirt. Antolick wound up and delivered a hard fastball that Kaufer took a wild swing at and fouled off. The second pitch was a little outside, but Kaufer once again lunged and got a piece of it. Once again, the ball ended up foul for strike two. There was nowhere to hide for these two Aggies. The crowd was deathly silent. Antolick threw one outside that Kaufer took for ball one. Before the fourth pitch of the at-bat, all Kaufer was trying to do was protect the plate so he wouldn't be a strikeout victim. He kept repeating over and over to himself, "Just put the ball in play somewhere—give Fischer on third a chance to score." As the pitch was thrown, Kaufer took what he admitted after the game "was an ugly swing."

Kaufer lifted a fly ball to left field that was caught for the second out. It was deep enough, though, for Fischer, who was perched on third, to tag up and score the winning run on the sacrifice fly. Kaufer and Brewster came out ahead to the delight of the largest crowd of the season for the home team.

Immediately after Fischer scored the winning run, the umpires halted the game due to darkness.

In a game shortened to seven innings due to darkness, it was celebration on for the "comeback Caps." It was the perfect ending to the day. Now it was time for all the players to head home and practice their new sleeping techniques. They would need to be well rested for the next day when they would travel to Wareham to play the Gatemen.

After the game Shevchik was overjoyed to say the least. When asked if he still wanted to have lights installed at Stony Brook Field, Shevchik proclaimed, "What a way to win a game. I'll take them any way I can get them. Cuvet gave us one heck of a homecoming celebration."

WHITECAPS AT WAREHAM GATEMEN

Next, Brewster traveled to Wareham to take on the Gatemen at Clem Spillane Field for the first time in 2024. Wareham entered the game in first place in the Cape Cod West Division with a record of 11–5.

Wareham jumped off to a 4–1 lead in the third. Brewster fought back and tied the score 5–5 behind Cuvet's two-run double in the top of the seventh. In the eighth Wareham put the game away when Triston Gray lifted a long three-run homer off Brewster's DJ Primeaux (LSU). The final score was Wareham 8 and the Caps 5.

The win improved the Gatemen to 12–5 and dropped the Caps to a disappointing 7–11.

In sports there is a saying that says, "Regardless of how good you are on paper, you're only as good as your record."

And right now, that's not very good for the beloved Caps.

While in Wareham, visit the Gateway Tavern for their yummy clam chowder.

ORLEANS FIREBIRDS AT WHITECAPS

The jinx is over! The Whitecaps broke an eight-game losing streak to Orleans to improve their record to 8–11 and move three games ahead of Orleans for the fourth and final playoff spot in the Cape Cod East Division.

This was a huge win for Brewster. The Caps had not beaten Orleans since 2022. It was not easy, though. Forbes started the game and breezed through the first four innings, giving up only one hit. This was Forbes's first outing since he returned from Team USA. He was looking forward to returning to the summer friends he had made before leaving. Forbes was back to his dominant self as he hit 95 mph on the radar gun several times during his work.

The Caps took an early one-run lead in the fourth. It looked for a while like the Firebirds were going to hang a ninth loss on the home team when they took a 3–1 lead through six innings. In the bottom of the seventh, it was all Brewster. Dumesnil and Kent came up big for Brewster combining for three RBIs. Ray closed out the game for the Caps, setting down the Firebirds in order in the ninth.

Shevchik was relieved to put any more talk about an Orleans jinx to bed. "We finally got the Orleans monkey off our back. They're the type of team that lulls you to sleep. Every team on the Cape is good. We keep coming back when we're down. That's a sign of a team going in the right direction."

Ray is starting to step up as the team's closer. Even though it's hard to give any pitcher on a Cape roster a specific role, Ray is starting to step up. "I felt good. I had two or three days off, so I was ready. I think today was my coming out party," Ray proclaimed after the win.

The Caps have played without star infielder Fischer for the past two games. Fischer has entered his name in the NCAA transfer portal and is leaving Ole Miss. He is visiting both Tennessee and

Florida. He is looking to improve his chances of winning a College World Series during his final year of NCAA eligibility.

Before the game a conversation was held between the three African American players on the Brewster roster. Boston Flannery, Ross, and Hylton were discussing the issue of why so few blacks are playing baseball in America.

"The biggest problem I see is that the African American athletes are not playing baseball in high school. They play in youth leagues, but when they get to high school, they devote their time to football and basketball," explained Ross.

"Breaker Series, a program designed to get more blacks from inner cities involved with baseball, is starting to grow along with Major League's RBI [Reviving Baseball in the Inner Cities] program, and both are free," Flannery pointed out.

Ross said, "Kids today think baseball isn't cool. They think basketball and football are cool. When I was growing up, I only played one year of Little League. The coach batted me last in the order the entire season because they didn't think I was any good, and yet I was the best player on the team. Racial profiling in baseball still exists. I grew up watching Ken Griffey Jr. and Marquis Grissom. I wanted to be like them. Today there aren't as many role-models on TV playing."

In 2022, for the first time since 1950, there were no African Americans playing in the World Series between the Houston Astros and the Philadelphia Phillies. There were several Black Latinos but no African Americans. Also, only 6 percent of all current Major League players are African Americans.

Flannery is a pitcher for the University of North Carolina in the ACC. Flannery said, "The NCAA just passed a change that starting in 2025, all NCAA Division I baseball players will be put on full athletic scholarships. No longer will they be given small stipends. This will help level the playing field and bring out more high school football and basketball players into baseball."

Hylton also added that "In the near future, more African American youth will start to play baseball again, which will only help the Major Leagues."

COMMUNITY DAY
Just what the good doctor ordered: a day off for some sun, fun, swimming, relaxation, and a little hoop. Nothing like getting away from the daily grind to recharge the batteries.

After winning a close game against Orleans the day before, the Brewster Whitecaps headed to the First Light Beach Community Pool in Brewster. There the fans and the community came out to meet their heroes. Autographs, smiles, handshakes were the order of the day.

Every player was in attendance. That's what families do. They work together and they celebrate together. Yes, Whitecap Nation is truly one big family.

World class baseball players are often elite all-around athletes. Many times, they played more than one sport growing up. Adjacent to the community pool was a basketball court. After the players were done signing autographs, basketball games started breaking out. The players were showing off their moves. Some were quite good, and it was easy to see they had once played basketball along with baseball.

Cuvet had game and had some smack talk to go with it. He kept challenging his teammates to a game of horse. Wouldn't you know it, the freshman All-American baseball player from Miami blew everyone away. Including this 72-year-old author.

After the meet and greet, the players had the swimming pool all to themselves. It was a grand day for all in attendance.

As people started to leave, Shevchik admitted he was still trying to figure out the best way to build the roster for the Brewster Whitecaps. He was heard telling long time Brewster fan Torrey Marshall, "I've tried many different formulas to bring college baseball players to Brewster throughout my ten years as the manager. It's tricky. I must admit I still don't know what the best formula is."

Shevchik is referring to building the roster with the very best players available. The danger of this is that sometimes, before the end of the season, their college coaches and personal advisors will make them return home. When this happens, a manager must start finding other players around the country who are not playing ball in the summer to replace them.

Another formula used to build a team is trying to find players who may be one small step from being the best. Looking for hungry, motivated players who will commit themselves to staying the entire summer has its advantages.

WHITECAPS AT COTUIT KETTLEERS

Long before the game at Lowell Park in Cotuit, the Caps were showing off their power in batting practice. Dumesnil, Macias, and Kent lit up the sky. Kent in particular put on a dazzling display. The slick-fielding second baseman is following in the footsteps of his dad, Jeff Kent. Jeff was selected to five all-star games and played second base for six Major League teams over a seventeen-year career. He also won the National League MVP playing for the San Francisco Giants. His highly competitive and very intense son, Kaeden, is also on his way to a long professional career if he keeps playing the way he is performing for the Whitecaps.

The most impressive batting practice performance came from switch-hitting shortstop Faurot. The talented power hitter extraordinaire was drilling shots out of Stony Brook Field from both sides of the plate. When word gets out about his pregame performances, there will be more people coming to watch Faurot take batting practice than there will be for the game.

Leaning against the fence on a beautiful, warm summer evening, Shevchik was shaking his head in wonder. "I have never had a team in my ten years managing Brewster that had this much power," said the manager.

After the pregame fireworks, the players relaxed in the dugout, enjoying the new friendships that they had been building. Suddenly the subject turned to the best ballparks on the Cape. Everyone had an opinion. The team's trainer, Bre Kender, suggested it was Brewster. The intern-trainer, Chloe Johnson, said it was Orleans. Some said Cotuit had the best, others said it was Chatham, others said Harwich, and others had Orleans. The final consensus was that Lowell Park in Cotuit was number one, followed by Stony Brook Field in Brewster. It was unanimous that Spillane Field in Wareham, home to the Gatemen, is the absolute worst.

During the game the dugout was in a festive mood. Schmolke was flirting with both female trainers. Pitchers Ray and Tomczak were chirping at the umpires. Everyone was bouncing around between innings giving each other fist bumps and encouragement. The Caps dugout has certainly come alive over the last few games. Winning has a way of lifting spirits.

The Caps are starting to gel. Everything is starting to come together according to the plan that Shevchik had in mind this winter when he put this team together at Keystone University in Pennsylvania.

The pitching performance against the Kettleers was the best it has been this season for the Caps. Ure Ryan (Oklahoma State) pitched the first four innings and gave up only two hits and one run. Guth followed and had his best outing as he gave up two hits and one run over three innings. Zach Johnston (Wake Forest) pitched the final two and worked out of jams in both innings to earn his first save of the summer.

The three pitchers showed tremendous command of where they were throwing the ball. Between the three, only four walks were given up, and they combined to strike out eight.

Helfrick once again hit a solo blast (his sixth of the season) in the first to get the Caps off to an early lead. One of the big highlights of the game was the absolutely mammoth home run that Cuvet, the tremendous prospect, hit in the sixth. The ball traveled an astonishing 455 feet. As it left the field, his teammates were falling all over themselves in amazement in the dugout. Everyone is starting to wonder if this phenom might just be the top MLB prospect on the Cape. This is the second mammoth home run hit by Brewster in the last few days. Brody Donay hit one 441 feet just a few games ago.

In all it was a great team win for Brewster. The final score was 4–3. The Caps are starting to get contributions from many players. They are starting to move up in the standings and are currently only one game behind Chatham for second place in the East Division.

Shevchik was full of praise for his team after the game. "The team is on schedule. We are playing the way we envisioned. If we don't have players leave and go home for selfish reasons, we could be in control of our destiny. This is without a doubt the most power hitters I've ever had on one of my Cape rosters. I get a little nervous this time of year. I just don't want to lose anyone."

The attendance at Lowell Park was well over 2,500 fans.

The Caps improved to 9–11 on the season.

BOURNE BRAVES AT WHITECAPS

The MLB draft is finally here. Every player who has ever received a baseball or a glove as a gift has dreamed of playing in the Major

Leagues. Every player playing on Cape Cod during the summer of 2024 has put themselves in the elite category of all players worldwide. They have waited and dreamed of hearing their names called during the draft. When and if that day ever comes, it's a moment they will cherish for the rest of their lives. Draft-eligible players are players attending four-year colleges who have completed their junior year or are turning twenty-one years old.

When the three days of the draft finally come, all thirty teams will take turns selecting their twenty players. The players that are drafted will all start their careers playing in the Minor Leagues. This is when the grind really starts. Many times, it takes players several years to get called up to "the show" (Major Leagues). All will play with the hopes that one day they will be called up to the Majors. During the time they will play in the Minors, the pay is usually well under $2,000 per month. Add to it the fact that Minor League teams all travel throughout their seasons by bus. Lastly, a season in the Minors lasts a total of 144 games.

In 2023, a total of 614 players were drafted by the thirty MLB teams. Of those players, 219 had at one time or another been products of the Cape Cod Baseball League. That's a whopping total of 36 percent of all drafted players. Every one of these elite athletes was showcased in the CCBL and evaluated by MLB scouts.

One in every six current Major League Baseball players have played in the Cape Cod Baseball League. There are annually over 370 active Cape Cod Baseball League alumni playing in the Major Leagues and more than seventeen hundred all-time.

The Brewster Whitecaps have produced nearly two hundred MLB players in their history. Remember, Brewster only became an expansion team in 1988. In 2023 alone the Caps had a total of twenty-three active MLB players. The currently playing name most familiar to baseball fans is Aaron Judge. He plays for the New York

Yankees and was named the American League's MVP in 2022 and again in 2024.

Draft-eligible players that are currently on the Whitecaps active roster for 2024 include Cooper Vest, outfielder (BYU), Ryan Ure, pitcher (Oklahoma State), Will Ray, pitcher (Wake Forest), Seth Tomczak, pitcher (Cal State Fullerton), Jacob Marlowe, pitcher (Florida State), and JD Rogers, outfielder (Vanderbilt).

Out of these five players, the possibility exists for Ray, Ure, Tomczak, and Vest to possibly get drafted. Of course, if any player gets drafted, they can still go back to school and use their remaining college eligibility. If they return to school and have a good year, they could possibly improve their draft position for the following year.

Matt Hyde, the Dean of Yankee scouting, was ranked in the top fifty most influential men in baseball by BATTER-UP in 2019. Before the game against Bourne, Shevchik had Hyde address the entire Whitecaps team. Hyde grew up in the Cape. He was once a bat kid for Chatham. While attending the University of Michigan, he played four years of college baseball. He then was on the coaching staff for Brewster at the Cape. Next, he spent nine years as an assistant college coach at Harvard, Michigan, and Boston College. It was after his college coaching that he joined the Yankees as their northeast regional scout. Hyde has been with them for the last nineteen years.

Hyde had the following to say to all the Caps players: "We want you to succeed. Scouts come to the Cape League to fish for players. If you want to be a great player, you must want to face the best players every day. We don't want guys who only want to be drafted. We want guys who want to be great Major League players. If you're a pitcher, we want pitchers who want to challenge the best hitters. If you're a hitter, we want hitters who want to face the best pitchers."

Hyde continued, "The Cape League is great. Don't get caught up in just your performance. How you handle failure is important. If we can watch you fail, we can then watch how you pick yourself back up. There are so many people who want to influence you. Your so-called advisors, agents, family members, college coaches, and friends often don't look out for your best interests. They tell you what you want to hear. I've never seen a great player who wants to leave the Cape early because he misses his girlfriend. We don't want players who just want to get drafted."

Hyde concluded, "The Yankees want guys who want to compete and win. We want fighters. We want guys who are obsessed with being champions. Everything we want to find out comes from the fields of Cape Cod. College coaches who say, 'Come home, you've played enough' are not doing you a favor. If you can't play a forty-game summer schedule, how can you possible play a 162-game schedule that they play in the Majors?"

After the important message that Hyde gave, a couple of Brewster players shared their thoughts. Macias, an infielder from Oregon State, was enthusiastic about what he heard. "I loved every word of what he said. Hyde's words were inspiring to me."

Vest offered up his ideas on what he heard: "When a Yankee scout speaks, you need to listen."

Tomczak, the starting pitcher against Bourne later in the day, had conflicting viewpoints about the message. "I don't want to fail just so someone can watch me become successful again." The point Hyde made was that baseball is a sport of failure. The Yankees want to measure success by making sure they don't have a quitter playing for them when things get tough.

Later Shevchik thanked his close buddy Hyde for speaking to his players. What Shevchik said afterward confirmed everything Hyde had just communicated. "Something needs to change here. The players surround themselves with people who are offering them some bad advice. Players who want to go home early are just wrong. There is no accountability," Shevchik added.

Andrew Fischer was back from his recruiting trip. After putting his name into the NCAA transfer portal, the former Ole Miss third baseman visited both the U of Florida and U of Tennessee. The twenty-fifth-ranked player in the MLB draft class of 2025 had committed to Tennessee. The Volunteers had just won the 2024 College World Series.

The outstanding left-handed hitting third baseman, who has been given several nicknames by his Caps teammates, was even more excited to play than usual. The nickname of "Kid Brett" seems best suited. George Brett was also a left-handed-hitting third baseman. Brett has now been inducted into the Baseball Hall of Fame. When Brett played third, he played with the same enthusiasm and fire that Fischer displays. Hence the nickname Kid Brett will be used for Fischer throughout the remainder of this story.

Kid Brett was really fired up after missing the last three games. He called out, "I used to hate Tennessee, but I love them now; look at my new Vols head band!" Just then a song by the music group Journey came across the loudspeakers at Stony Brook Field. He started singing along, and everyone sitting around him in the dugout joined in. "My boy Kid Brett is back in Brewster—let's play ball!" shouted Vest.

Bourne came into Brewster tied for fourth in the West Division. When Tomczak took the mound, he seemed to be thinking more about the MLB draft in four days than the Bourne Braves. The tall, lanky right hander gave up six runs on six hits in 4⅔ innings in his last start before the draft.

After falling behind 6–0, the Caps were never able to catch back up. The only offensive spark for the Caps came off the bat of Donay. The big slugger accounted for a solo home run and a two-RBI single.

Sixth Inning—MLB Workout Day, Fenway Park

A pitching bright spot came from Jacob Marlowe, who was making his fourth appearance of the summer. After two heart surgeries, the lefty from Florida State continues to make the long climb back. Marlowe had his longest outing of the summer, going 2⅓ innings.

After the 9–4 loss, the Whitecaps fell back to 9–12 on the season.

Camden Kozeal (Vanderbilt), now playing for Bourne, had a big night against Brewster, going three for five. A shortstop, Kozeal spoke about his season after the game while dining with his family and girlfriend at the famous restaurant in Brewster called the Brewster Chowder House. "I got off to a slow start at the plate with Bourne, but with great coaching from Jarrod Saltalamacchia (former Red Sox star catcher), our hitting coach, I got back on track. I love playing against my college teammates at the Cape like I did tonight when we faced JD Rogers of Brewster. It's fun. As teammates in college, we know the guys on the other side better than anyone else does."

Kozeal pointed out that "It's hard to build rivalries among the teams because on most nights, we have friends on the other team." The slick fielder turned down a lucrative offer out of high school in Omaha, Nebraska, to go pro. Instead, he now enters his sophomore year at Vanderbilt and will be eligible for the MLB draft in July 2026.

WHITECAPS AT YARMOUTH-DENNIS RED SOX

They say in sports that a tie is like kissing your sister. Well, tonight Mr. Whitecap kissed his ex-wife. (I think I know what that might feel like.) The Whitecaps wasted their best pitching performance of the season. Clemente, Guth, and Ray combined to pitch a four-hitter against the first place Yarmouth-Dennis Red Sox.

On an overcast night with a steady drizzle at Dennis-Yarmouth High School, the Caps let one slip away. The tie could have been prevented. An Achilles' heel in Brewster's losses this summer has been the inability to put together a string of hits that would have put a game away early. The other problem has been some poor baserunning. Well, those two crucial pieces reared their ugly head once again. The result was a disappointing tie.

Just when it looked like the win was within reach for Brewster, Easton Carmichael launched a solo shot over the left-center field fence to bring heartache to the visiting team. All night the Caps pitchers were dazzling. They challenged the hitters by throwing fastballs right at the Red Sox. Even the big slugger for the Sox, Ethan Petry (South Carolina), struck out three straight times. In the end it was a game that the Whitecaps can build on.

The tie was not lost on Shevchik.

After the game Shevchik had nothing but praise for his pitching. "To go against a team as good as Yarmouth-Dennis and control their hitters is something we should be proud of," Shevchik told his players.

The Caps record now sits at 9–12—and one tie.

Seventh Inning—Morning Clinics: Sharks and Minnows

EVERY SUMMER THE BREWSTER WHITECAPS get the children in the community involved with their baseball program. The Brewster Whitecaps Summer Baseball Clinics start on June 24 and run for six weeks, five days a week. The clinics are held each morning at Stony Brook Field for children ages five through thirteen. The baseball players for the Caps work as counselors.

Let the fun roll! The morning of the game versus the Chatham Anglers, close to sixty boys and girls showed up early to learn the basics and have a blast with their heroes. My oh my, what fun they had. It was impossible to say who was having the most fun. It was a toss-up. The famous coaches had bought in hook, line, and sinker. The kids were in heaven. It was the perfect storm coming together. Playing games of pickle dodge ball, practicing their hopefully soon-to-be-famous home run trots, hitting in the same batting cages that the future Major Leaguers use: These are memories the youngsters will surely always remember. Oh yes, on Fridays the waterslide comes out at the end of camp. The morning was full of nothing but joy and laughter.

Tracey Tomkins, the mom of five-year-old Connor, was gushing with happiness in sharing how much her boy loves the clinics. "Connor just finished his first year of T-ball. He is in total heaven coming here. Just last night he was pretending to be Cooper Vest. That's his favorite counselor."

Sabrina Eberhardt, the mom of Rilo, shared that this is her son's second year coming to the clinics. "My son Rilo just loves this clinic. He thinks these Whitecaps are superheroes. He has improved so much in a year. He is thriving and just loves everyone here."

Melissa Sinkiewicz has brought her son Caleb to the clinics for three years. "We come from out of state. My son just loves this clinic so much. The counselors do a great job of teaching them the game and keeping it fun. Once he builds a relationship with a player, he follows them in the draft and then follows their career."

A few youngsters were thrilled to share their day's activities. Some said their favorite activity was scrimmaging, others said it was hitting in the batting cages, and several others said they couldn't wait for the waterslide. A six-year-old boy claimed that he had been coming to clinic for eight years. Cute little Emma won the pickle dodge ball contest. No one could catch this rising star with a personality that could melt anyone's heart.

When it came to their favorite coaches, Vest was the runaway winner. Other favorites were infielder Kent, pitcher Guth, pitcher Marlowe, pitcher Huesman, pitcher Johnston, and pitcher Primeaux.

Kent did not feel the aftereffects of losing a tough game the night before; he was ready to go early on. "This is fun. I love helping the next generation. We even have two eight-year-olds who already know how to switch-hit. This is a great way to give back to the great baseball fans of Brewster."

Vest, the fun-loving and popular player, never has a bad day. He was proud to know that he was beloved by the children. "I love these kids as much as they love me. The feelings are mutual. In the morning, I sometimes feel a little tired, but once I have a cup of coffee, I'm ready to go."

Coaches Rocco DePietro and Del Rosso are the clinic directors. DePietro explained his philosophy of working with youngsters: "We get a lot more children as the word of the clinics has grown. The counselors do a great job. We break the kids up into groups by age. We make sure to keep everything as fun for them as we can. It's important that they use this clinic to practice, to learn, and to get better."

Another important aspect that DePietro pointed out is that "The Brewster players who do work earn a little extra spending money. It used to be that the players, when they came to the Cape, had part-time jobs waiting for them. This isn't the case anymore. There isn't enough time for them to do their workouts, practice, and play every night."

Just about at this point, the waterslide was rolled out. The kids (and this seventy-two-year-old author) had a giant blast. The weather was perfect as the children went bonkers going down the slide.

As the morning was coming to an end, a five-year-old little boy whose front teeth were missing was asked what his favorite part of the clinic was. Without hesitating the cute little guy shouted out, "Sharks and minnows!"

Once the players started arriving for the game that evening, it was time to put the children's clinic to rest.

CHATHAM ANGLERS AT WHITECAPS

Chatham was the opponent on this day. As the Anglers started taking batting practice, it became obvious immediately that their batting practice pitcher wasn't in the same class as Scott Grimes. Grimes is the Caps hitting coach who also throws batting practice. In fact, they weren't even in the same hemisphere.

The mood was festive in the dugout before the game. Several players were enjoying chatting about the pretty young ladies they have gone out with in college. Livvy Dunne's name came up a few times. She is the gymnast from LSU who has gathered several million followers on Instagram. With the changes that have taken place that allow college athletes to get paid, Ms. Dunne is currently earning a couple of million dollars a year. That's more than Cooper Vest is getting paid by BYU.

Del Rosso and catcher Donay were huddled together planning the game's strategy. Del Rosso was explaining to Donay the best way he wanted the Caps pitchers to pitch to Chatham's hitters during the game.

Shevchik was asking his players if they pray before games during the year. He was wondering what approach to take with his players at Keystone if in fact he were to suggest the idea. At this point Shevchik has mixed feelings about team prayer.

Huesman (Vanderbilt) started the game for the Caps and struggled to get through the first two frames.

The firepower of Brewster struck twice. First, Cuvet hit his longest tape measure job, a blast that traveled 477 feet in the second. That's even longer than any major leaguer has hit a ball this season. As the Herculean shot went into orbit, the entire dugout were all left gasping and chasing each other around, jumping on each other's backs. When the future MLB player rounded the bases, he displayed a sly grin. When told how for the ball traveled, Cuvet shyly said, "That's the longest home run I've ever hit." Next, Helfrick hit his second grand slam of the season in the third. The Caps, win or lose, are fun to watch as they have some serious firepower.

It wasn't enough on this night as the Anglers had their way with the Caps pitchers. The Whitecaps pitchers once again gave up nine walks in the game. That's just way too many.

After the 9–6 loss, Shevchik had this to say: "I think it was nine free passes today. And then you start mixing in all the bases that go along with it—that turned out to be the big difference in the game today."

Chatham improved to 12–11.

The Caps fell to 9–13 with one tie on the season.

WHITECAPS AT WAREHAM GATEMEN

So much has been said regarding JD Rogers's incredible weight-training program. On the Vanderbilt baseball team, they have an established competition that they hold every year called the Omaha Challenge. For the three years Rogers has been at Vanderbilt, he has won the competition each year. The morning of the game against Wareham, Rogers put himself through his weight-strength routine. It was extremely impressive. Rogers brought the same hard-nosed grit he displays on the baseball field while playing for the Caps to Nauset Fit Company in Orleans. Nauset Fit offers a generous discount to all the Caps, so they have a place to work out every day.

Rogers's career at Vandy can be categorized as a disappointment so far. His summer playing for Brewster can be considered his breakout. There is no question Rogers has turned the heads of several scouts who have been watching this summer. The possibility exists that there may be an all-star appearance in the not-too-far-off future in Falmouth coming up.

It poured all day on the Cape. Every game in the league was postponed except for the Whitecaps playing at Wareham. The Wareham Gatemen have the best record in the league at 15–7. They have a great team with tremendous tradition, top-notch coaches, and a great support staff. They also have the worst field and facilities in the league. When the term "sandlot" is used, it refers to the run-down field in Wareham better known as Spillane Field.

Before the team was bused to Wareham, hitting coach Scott Grimes pulled all his hitters aside for a meeting. The rather reserved Grimes called a meeting to get the attention of his powerhouse lineup that had been greatly under achieving. He used the opportunity to get their attention before any more games went by the boards. He let them know that if they didn't stop going through the motions, they would someday regret that they missed one of the greatest opportunities they were ever going to get. He emphasized that playing in the Cape League could be life-changing for many if they take advantage of it.

Well, what do you know. Here come the Caps! Grimes's words and the timing were prophetic. After losing to the Gatemen in Wareham just one week earlier, the Caps woke up. Everyone knows the Caps roster is loaded. Even the players know they have been underachieving.

With Ure making his last start for Brewster, the tall left-hander from Oklahoma State was brilliant. With the MLB draft one day away, Ure had one more opportunity to show the scouts what he could do. Don't be surprised if someday you see Ure on a major league roster. Guth and newcomers Kellan Oakes (Oregon State) and Colby Frieda (Kentucky), both making their first appearances of the season for Brewster, all contributed to shutting down the Gatemen.

Cuvet led the Brewster offensive onslaught once the weather cleared with two long blasts. Helfrick, the league's home run leader with eight, once again belted one. Faurot got into the act by blasting a three-run homer, his first of the year. Faurot was overdue. Don't be surprised if this slick-fielding, switch-hitting shortstop from Florida State goes on a tear. Using the ten run and seven inning mercy rule, the game was stopped after seven. The final score was the Caps 11 and the Gatemen wishing it had never stopped raining.

After the game, Grimes was all smiles as he was asked about the timing of his pregame inspiration. "You get a sense of what they're capable of. I don't make a lot of speeches. I'm not a rah-rah guy by nature, but I thought today was the right time. The offensive potential has always been there, but we just haven't been consistent. I have no doubt about this lineup. I know what they can do."

The league knows also. The Caps might be underperforming, but if this was their wakeup, the rest of the league better take notice. Once the Caps start rolling, there may be no stopping them.

On the season the Caps are now hitting .260 with twenty-four homers. The team's era stands at 4.95.

With the shutout win against the team with the best record on the Cape, the Caps moved to 10 wins, 13 losses, and 1 tie.

FALMOUTH COMMODORES AT WHITECAPS

It was the pitchers' turn to take batting practice on a picture-perfect Sunday evening. When the pitchers have tossed a shutout the previous day, like they did in their 11–0 win against Wareham, the reward is that they get to swing their bats. Primeaux and Schmolke each connected to belt one over the fence. Each homer brought a large round of applause from their pitching teammates.

Host families of the Caps players were honored before the home game against the Falmouth Commodores. Host families play one of the most important roles in the Cape League. Without them the league would not be able to operate. For the players, other than their teammates, it's one of their most treasured memories of playing in the Cape Cod Baseball League.

The players, many times, take the roles of big brothers to the younger children with the families that host them. Family dinners include the players. The relationships continue long after the season ends. A highlight for the families is that they get up close to the future Major Leaguers and can enjoy following their careers in and out of baseball.

Sullivan, who wears many hats for the Caps, coordinates the housing for the Whitecaps. The responsibility for Sullivan is massive, and it is a twelve-month job to place all the players with the right hosts. Remember, during the season there is a large amount of coming and going with the players. This can become taxing for the hardworking Sullivan, who wears her Brewster pride on her sleeve.

Sharon and Tim Kautz hosted Hylton, Tomczak, and Helfrick throughout the summer. Their experience with the players living in their home was wonderful. Sharon had this to say: "We have four children, so we have a large family. The players joined right in. They became excellent role models for our children. When we would all sit down and eat, they would even teach our kids life lessons and talk about their education. They have become part of our family."

The SEC Network came into town to chronicle the league and the Caps. They are highlighting the many players who play for programs in the SEC. Brewster has several players who are playing in the SEC Conference. Kent plays for Texas A&M, Primeaux plays for LSU, Donay, Colby Shelton, and Clemente all play at Florida, Helfrick plays for Arkansas, Kaufer is transferring from Texas A&M and will be attending the University of South Carolina in the fall, Fischer transferred to Tennessee, Rogers plays at Vanderbilt, and several other Caps play for other SEC schools.

Just before the game began, the players were all talking in the dugout about the start of the Olympic Games that was on the horizon. It was unanimous: Women's beach volleyball was the sport everyone was looking forward to watching the most.

Once the game began, the red-hot bats of the Caps gave them a quick 5–2 lead after two innings. In the bottom of the second,

Helfrick, who leads the league in homers, continued his onslaught with a two-run bomb. Helfrick, a quiet and modest young man, admitted afterward that he hasn't been on this kind of tear for a long time.

In the bottom of the fourth, Faurot continued where he left off the day before and drove a double to right field to score all three runners on base and increase the lead to 8–2. From there the Caps scored two more in the bottom of the fifth when Kent doubled home two runs.

Two Wake Forest Demon Deacons, Schmolke and Ray, who have pitched well for Brewster all summer, combined to slow down the Commodores. The Caps would hold on as their closer Ray finished off Falmouth with a perfect ninth, and the Caps would go on to win by a final score of 10–8.

After the game Shevchik was asked how he felt about his offense scoring twenty-one runs over two games. His four-word answer summed up the day perfectly: "Let it ferment, baby," Shevchik said with a catlike smirk.

Brewster improved their record to 11–13 with 1 tie. They now have a solid grip on third place in the East Division with a razor focus on second.

Falmouth dropped to 8–16 and remains at the bottom of the West Division.

Fischer missed his third straight game with a sore back.

Seventh-Inning Stretch— "Sweet Caroline"

2024 MLB Draft

THE CAPE COD BASEBALL LEAGUE came to a standstill on July 14 as the 2024 MLB draft took center stage. Games were still ongoing, but all eyes were locked in on the MLB draft. An astonishing record of fifteen Cape Cod alumni were selected during the first round of the MLB draft. This number is unlike anything the CCBL had ever experienced in their proud 101-year history. These fifteen future MLB players are only from the first round. The entire draft has twenty rounds. In total 197 Cape Cod alumni were drafted from all the ten organizations combined. In today's world of drafting college baseball players, if a college player is holding on to the dream of playing in the Major Leagues, he better make his summer plans of playing baseball on Cape Cod.

Travis Bazzana, an Australian-born, left-handed-hitting second baseman (Oregon State), hit .382 in the summer of 2023 playing for the Falmouth Commodores in the CCBL. Bazzana came away with the league MVP honors at the end of his glorious summer on Cape Cod, and he was selected first overall in the entire draft by the Cleveland Guardians. This was the sixth time in the last seven MLB drafts that the number one overall draft pick found his career path starting on the Cape. The legacy remains intact year after year.

Sullivan, the do-all queen of Whitecaps Baseball, was prancing around Brewster as proud as a prom queen. One of her many favorite sons, James Tibbs (Florida State) had been selected in the first round of the 2024 MLB draft by the San Fransisco Giants. Tibbs played for Brewster and Manager Shevchik in the summer of 2023. The overall thirteenth selection in the draft hit .303 for the Caps that summer. This past college season (2024), the right fielder hit .360 for Florida State. Shevchik was elated when the news of Tibbs reached Brewster. "Tibbs is one of the best players I've ever been around," proclaimed Tibbs's former manager.

In all twenty-two Whitecaps alumni heard their names called over the three days of drafting. Tibbs wasn't the only Whitecaps and Florida State alum drafted high in the 2024 draft. Drafted in the fourth round was Tibbs's best friend and fellow outfielder Jaime Ferrer, who was selected by the Milwaukee Brewers with the overall 126th pick. Ferrer hit .313 for Brewster in 2023. He finished his three-year career with the Seminoles with an impressive .320 average.

Two players who suited up for the Caps in 2024 heard their names called. Pitcher Rocco Reid (Clemson), who was with the Caps early in the summer of '24, was selected by the Arizona Diamondbacks in the fifteenth round. Reid also had a stint in Brewster in 2023. He logged twenty-six innings in '23 and only six innings in 2024. He was released early on in 2024 with a 12.79 ERA. Obviously, the Diamondbacks saw something they must have liked.

Smiles were everywhere in Whitecaps Nation as fan favorite Ure (Oklahoma State), who pitched parts of two seasons (2022 and 2024) with Brewster, was selected by the San Francisco Giants in the nineteenth round. The six-foot, nine-inch, soft-spoken Ure was also drafted out of high school by the Texas Rangers in 2021.

The remaining 2024 draftees with Brewster ties are:

Mike Sirota (Caps 2022)—third round, Cincinnati Reds
Austin Gordon (Caps 2022)—fourth round, Los Angeles Angels
Carson DeMartini (Caps 2023)—fourth round, Philadelphia Phillies
Clark Candiotti (Caps 2023)—fourth round, San Diego Padres
Payton Green (Caps 2023)—sixth round, Miami Marlins
Will Turner (Caps 2023)—seventh round, Boston Red Sox
Greg Farone (Caps 2021)—seventh round, San Francisco Giants
Ivan Brethowr (Caps 2023)—seventh round, Chicago Cubs
Davis Diaz (Caps 2023)—eighth round, Oakland Athletics
Sam Garcia (Caps 2023)—eighth round, Milwaukee Brewers
Fisher Jameson (Caps 2023)—tenth round, Colorado Rockies
Brendan Girton (Caps 2021)—tenth round, New York Mets
Cameron Leary (Caps 2022)—tenth round, Oakland Athletics
Derek Berg (Caps 2023)—tenth round, Pittsburgh Pirates
John West (Caps 2022)—twelfth round, Arizona Diamondbacks
Brock Tibbitts (Caps 2023)—thirteenth round, Toronto Blue Jays
Najer Victor (Caps 2022)—fourteenth round, Los Angeles Angels
Colby Shelton (Caps 2024)—twentieth round, Washington Nationals

The remaining undrafted players for Brewster who were eligible to be drafted will be returning to school in the fall of 2024 with the hopes of having another opportunity to open the eyes of MLB scouts. Vest, Rogers, Ray, and Marlowe will be working toward the 2025 draft.

Whitecaps at Hyannis Harbor Hawks

Brewster bused their way over to Hyannis to face a tough foe in the Harbor Hawks.

The torrid home run barrage continued for the powerhouse Brewster Whitecaps. Rogers showed off some of his strength from his monstrous weightlifting regimen when he shot one over the right-center field fence for his first homer of the season. Donay followed Rogers to hit his fourth round-tripper of the summer to tie the score at two apiece.

In the fourth, Faurot showed why he is emerging as a real star in the league. He blasted his second homer in three games that brought around Donay in front of him. Faurot wasn't done making noise on the night. In the sixth he also fired off a solo shot to put the Caps ahead 5–3. The switch-hitter did something only three other players in the history of the Cape Cod Baseball League have ever done: hit a home run from each side of the plate in the same game.

Hyannis came right back in the bottom of the sixth to retake the lead 6–5. The game was turning into a classic Cape slugfest.

Pitchers Guth, Primeaux, Huesman, Flannery, and Marlowe all had a tough night for the Caps. All got hit around hard on this beautiful evening in the town that many consider the capital of the Cape.

When a team hits four home runs on the road, it's critical that someone on the pitching staff steps up. The inconsistency is still troubling. The Caps have enough talent to put together a solid winning streak, but through twenty-six games, it hasn't happened. It's one win and then two losses. Or it's two wins and one loss. The efforts to reach the elusive goal of evening off their record at five hundred are still coming up short.

A SEASON WITH THE BREWSTER WHITECAPS

Seventh-Inning Stretch—"Sweet Caroline"

The final score was Hyannis 8 and Brewster 6. Dalton Bargo and Kane Kepley each had a home run and combined for five RBIs for the Harbor Hawks. Hyannis improved their record to 15 wins and 9 losses. Brewster dropped to 11–14 with 1 tie on the season. The Caps now only have a one-game lead over Harwich for third place in the East.

Frustration is starting to creep in throughout the Whitecaps Nation. If the trend continues, frustration may not be a strong enough description. Shevchik, who shares his positive outlook with everyone around him, said after the game, "The guys battled it out. The sixth inning just killed us. It took away all of our momentum." As much as Shevchik appears to remain unfazed on the outside, the manager is doing all he can to hide his true emotions inside.

As New York Yankees scout Matt Hyde points out regularly, "Even though a team like the Caps, who play with a loaded roster, might not match the expectations of them on the field, you never know how each player is going to take advantage later on of the experience they gained."

WHITECAPS AT HARWICH MARINERS

Welcome to the continuing saga of Dr. Jekyll and Mr. Hyde. Just when you think the Caps are rolling away from shore, here comes another tidal wave. In a must-win game against their divisional rival the Harwich Mariners, the Caps came storming back in.

Before the game the Whitecaps were given some tough news. In a heartbreaking development, the fun spirit of the entire Caps Nation had left and gone home. Andrew Fischer, the preseason favorite to become the league's Most Valuable Player, succumbed to a back injury. The infielder, who is ranked twenty-fifth in the 2025 MLB draft class, was the spirit of the Brewster Whitecaps. Others like Helfrick, Dumesnil, Kaufer, Kent, Rogers, Vest, Guth,

Schmolke, and Ray will step up, but "Fisch," also nicknamed "Kid Brett," will be sorely missed.

Fischer transferred over the summer to the 2024 College World Series Champion Tennessee Volunteers from Ole Miss. Just like that, Fischer was gone.

In sports as in life, change is inevitable. Very few athletes in any sport are irreplaceable. With the exceptions of athletes like Larry Bird (Boston Celtics), David Ortiz (Boston Red Sox), Tom Brady (NE Patriots), and Bobby Orr (Boston Bruins), all icons who won multiple championships in Boston, almost all players come and go. Of course, Fischer will never be in that category. Here is the thing about Andrew Fischer. As great a talent as he was on the field, his value off of it may have even been greater.

There are certain intangibles that will never show up in the box scores. Leadership, personality, swag, charisma (rizz), and the 'it' factor are a few of them. To have a successful and fun environment, almost every team must have a player that everyone wants to rally around. Fischer brought all that and more to the Brewster Whitecaps.

There should never be a question that if Fischer did not hurt his back, he most certainly would have stayed and would have wanted to be in the lineup every day. The term they use in baseball, "gamer," is a perfect description of this top 2025 MLB prospect.

Upon his departure, the whispers were there. Did Fischer find an excuse to leave early? It was an old injury that came back and reared its ugly head. During the first several days after he stepped away from playing, he tried to work through it by continuing his daily stretching and conditioning program. After just transferring to Tennessee, though, he felt it best to get home and get some rest.

Here is what Shevchik had to say upon Fischer's departure: "Fisch was a high-motor-energy kid. The type that everyone needs on their team to build the chemistry around. The dugout was different after he left. Once he got hurt, he tried to play through it. He never wanted to really leave. He needed to get himself right before he started school at Tennessee."

For me, the author, watching Fischer leave was like saying goodbye to a younger brother as he leaves for his freshman year in college. Fischer spoke to me on the phone from the University of Tennessee. "Developing a friendship with you was easy for me, Pathfinder [my nickname]. I never looked at you as someone who was fifty years older. You are my buddy. They should have given you a team jersey with a number on the back. You were part of our team, and I wanted you with us everywhere we went. You're a funny guy with some great stories. After I accepted you as my friend, it made it easier for the other players like JD Rogers to do the same. For me it was just two dudes hanging out together at the ballpark this summer."

"Yes, we were just two dudes hanging out together at the ballpark," I replied.

Fischer concluded, "Brewster will always have a special place in my heart. My manager 'Shev' was like a second father to me."

See you in the Major Leagues, Andrew "Kid Brett" Fischer.

Once the Caps got over the shock of continuing without Fischer, the players put their game faces on. There will never be any quit found in the Brewster Whitecaps.

On a beautiful night at Stony Brook Field, a crowd of over nineteen hundred fans circled the field.

Clemente took the hill for Brewster and pitched the game of the year for the Whitecaps. The tall right-hander was absolutely brilliant. He faced one batter over the minimum during his seven innings of work. Clemente gave up one hit, and only one other Mariner reached base on an error. Clemente was followed by Oakes (Oregon State) and Detmers as they each pitched a perfect inning. This was the second shutout in four games for the Caps.

Clemente lowered his team-leading ERA to an eye popping 1.93 on the season.

After the game Clemente described his success. "My biggest thing today was just to come out and attack the zone. Just being able to do that was something I've been trying to do."

Clemente came to Brewster as a relief pitcher with the University of Florida. In 2024 Clemente made nineteen appearances. Seventeen of those came out of the bullpen. When he arrived in Brewster, he asked pitching coach Del Rosso for the opportunity to pitch for the Caps as a starter. Well, when Clemente returns to Gator land this fall, it's reasonable to think that he has shown that in fact he is very capable of being placed in Florida's starting rotation for the 2025 season.

The game raced along at a fast clip. The game started at 5:00 p.m. and ended exactly two hours later. Afterward the players were giddy as they were looking forward to hitting the town to introduce themselves to some of the pretty college girls who also spend their summers on Cape Cod.

There are not too many games where the thundering bats of Brewster don't hit home runs. Donay gave the Caps all the runs they would need when he slugged another blast, his fifth of the summer, in the second with no one on. Helfrick added two RBIs to his league-leading thirty-three.

With the win the Caps took control of third place in the East with a two-game lead over Harwich. Shevchik was full of praise for his star pitcher after the stellar outing. "Every pitcher should have paid attention to why he turned seven innings and the success he had. Today Clemente threw strikes and competed at a high level."

With the MLB draft in the rearview mirror, a former Whitecaps player, Spencer Jones, participated in the MLB All-Star festivities. The Futures Game is designed to showcase the next group of young minor leaguers who are excelling in Minor League Baseball. The game is played the day before the MLB All-Star Game. Jones was invited to play and represented the Yankees. In 2021 he played for the Brewster Whitecaps and batted .312. Jones was drafted in 2022 in the first round by the Yankees out of Vanderbilt.

Before the Futures Game, Jones announced to a throng of media that "the Brewster Whitecaps is my happy place. I owe so much to Cape Cod baseball. The league taught me how to prepare myself for playing baseball every day."

There are a lot of multimillionaires running around the United States saying the same exact words, Mr. Jones.

FISHING TRIP WITH CAPTAIN JON MECCA AND CAPTAIN DAN

When there is an off day for the Caps, there is only one thing to do. Jon Mecca is one of the most renowned deep-sea fishermen on the East Coast. Mecca has captured several first-place deep-sea fishing prizes during his illustrious career on the water. Recently he earned his certification as a fishing instructor. The general manager of the Caps has remained humble about his national reputation. Mecca decided to organize a one-day fishing trip for the Caps coaching staff.

Captain Dan was called in, and off went the boat called *Hit the Waves*. Mecca enjoyed describing the Caps adventure. "The group of fishermen that chartered the boat included Manager Shevchik, Scott Grimes, the hitting coach, Steve Meinelt, who assists with running the Caps team store, and myself. The day started out really rough. The ocean caps on top of waves were coming at us with fury. There was thick fog, hard rain, and large swells. No one could see outside of five feet. Captain Dan saved us several times from going over. At one time on the way out to our fishing spot off the coast of Chatham, the boat was tossed completely out of the water. We thought the end was near, but in the end, nobody got sick," Mecca said.

Mecca continued, "The risk was worth the reward. The fishing was unbelievable once the weather cleared. The only problem that occurred once we started fishing was when a large bluefish almost pulled Shevchik overboard. He was petrified. It took all of us to keep him in the boat. Of course, the fish got away and took his fishing pole with him. It turned out to be a perfect day for fishing. In all we caught over thirty striped bass. We pulled one in that was close to forty-eight inches. We threw all of them back except for one that Meinelt brought home to his family that night for dinner. What a great way to spend an off day."

The Caps roller-coaster ride on the waves will continue in their next game when they visit Bourne. This time it won't be in a boat.

WHITECAPS AT BOURNE BRAVES

The Whitecaps' trip to Bourne to play the Braves turned into a disaster. The entire team played like they had just got off the boat *Hit the Waves*. Everyone played as if they were seasick.

The Caps picked up three players to fill out their ever-changing roster. They were brought on by the sharp eye of Brewster's Director of Baseball Operations and Analytics, Ethan Kagno. Kagno works in the same position at Keystone College under his mentor and boss Shevchik. The new players that reported are pitchers Noah Samol (Clemson) and Bobby Lasbury (Iona) and infielder Colby Shelton (Florida).

Brewster starter Samol made his first appearance of the summer and pitched a perfect first two innings. In the third inning, the wheels came flying off, and from there it was all downhill for the Caps the rest of the night.

Bourne shut out Brewster 5–0. It was the first time Brewster was shut out all summer.

"Their pitching was decent, but we also had opportunities to score runs. We had guys on base every inning, but we couldn't come up with a big hit when we needed it. I told the guys that we have two big games coming up this weekend and I need more out of them," Shevchik said.

The roller-coaster season continues. Brewster is now clinging to third place in the East with a record of 12–15 and 1 tie.

Soon the Cape Cod Baseball League All-Star rosters will be released.

Brewster All-Stars Announced

The Cape Cod Baseball League All-Star rosters were released. What jumps out is the incredible number of Whitecaps selected. A total of nine Caps will be heading to Falmouth for the big event on Saturday, July 27. Five will be starters, and two are pitchers. The other three will be reserve position players. The Caps will have more All-Stars playing in Falmouth than any other team.

What this means is that the 2024 Brewster Whitecaps, if things don't improve quickly, will possibly go down as one of the biggest disappointments in Cape Baseball history. Nine all-star players show tremendous individual starts, but the record of 12–15 and 1 tie is disappointing.

The Caps that highlight the East All-Star roster include these starters: catcher Ryder Helfrick (Arkansas), third baseman Daniel Cuvet (Miami), outfielder Nick Dumesnil (California Baptist), and first baseman Brody Donay (Florida). Infielders Kaeden Kent (Texas A&M) and Drew Faurot (Florida State) were selected as reserve infielders. Donay has come on strong in the last couple of weeks. Also selected are pitchers Jake Clemente (Florida) and Will Ray (Wake Forest).

If Andrew Fischer, Nolan Schubart, and Patrick Forbes had not left early, Brewster possibly could have had twelve all-stars.

For Ray, Dumesnil, and Rogers, their selections are a reward for three unsung players whose determination throughout the summer has not gone unnoticed. They battled and fought and now have reached great personal milestones.

Helfrick, who leads the league in both home runs (ten) and RBIs (thirty-four), and Cuvet, who is close behind, were considered automatic locks to be named. The two sluggers are enjoying the challenge of playing together and pushing each other. They are challenging each other toward greatness. Cuvet had this to say about the personal challenge. "It's fun," Cuvet said with a big smile. "Helfrick is a great friend, but I enjoy the challenge of trying to keep up with the great things he is doing." Helfrick had this to say about Cuvet: "Danny is a great player, so to be compared to him is a great honor."

Kent and Faurot also give the Caps great reason to believe Brewster will finish the season strong. There is nowhere left for Brewster to hide. The word is official. The roster is loaded. Now all the Caps have to do is finish the season with some wins.

In 2023 the Brewster Whitecaps placed seven players on the All-Star roster. They were:

Pitchers—Joey DeChiaro and Patrick Forbes
Catchers—Brock Tibbetts and Ike Irish
Infielder—Davis Diaz
Outfielders—James Tibbs and Will Turner

The MLB draft bonus pool was formally announced for the recent 2024 draft. The amount of bonus money awarded to the players is staggering. The bonus system has changed over the years. It used to be that agents would negotiate until an agreement was reached. If there was no agreement, the players who had NCAA eligibility left would return to school.

Today all the teams have a set money arrangement prior to the draft. They have a set amount put aside for their bonus structure.

This money pool is divided among the players that a team drafts. The largest amount of bonus money per team goes to the first-round draft choices. The bonus structure drops considerably according to the round a player is drafted.

An example of this is as follows. The Cleveland Guardians have the largest amount of bonus money available in their draft pool. They have over $18 million put aside to divide among their newly drafted players. Out of this amount, a predetermined cash payout of $10.5 million went to Travis Bazzana, the first player taken in the draft by the Guardians.

The popular first-round pick that played for Brewster in 2023, James Tibbs from Florida, was awarded just under $5 million from the San Francisco Giants.

To say that showing up on Cape Cod and proving that you can hit with a wooden bat or successfully pitch against the best college players will pay dividends is an understatement.

WHITECAPS AT ORLEANS FIREBIRDS

Losing hurts. Losing when you know deep down that you're the better team hurts even more. Losing when you know you're underachieving is the worst. Then when you lose 12–2 to Orleans, it's downright heartbreaking and gut-wrenching.

Even though Brewster doesn't have a true archrival, the whispers are there. In fact, sometimes the whispers aren't really whispers. To a man there is no love lost in the good guys' (you pick who the good guys are) dugout.

It's quite reasonable to believe that the Firebirds feel the same way about the lovable Caps. The Firebirds have gotten the best of Brewster in 2024. They have taken the first three out of four. The season is not over yet.

All you can do is get ready to play tomorrow and not dwell or analyze it too long. That's the beauty of playing baseball on the

Cape. You play every day, and the players must learn to flush out any lingering effects of slumps and losses. In fact, this lesson is a must before the players move into professional baseball, when the season lasts 162 games.

Shevchik shared the following sentiments after the brutal loss. "Today we just beat ourselves. Let's see what type of team we are made of tomorrow. If we go out and play the same, then all we are is a talented team on paper that is not playing well on the field." The stress of managing an underachieving team can be tough, even for an experienced manager.

Let's get ready to play the Anglers and roll Caps!

THE CHILDREN

The Whitecaps are all about children. You can hear the children's laughter all game long, coming from the playground adjacent to the ballfield.

Let's not forget the long lines of families waiting at the tables set up for players' autographs before every home game. The daily morning clinics run by the players have become popular for teaching and practicing baseball skills. The hundreds of kids racing each other as they chase down foul balls throughout every home game at Stony Brook Field are a sight to behold. The Brewster Whitecaps are about children.

The players love their interaction with the next generation of Whitecaps. They enjoy it as much as the children do. Attending a Whitecaps game during the summer months is truly a family affair.

The children of host families enjoy the relationships that are formed. These relationships become lifelong friendships between the players and their host families. Host families often enjoy not only following the future careers of their guests but also becoming part of their lives when the players settle down and have their own families.

A SEASON WITH THE BREWSTER WHITECAPS

Seventh-Inning Stretch—"Sweet Caroline"

The Brewster Whitecaps are at the heart of what makes our great country so special.

BREWSTER WHITECAPS BUDGET

Robert Tobias is another dedicated board member. He is the Vice President of Finance for the Whitecaps. Tobias has had a successful career as an accountant. Before the game Tobias took some time out to explain the annual costs to run the Brewster franchise. "Our annual budget with all our revenue and expenses comes close to about $400,000. That does not include a beautiful scoreboard. We received a wonderful contribution for it. It came to about $70,000. The league contributed $10,000 for it. We pay our coaches a fair amount of money. It's enough to pay for their housing costs and a little salary. They're not here to make a lot of money. They really have to love what they're doing. We've been able to make improvements every year. This year we bought an eight-seat golf cart to help transport our fans from the parking lot to the front entrance. Also, we put up fencing around the field for the safety of the fans. We work hard every year to keep making improvements. We keep our finances structured for each department of operation. I love baseball," Tobias said.

Tobias added, "I'm glad we're able to do what we do for the Brewster community. A lot of people come out to the ballpark to watch baseball. This is a great way for our community to work together and then come together in the summer months."

CHATHAM ANGLERS AT WHITECAPS

Definition of Consistency: noun (Being the same)—Cambridge Dictionary
The quality of behaving or performing in a similar way or of always happening in a similar way. (They've won a few games this season, but they lack consistency. It's important to show some consistency in your work.) Opposite of inconsistency.

There is zero question the biggest problem for the Caps over the last few games is inconsistency. They have not been playing a complete game. Only a few times this season have all their parts been running on full throttle. One day their hitting is going well and their pitching is struggling. Another time it might be that their pitching is on and they can't manage the big hit to turn the game around. Another time it might be careless base running, and another time it might be a costly error.

Baseball is one of the most difficult games to compete in. It can be brutal when things are not going well. A player will tighten up, and that will only make things worse. Because baseball players play so many games, it's critical that the game remains fun.

Players not only have to be relaxed, but they also must enjoy their teammates. During a season the team becomes an extension of their family.

The Caps have tremendous team chemistry. That should never come into question. Some coaches feel that team meetings when things aren't going well are the answer. Team meetings occasionally can help, but too much talking can be counterproductive. Staying relaxed, having fun, enjoying your teammates, working hard, and believing in one's ability are the best ways to get back on track.

Hyde, the Northeast Area Scout for the New York Yankees, explained to the Whitecaps in a speech a couple of weeks before what the Yankees are looking for when they scout a player. "We want to see how a player reacts when he fails. Baseball is a game of failure. The Yankees want to see if a player is going to fight through the tough times, or is he going to sulk and give up? We're not only scouting talent; we're scouting character."

Chatham beat Brewster on a beautiful evening at Stony Brook Field, 7–3. A crowd of over twenty-two hundred fans turned out. Pitcher DJ Primeaux gave up one hit in four innings of relief. With ten games left, anything is possible.

The Whitecaps now stand at 12 wins, 17 losses, and 1 tie on the season.

At the end of the game star pitcher Patrick Forbes notified the Brewster Whitecaps that he was leaving.

WHITECAPS AT YARMOUTH-DENNIS RED SOX

"At least we didn't lose," and so the saga continues.

Before the game at Yarmouth-Dennis, a few of the Caps players were lamenting how long they had been playing baseball during the first seven months of the 2025 calendar year. Between the college season and the Cape season, they have played close to one hundred games. The sheer mental and physical strain can take a toll on a player.

Primeaux commented, "We're wearing down. The guys are tired. We're losing our spark a little. We're at the ballpark day and night."

Boston Flannery, another pitcher, said, "We're fighting to make the playoffs. It doesn't matter if we finish first or fourth in our division. You don't get a trophy for finishing first. The top four teams in the East make the playoffs. Just making it gives us a chance for a championship."

At this juncture, after thirty-one games, the Caps are in third place, with Harwich breathing right down their backs.

The players were loose before the game. There was an announcement that Jake Clemente was slated to be the starting pitcher for the East team in the all-star game coming up. This will make five players wearing the Brewster uniform named as starters. He'll be joined in the starting lineup by Donay, Helfrick, Dumesnil, and Cuvet.

Also, it was announced that Ryder Helfrick was named the MVP for the first half of the Cape Cod Baseball League.

There was no pouting during warm-ups. The all-stars from

Brewster were ecstatic. Rogers, who came out of nowhere to become a Cape All-Star, was overjoyed. "It was shocking," said Rogers. "It was exciting to know I had been named among the best of the best. I proved to myself I can play against the best. I tried to keep it in. My parents were thrilled to find out. They were as excited as I was."

Dumesnil, another player who turned the heads of several scouts this season, couldn't contain himself. He also was honored with his news. "I was very excited—it's cool to be among the best in the all-star game. I set my goals high. Now I have to keep it going."

Donay, the laid-back starting first baseman, also was honored. "It will be really cool to look back at this summer and know I played against the best college players in America. This is the best summer league. It's awesome to be part of this history."

Kent shared his joy. "It's great—it's awesome. It will be fun. I'm really looking forward to the entire event this coming Saturday."

Shevchik experienced a tough week as his Caps lost four out of five games. Regardless of his roller-coaster grind, he found time to look back with optimism. "This was the hardest week of the season. We put together the best lineup on the field that we possibly could. In back-to-back games, we struggled to find hits. Usually, I let everyone have a chance to play without sitting out more than two games in a row. For the rest of the summer, I'm going to go with our best players and see if we can't figure this out. I had to explain this to a few guys today, and they seemed to handle the news well. These kids don't want to take a day off. They want to play every day. This new playoff system, with the first round being one loss and you're done, is a complete disaster. We can't just settle to make the playoffs as a third or fourth seed. We need to be playing our best baseball when the season rolls around."

With the score the Caps 3 and the Y-D Red Sox 1, and with darkness creeping in, the Caps were about to experience their best win of the year. A huge win was within the grasp of the Caps. Then, with two outs and two strikes on the hitter in the bottom of the ninth, the win was snatched away.

Anthony Martinez, the first baseman from Cal Irvine, lined a double, knocking in two runs for Y-D. What was about to be a feel-good moment turned into another heartbreak for Brewster. The final score was Brewster 3 and Y-D 3. It was the second tie with the best team in the league for Brewster in as many games between the two East Divisional rivals.

Guth, Colby Frieda (Troy), and Oakes all pitched brilliantly for the Whitecaps. Kaufer, a hard-nosed catcher, let out the frustration for the entire Brewster team in the dugout after the game. A beautiful evening at Red Wilson Field in front of almost three thousand fans ended with a thud.

Shevchik sat motionless, alone, for fifteen minutes. Finally, he stood and took a deep breath while turning to his assistant Scott Grimes and said out loud, "At least we didn't lose." This was going to be a tough ride home for Shev.

Within minutes after the game, several players, including Cuvet, Faurot, Vest, and a few others, were all enjoying clam chowder with Ms. Whitecap, Jane Sullivan at Royal 11 Restaurant and Grill in Yarmouth.

The Caps know how to roll with tide. Or at least on the surface they do.

Wareham Gatemen at Whitecaps

Walking into Stony Brook Field for a Whitecaps game, every fan gets greeted by some of the kindest and most talented student-interns in America. For a friendly person, becoming an intern with the Caps is the perfect setting to meet new friends and establish lasting relationships.

For Maeze Myles, the coed from Holy Cross, her favorite part of working at the front entrance is getting to know the names of the many canines that are brought in on a leash by the dog owners.

For the good-natured Giani Shevchik, she enjoys the sport of baseball that was handed down by her dad that she is so proud of, Manager Jamie Shevchik.

Tommy Higgins and Elise Prodanov round out the group of interns who collect donations and hand out the daily rosters to the Brewster fans.

The professional interns who work tirelessly to support the Brewster organization are second to none. They all have experience and savvy that places them way beyond their years. If they're any indication of the future workforce in America, our nation will be in great hands.

Austin Barach and Max Gifford are students at Syracuse University majoring in Broadcast and Digital Journalism. Syracuse has produced some of the finest sport broadcasters in the business. Add the names of Sean McDonough, Bob Costas, Mike Tirico, Dave O'Brien, Marv Albert, Len Berman, and Dick Stockton, to name only a few.

Soon the names of Barach and Gifford will be added to the list of greats who graduated from Syracuse.

For Gifford, broadcasting Whitecaps games has given him a chance to gain some valuable experience while networking and building relationships. "My dad worked in the minor leagues while I was growing up. Sports broadcasting is something I have always wanted to do. My career is just at the beginning stages. I'm trying to learn my craft. Austin and I are constantly trying to send out our tapes so they can be critiqued. Right now, people in the industry are being patient with us when we make mistakes because we're college students. My intern experiences this summer have been tremendous."

Barach has his sights on someday becoming a member of the

number one or two broadcasting team for the NBA on ESPN or FOX. "The Whitecaps are an awesome platform for college students. There is nothing like a close nine-inning game that comes right down to the end. I live for that. Being around great baseball players on the Cape has been wonderful. The Whitecaps are all great guys and have been wonderful to us. Syracuse doesn't have a baseball team, so this has been a valuable experience this summer."

Mitchell Fink and Aiden Stapansky are two more interns who spent their summer of '24 gaining experience in their college majors. Both are the baseball daily beat writers for the Caps. They write all the online articles that appear on the Whitecaps website. They both have incredible talent and have gained immeasurable experience over the summer.

For Fink, who is majoring in Journalism at Boston University, the summer with the Caps has given him a chance to write not only the postgame summaries for each game but also a variety of other stories as they relate to Brewster.

Fink explained what some of the biggest challenges are for a baseball beat writer. "Trying to keep a new storyline every day is something I try and pay attention to when writing our daily articles. I want to keep everything fresh for our readers. I feel fortunate to go to school in Boston, which in my opinion is the number-one sports city in America. One of my mentors is Sherrod Blakely. I've taken a course from him. He covered the Celtics for many years. I'm a huge sports fan. I cover the Boston University hockey team for the school newspaper. This summer has been invaluable. Jamie Shevchik has been incredible to work with. I want to give a career as a beat writer a shot. It's not just a career; it's an incredible way to live."

Stapansky also attends Syracuse. He is currently majoring in digital journalism and minoring in sports management. Stapansky shared his future career goals: "It's important not to have the readers follow the same chronological order every day when they read about their favorite baseball team. This will make them go stale, and they'll stop reading your articles. I would love to be a beat writer for a professional team after I graduate. This summer has given me the opportunity to ask Shevchik some tough questions after a loss. He's been great. I cover the Syracuse basketball teams for the Syracuse school newspaper. I also cover the women's soccer and hockey teams. They haven't been very good in recent years. They have given me a chance to be around coaches who may not be pleasant after a game. It's important to have a variety of experiences. One of my mentors is Jason Stark, who covers the Philadelphia Phillies for the *Philadelphia Inquirer*. This has been a great experience. I want to cover baseball. There are always teams looking for online beat writers."

Another intern grew up in Brewster. Henry Blanchard, a rising senior at Suffolk University in Boston, describes his summer as "the best experience of my life. I couldn't ask for anything more. Watching baseball, this doesn't even seem like a job. I'm living at home and I'm getting to watch the best college baseball players in the world. I can't ask for anything more. I've always been around baseball. I went to Stony Brook Elementary as a student. I even grew up playing on this field. Everything is coming full circle now. I've always been a fan of Cape baseball. Working for the team adds new perspective. I've been around this field for sixteen out of my twenty-two years. I'm working as the MLB scout liaison for the Whitecaps. I get to talk with MLB scouts and agents. I feel like the luckiest college student in America."

Courtney Faber is a rising sophomore. She attended her freshman year at High Point University in North Carolina. Faber is studying sports media with a minor in photography. With her talents, she will go a long way in her career.

A SEASON WITH THE BREWSTER WHITECAPS
Seventh-Inning Stretch—"Sweet Caroline"

There were over thirty scouts on hand for batting and infield practice at Stony Brook Field prior to the game against Wareham. Immediately after the Caps were finished with their pregame routines, the players all bolted across the street for their pregame nutrition. This usually takes place ninety minutes before each home game.

Pico's Taco Shack on Underpass Road in Brewster is the pregame home for the Caps' favorite shrimp burrito. Oh my, they are out of this world. Ferretti's Market is also the "in" place for all types of the Whitecaps' favorite foods. Each player returns before each game and sits in the dugout as their favorite delicacies make their eyes water. It's important to understand that without a locker room, the small dugout on the third-base side at Stony Brook Field serves as the team headquarters for almost twelve hours each day.

Before the game, baseball umpire Ryan DiMari was sharing his experiences as an umpire in the Cape Cod Baseball League while putting on his protective equipment. It was his turn to call the balls and strikes behind the plate for the game between Brewster and the Gatemen.

DiMari, who has been umpiring for twenty-five years, is in his seventh season of umpiring on the Cape. For the past seven summers, he has been traveling back and forth from his home in Foxboro, MA, about fifty miles away, six nights a week. DiMari works as a client service insurance representative in Boston for his full-time job. "It's been a progression in my umpiring career to finally get a chance to umpire on the Cape. It's a much more relaxed atmosphere here. The fans, players, and coaches aren't on you as much here. The players are the best of the best, so you must stay on top of your game. A lot of umps come here to stay sharp for when they work college games. Others use it to advance into the professional ranks. It's a tough way to make a buck. The daily grind of working six games a week and the travel can wear you down," said DiMari.

Technology has become a key element in baseball, as it has in all parts of our daily lives. DiMari pointed out that "Baseball should always have the human element as part of the game. I use technology to help me evaluate my performance. Everything we do here is evaluated and observed. I love the game, and it's an honor for me to umpire here on Cape Cod."

After the game several players enjoyed a postgame dinner at the Brewster Chowder House on Main Street in Brewster. This old-fashioned restaurant is a mainstay for all who live or vacation in this quaint Cape Cod hideaway.

Of course, each player enjoyed a bowl of their famous clam chowder as an appetizer. The banter among the players and this author did not represent the final score of the game that the Caps had just lost. This was a payback to the Caps for the thrashing they had put on the Gatemen ten days earlier.

The wide range of topics included everything from the new policy of paying college athletes (called "NIL" for "name, image, and likeness") to the importance of having a great host family to the coaches of the Caps to the incredible summer the players were all experiencing, and of course, finally, to pretty girls.

Luke Schmolke, the pitcher from Wake Forest, told of his stories about waking up at dawn every morning so he could take the small boat that his hosts were letting him fish with out on the lake.

Will Ray, another pitcher from Wake Forest, was sharing his experiences of getting to play on some of the Cape's nicest golf courses.

Ryder Helfrick, the Arkansas catcher who has taken Cape Cod baseball by storm, talked about how he must break out of his three-game slump.

JD Rogers, the Vanderbilt outfielder, announced that his

college coach would be attending the Cape All-Star game in Falmouth that he was selected to play in.

Cooper Vest, the star of Brigham Young, spoke about this book, *CAPE DREAMS: A Season with the Brewster Whitecaps*, and how someday he hopes it will become a movie.

Dallas Macias, the lovable and friendly hotshot from Oregon State, explained that the host families were the key to a successful summer experience for the players on Cape Cod. He was quick to add, "The reason the players in Brewster are enjoying themselves is because of Jane Sullivan, who organizes the host families for all the Whitecaps players. Some other teams have had problems where players were not happy and went home. At Brewster, if a player leaves, it has nothing to do with not being happy. There may be other reasons such as injuries or a family situation."

Yes, in case you may have wondered, the score of the game was Wareham 8 and Brewster 1. The game was called after seven innings due to darkness.

As the great former Patriots coach Bill Belichick might say if he were coaching the Brewster Whitecaps, "ON TO HARWICH!"

WHITECAPS AT HARWICH MARINERS

Winston Churchill once said, "Success is not final, failure is not fatal: It is the courage to fight on that counts."

Harwich nipped Brewster 2–1 at Whitehouse Field. The Caps fell to 12–19 and 2 ties on the season. They remain one game in front of Harwich for third place in the East standings.

Shevchik represents all that is good about sport. For him to experience what his Brewster Whitecaps are experiencing is something that even Shevchik has a hard time putting into words. "I feel I'm letting the entire organization down. Jane Sullivan, Luke Dillon, Jon Mecca, and the entire Whitecaps community deserve better. We have a tremendous group of guys. I have never had a team that I enjoyed being around as much as this group. When I took over this organization, they were complacent. Now we have a championship-caliber ball club that we have put together to bring more glory to Brewster. This should be the best team in the league. They are coming to work every day and are busting their butts. Their work, effort, and attitude are exactly what they need to be. This is a results business, and we are not getting the results that this team was built for. I cannot ask them to give any more of themselves than they have given. I know when tomorrow comes they will be up for the challenge. When 1:00 p.m. comes back around and I get back to the field, I'll put this behind me. I'll come back even more determined."

So, the fighting Caps will never be quitters. They are underachieving, yes. The players are more determined than ever to get back on track. With seven games remaining, the other nine teams still don't want anything to do with the fighting Caps.

Today's game was a microcosm of the entire season. The Whitecaps fought the Harwich Mariners tooth and nail. Evan O'Toole, the newly acquired pitcher (Oklahoma State), and Detmers pitched brilliantly for Brewster. Each pitched four full innings and gave up only three hits each. In fact, Detmers may just be the most improved pitcher since the beginning of the season on the Whitecaps pitching staff.

As great a pitching performance that came from both teams, the Caps just couldn't land the knockout punch. They have been so close in several games that the strain they are putting on themselves is starting to show on the players' faces.

Hitting is contagious. The Caps' hitters have grown silent of late. Dumesnil has been the only consistent hitter during the last few games. His batting average climbed to over .330 after his two doubles against Harwich.

A SEASON WITH THE BREWSTER WHITECAPS
Seventh-Inning Stretch—"Sweet Caroline"

Take nothing away from the Mariners' Donovan Burke, the pitcher out of James Madison. Burke gave up only four hits in his seven innings of work. Sam Tookoian (Mississippi) came in for the top of the eighth and struck out five of the six batters he faced to earn the save.

Just when things seem to be at the bleakest, this Brewster Whitecaps team that was built for championship success will be there giving every ounce of energy they have till the very end.

After the game Shevchik shared his sentiments. Shevchik said he wonders if the team is "forcing things or doing too much," as he put it. Whatever issues may exist, he emphasized the fact that there remains time to work through them. "We're still holding on to the third spot in our division," he said. "There's still life. We're still breathing. Until that breath is gone, this team needs to keep fighting. I just can't be the only one that thinks this team is good."

Indeed 'Skip", you are not the only one who feels this way!

The Caps picked up a few more players for the stretch run. Andrew Koshy, a right-handed pitcher from Maryland, was "ecstatic" to be added to the roster.

Noah Samol, a big right-handed pitcher from Clemson, talks proudly about the college he plays for. "When a player puts on the Clemson Jersey, they can feel the history of the program. There is a weight of the jersey that you can't explain."

Another pitcher brought in to replace the recently departed pitchers was Alex Valentin from Texas State. Valentin is a teammate of Chase Mora, who had to leave Brewster when he was beaned earlier in the season.

Shortstop Colby Shelton, a rising redshirt junior out of Florida, was also added a few games ago. Shelton, a twentieth-round draft choice by the Washington Nationals last week, decided to go back to Florida in the fall instead of turning pro. The decision to return to school made him eligible to get picked up by a Cape team.

COMMISSIONER OF THE CCBL—JOHN CASTLEBERRY

There is an expression used frequently that home is where the heart is. So for first-year Cape Cod Baseball League Commissioner John Castleberry, when he rests his head on his pillow after a long day of traveling to as many Cape games as he can visit in an evening, Castleberry can smile. He is back home where he belongs.

The Commissioner is a baseball lifer. Make no mistake about it. Growing up on the West Coast and playing collegiately at the University of San Diego, Castleberry decided right out of college that a career in baseball was going to become his career journey. What a ride it's been. From starting off as an assistant coach at the University of Washington in 1983 to managing the Orleans Cardinals and Hall of Famer Frank Thomas to becoming the head coach at George Washington from 1985 through 1991 to spending over thirty years scouting for the Marlins, Reds, Phillies, Rangers, and Giants, Castleberry was the ideal choice to carry on the glorious tradition that is the CCBL.

Castleberry had been working hard since he first was named the commissioner. Finally, there was a short break for him to speak about his first season as the leader of the finest amateur athletic organization in America. "I started here, I met my wife here, I got married here, I have a home in Orleans. It feels great to come back home. It's a bigger league than when I was here as the manager for Orleans in the early eighties. When the league went to wooden bats in the mid-eighties, the league really took off. Recruiting players for the managers is a little tougher with the new NCAA rules they have now. Recruiting starts in the fall. The position players are better now than they ever have been. The transfer portal is just one obstacle the Cape organizations must deal with.

The changing of the MLB draft from early June to mid-July is another. Our coaches do a great job of building their teams. Housing is another important aspect that the teams do a great job of. The Cape is drawing bigger crowds than ever," Castleberry said.

The commissioner continued to enjoy talking about his favorite life's passion. "There are some things we can't control. What we can control is getting out here every day and making sure we play baseball for the fans and give the players a great experience. To lead this great tradition is a tremendous honor. This season alone we have 388 former Cape players playing in the Major Leagues. One hundred and ninety-seven more just got drafted. This is where the scouts come. These are the best players. This is the future of the Major Leagues. This is where the draft starts. We need to make people aware that this isn't just a Cape league, this is a national league. We have to work a little harder to get the word out across America to people who may not know that much about us. We have a great president in Andrew Lang. The future of the Cape Cod Baseball League is in great hands," Castleberry ended.

The great American tradition will carry on.

Hostess Nancy Sveden

One of the most special aspects of playing baseball on the Cape is that the players live with host families. It's been a long-standing tradition that goes back many decades. Many players feel that the host family plays the most important part of their summer.

Once a player bonds with their host, the relationship never ends. This is especially true with host families in Brewster.

Sullivan is the coordinator for the host families along with all her other responsibilities. When Sullivan does something, she puts her whole heart into it. She places, screens, and monitors everything that goes on throughout the summer. It's no wonder that Brewster has a group of loyal hosts that volunteer every year.

One of the sweetest hostesses in the history of Cape Cod baseball is Nancy Sveden. She has been the 2024 host to JD Rogers and Levi Huesman, two Whitecaps who are also teammates at Vanderbilt University. Nancy is everything a ballplayer could possibly ask for: kind, gentle, motherly, generous, and loving. The two players landed in a great big giant pot of honey when Ms. Whitecap (Sullivan) placed the two ballplayers with Nancy.

Nancy's home is dressed in New England charm. Sitting on her deck on a beautiful July morning, watching the different types of birds eat their seeds, is something out of a fairy tale.

Getting served a breakfast of quiche, fruit, juice, and coffee in that setting is almost too good to be true. Each player just adores Nancy. Rogers felt at home in his summer home. He was appreciative and had this to say about his summer hostess. "I love it here; Nancy has opened her home to Levi and myself like we are her own children. We get up every morning and make our own breakfast and sit out on the patio and enjoy the beautiful nature. We just love it here. We each have our own room. We could never have asked for more. Nancy is a big reason I have loved playing in Brewster."

Huesman has also been made to feel at home. "This has been a lot of fun. Nancy treats us like family. I've become really close to her. This is the most special summer I've ever had. Being with the team at the field and spending time with the guys is a lot of fun. I'll always remember this summer. Before we got here, JD and I were teammates at Vandy, but we were never too close. After this summer we've become good friends. It's really cool I've spent this summer playing on the Cape."

This is Nancy's eighth year of hosting players. Nancy has a

deep feeling for everyone who has ever stayed with her. "I love my players like my kids. Our pastor got me into this. I've always been given the best kids on the team. I love being a host. I stay in touch with all my players. I send them birthday cards every year. They even invite me to their weddings. I'm getting a little older, so I'm not sure how many summers I have left hosting."

Nancy Sveden is everything that the Cape Cod Baseball League stands for. Let's hope she continues hosting for many more years to come.

THE MIRACLE COMEBACK
Tonight's game against the Hyannis Harbor Hawks centered around the best feel-good stories of the summer in the CCBL. Jacob Marlowe is the comeback player of the last decade.

Marlowe underwent two open-heart surgeries in the past seven months. Shevchik has used Marlowe sparingly this summer. Shevchik was being very careful with how much Marlowe was going to be sent to the mound. Marlowe had pitched a total of eight innings all summer.

Tonight was the night that Marlowe was going to be tested. It was to be his first start of the summer. When he took the mound, he felt the adrenaline pumping throughout his body. No one knew what to expect. The players were all excited for Marlowe. Every fan at Stony Brook Field was saying prayers and wishing him good luck.

Marlowe settled in early and established a comfortable rhythm. As the game went along, the comeback kid fell into a nice groove. Soon he was pitching into the fifth inning. Suddenly five innings were in the books, and Marlowe was back! Five innings and only one hit. Fifteen Harbor Hawk batters out of sixteen he faced were retired. No one saw this coming—including Marlowe.

Marlowe was elated after the game and spoke about his

long-awaited milestone. "It was a lot. I didn't expect to pitch this many innings. I'm overjoyed. I thought I was going to go three innings. My stamina felt good. It means a lot to pitch again in a game with an umpire behind the plate. I was scheduled to throw fifty-five pitches, and I threw fifty-nine."

Shevchik was very proud of Marlowe. After the game Shevchik made the following comments. "For that kid to go out and do what he did tonight is huge for him. I'm thrilled for him. We babied him this summer. There was no set formula for someone who is in his situation."

Andrew Koshy, a pitcher from Wake Forest, followed Marlowe to the mound for the Caps in the sixth and gave up three runs in one third of an inning. Those were all the runs that Hyannis would need on this picture-perfect evening in Brewster.

In the bottom of the ninth with two outs, Kaeden Kent hit a two-run homer. Those were the only runs scored for the Whitecaps.

Hyannis would go on to win 3–2. It was a four-game season sweep for the Harbor Hawks over the Whitecaps.

Brewster fell to 12–20 with two ties.

The all-star break couldn't have come at a better time. "These guys need a day off; it's a welcome day off," Shevchik said. "Forget about everything that happened the last seven days and hopefully start a whole brand-new season starting on Monday."

It's not just the players who need to get away from it all for a few days.

Eighth Inning—2024 Cape Cod Baseball League All-Star Game

ALL-STAR SATURDAY IN FALMOUTH IS as close to having a slice of grandma's apple pie for desert on Thanksgiving as you can get. Nothing could be more American than this sacred tradition. This was the eleventh Cape Cod Baseball League All-Star Game to be held in Falmouth.

This gorgeous beach town located only a few miles over the Bourne Bridge was full of anticipation leading up to this annual celebration of the national pastime played on the Cape. Falmouth and Guv Fuller Field were decked out in all their glory. The upgrades to Fuller Field have been significant. The condition of the field itself and the fencing around it have placed Fuller Field among the top baseball fields on the Cape.

There are certain traditions in sport that are magical. There is nothing like bringing the best of the best of the best college baseball players that are playing on Cape Cod to Falmouth for the Cape's annual midsummer classic.

It's impossible to write a narrative to describe the love affair the town of Falmouth has for their Commodores. It's like a rite of passage passed on at birth from one generation to another.

Starting in 1923, the year that the Cape Cod Baseball League was formed, Falmouth has been at the very forefront of Cape Cod baseball.

From the legends of longtime Falmouth resident Al Irish, who attended his first game at the age of five in 1926 (and who didn't miss many, right up until he passed at the age of 101 years in 2021), to the greatest pitcher of his era, Paul Mitchell (1969–1971), to the current manager, the beloved Cape Cod Baseball Hall of Famer Jeff Trundy, Falmouth's pride for their rich baseball tradition has thrived.

Chuck Sturtevant began serving the Commodores in several leadership roles starting in 1986. Sturtevant is currently the general manager of the ball club. He has also served as the CCBL president for seven years. He was beaming with pride when asked what this all-star game means to Falmouth. "We're thrilled to be able to host this one. We wanted to wait until we made some upgrades to our facilities before we hosted another one. I have so many unbelievable memories from my thirty-nine years. One of my favorite memories is that of Darin Erstad. He played for me in both 1992 and '93. Erstad was the league MVP both seasons in Falmouth. He went on to have a twelve-year MLB career that included two MLB All-Star appearances. What a beautiful man. Then we have Jeff Trundy, the manager who has been with us for over twenty-five years. That's what means so much to me. Sure, we all want to win, but when you get right down to it, this league to me will always be about the relationships." Within a short time after this interview with Sturtevant, he resigned from his position with Falmouth. He was not available to speak about what caused the sudden turn of events.

Bob Curtis, the friendly president of the Commodores, was sitting back enjoying the fruits of his labor when I approached to talk about what this day means to his Commodore family. "We've worked hard for the last year to plan for this. This is so much fun.

A SEASON WITH THE BREWSTER WHITECAPS
Eighth Inning—2024 Cape Cod Baseball League All-Star Game

This is so wonderful to watch these college players perform. We have perfect weather for it. We expect a crowd of over five thousand fans. What a glorious celebration. I'm meeting a lot of parents of the players today. Don't forget that this is a big fundraiser for the league. We're entirely a nonprofit organization. Peter Gammons, the American baseball icon, is even here. Everyone wants to come to this game. I'm still a host for players in my home every summer. The one thing that makes me prouder than anything else is the volunteers who give up so much to make this league run. The three most important elements to run a team in this league are number one: money, two: the volunteers, and three: the players."

Fifty-four players were selected for this year's extravaganza—twenty-seven from the East squad and twenty-seven from the West squad. The Brewster Whitecaps led the way with nine players selected to play on the East squad.

Getting to interview the beloved baseball icon Mr. Peter Gammons for this story was my biggest thrill while working on this project. Mr. Gammons was interviewed while watching the all-stars take batting practice and while chatting with his dear friend, Yankee Scout Matt Hyde. Gammons entire interview was used as the foreword for this book.

Over one hundred scouts watched carefully as the all-stars took turns taking their batting practice swings. It's not just the games that the scouts come to see—it's how hard the players work before the games that is also of great interest to all the scouts.

Tyler Stubblefield, a scout with the San Diego Padres, was on hand to take a close look at the top prospects for the upcoming 2025 MLB draft. Stubblefield said, "This is the best way to get all the top college players together. This group is the best of the best of the best. I'm here to evaluate everyone. We want to not only evaluate the players' skills, but we want to see who truly understands how to play this game. We've seen almost all these players over the past season at their colleges. So we know who they are. The skill the Padres value in a player more than anything are the players that can really hit. That's my priority over the other five-tool skills."

It was time for the annual home run derby contest. Two Brewster All-Stars took center stage. Donay and Helfrick represented the Whitecaps family. Each represented themselves admirably.

The derby was won by Yarmouth-Dennis outfielder Ethan Petry (University of South Carolina). The big slugger out-blasted Nate Earley of Wareham (University of Louisville) in a playoff round to take the crown.

Petry was overjoyed to become the winner of this historic tradition. Afterward Petry had this to say: "This means a ton to me. The history of this league is incredible. So many great players have come through here. Both Major Leaguers and Minor Leaguers have made so much history here in the past 101 years. I'm so blessed to be a part of this. I'm so honored to be able to celebrate with my family here and my host family. I was wearing down a bit from the heat at the end. I'm South Carolina through and through. My whole family are Gamecock fans now. It's an honor to represent Carolina on the Cape. It's also an honor to wear their colors of garnet and black."

Nate Earley of the Wareham Gatemen, who was runner-up in the derby, was coming off a hamstring injury but still participated. He was thrilled to receive the second-place prize. Earley had nothing but praise for the Gatemen. "We're having a great season in Wareham. Everyone loves each other, and the coaches are great. We've put up a lot of wins. I've been working hard every day to get better. Even though our facilities at Wareham aren't the best, we put that out of our minds and just focus on just winning games."

A SEASON WITH THE BREWSTER WHITECAPS
Eighth Inning—2024 Cape Cod Baseball League All-Star Game

An overflow crowd of over five thousand fans was on hand when Jeff Trundy, the longtime manager of the Commodores, was honored just before the first pitch. In attendance to help honor Trundy was his friend and colleague, the manager of the Brewster Whitecaps, Shevchik. With well over five hundred wins, Trundy will be inducted into the CCBL Hall of Fame in November of 2024.

The Brewster Whitecaps had eight players that were in uniform in Falmouth. (Pitcher Will Ray would have been the ninth, but he had to tend to a personal situation back at his home.) Five were starters. Longtime Yankees scout Damon Sturtevant leaned over just before the game and could be overheard saying, "Brewster has the most talent in the League. It's a mystery why they're not winning." (It's a mystery to several others also.)

Jake Clemente, the big right-hander for Brewster, was the East starting pitcher. Before the game he said, "This is so cool to be part of such a rich history. It's almost surreal."

Every pitcher for each team usually pitches just one inning. Clemente took full advantage of his inning. He topped off his fastball at 94 mph on the radar gun. Clemente struck out two of the four batters he faced. He gave up one walk and no hits in his inning of work.

Dumesnil from the Caps, the starting center fielder in the game for the East squad, blasted the only home run of the game. His two-run shot came in the fifth.

In all the seven position players who represented Brewster Nation played very well. Kent had two hits in his appearance. Helfrick did a tremendous job behind the plate as he threw out a runner trying to steal second for the West team. Starting third baseman Cuvet knocked in a run for the East. Donay, Faurot, and Rogers also contributed. Ray was also on the all-star roster but was unavailable to play.

In dramatic fashion the West team won on the first walk-off hit in Cape Cod Baseball League All-Star game history. With one out and runners on second and third for the West team, Kane Kepley (Liberty University) from the Hyannis Harbor Hawks came to the plate. The rest is now a new historic event that can be added to CCBL lore.

Eight pitches into his at-bat, Kepley drilled the game winning walk-off single into right field to score Falmouth's Jaxon Willits. The entire West dugout poured onto the field to celebrate with their new hero.

The final score was the West 9 and the East 8.

MVPs of the game were given to Ethan Conrad representing the Bourne Braves from the West Division and Easton Carmichael representing Yarmouth-Dennis of the East.

The Brewster Whitecaps have had several of their players capture the MVP honor of the CCBL All-Star game in previous years:

Will Scalzitti—1991
Billy Wagner—1992
Geoff Blum—1993
C. J. Ankrum—1996
Reid Detmers—2018
Gage Workman—2019
Grayson Tarrow—2022

After the game the East manager, Scott Pickler from Yarmouth-Dennis, said, "It is so neat to watch the players in the dugout. They compete against each other, and now they get to compete together and enjoy getting to know each other."

"The all-star game, I think, should be a privilege for each one of the players to play in. They will remember this day for the rest of their lives," said West manager Mike Roberts from Cotuit.

A SEASON WITH THE BREWSTER WHITECAPS

Eighth Inning—2024 Cape Cod Baseball League All-Star Game

COTUIT KETTLEERS AT WHITECAPS

The Whitecaps played another game today. The result was another win off the field. Every single game that is being played by the Brewster Whitecaps in the Cape Cod Baseball League during the summer of 2024 is a victory. What will never show up in the standings are the values and life lessons that are being taught and experienced. Every single player, coach, intern, and volunteer is a champion.

The love that is being shared is priceless. The bonds that have been formed are eternal. The memories are forever. Friendships are beyond magical. The laughs will never end. The values learned are life-changing. Age has no boundaries. Entitlement doesn't exist.

The wins are not measured on scoreboards. The summer of 2024 will stay forever in everyone's spirit who has experienced being part of a family that was formed by people who truly love unconditionally.

Forever, the unbreakable magic of being a Brewster Whitecap has changed the souls of each person (including authors) who came and was part of something incredibly unique.

The Brewster Whitecaps of 2024 will forever be CHAMPIONS!

Whitecaps fan Patrick Toner brought his son, Peter, to Stony Brook Field for the first time today to watch the Caps. Like so many others who came to watch, they stopped at the concession stand and bought popcorn, a Diet Coke, and an Airhead from Franny Mendoza. Mendoza is a hardworking rising ninth grader in Brewster who has been serving customers all summer long. She spoke about her job in between customers. Mendoza said, "This job is about a six on a scale of ten as far as the level of difficulty. I stay pretty calm when the line gets long. The line can get quite long at times, but it moves along quickly. I really haven't had any major problems this summer. I work at every game. I get tired, but it's fun." Mendoza is another worker who helps make the Brewster Whitecaps a special part of the community.

Immediately after infield practice, Kent, the second baseman, came into the dugout ready to play. He let his teammates know he wasn't happy with their effort during infield practice and that they had better step up their game. The fiery Kent let out his frustrations.

Clemente and Dumesnil were still smiling about their performances two days earlier in the all-star game. Clemente was happy to share his memories. "I came to the Cape hoping to make the all-star game. I never expected to be the starting pitcher. That was a very cool honor. On the day of the game, I felt like it was just another game I had to prepare for."

Dumesnil couldn't wait to talk about his two-run homer (the only home run hit in the all-star game). "The whole day was an awesome experience. To hit a home run was sick. I wasn't sure it was going out. It was more like a liner that just made it over the left field fence."

Cotuit took control of the game with the Caps early by scoring six runs in the second. The Caps had a big inning of their own, scoring five in the third. The Caps just couldn't catch up on a beautiful Brewster evening. Cotuit won going away 9–5.

After the game Shevchik gathered his players around and spoke quite frankly. With fire in his eyes, he wanted to make sure they stayed engaged. "There are still a lot of people in this organization who believe in this team. I think we owe it to them to give it our best. If we lose, we lose. We don't want to die, and we certainly don't want to quit."

The Whitecaps are now in danger of falling out of playoff contention. Tomorrow night is a big one as the Caps travel to Chatham.

Cotuit has taken over the top spot in the West with an overall record of 21 wins and 11 losses.

On the way out of Stony Brook, Cotuit's Ethan Winfield, the right fielder from the University of Texas, was explaining how important it would be to win the Cape championship. "It would be the seventh or eighth championship for Cotuit. We'd love to win another one for the town and our manager, Mike Roberts. Playing on the Cape is better than I thought. I come from Texas, so coming to Cotuit has been different, but I really like it. The town and the fans really come out and support the Kettleers. The guys I'm playing with are all great guys. We'll all be friends for life."

WHITECAPS AT CHATHAM ANGLERS
Before the game at Chatham, I walked over to the Whitecaps manager and asked a question. The question was "How are you feeling, skipper?" (The concern was the tough season he has had to endure.) The one-sentence answer summed up the entire season. Brian Del Rosso, the pitching coach for the Caps, was standing nearby and answered the question for his close friend Shevchik. "He's feeling much better since he just left the office of Dr. Jonathan Katz." Dr. Katz is the Whitecaps' sports psychologist.

Kent got the team excited for the infield and outfield pregame workout. The ball club looked extremely sharp. For the first time all season, there wasn't one missed play by one of the position players. Kent has been doing a great job of taking over for the rallying cry of Fischer since he left.

Pitcher Darien Smith (Southeastern University) was called on by Shevchik to make the start. Smith is back with the team after being released earlier in the season.

There were over three thousand fans on a picture-perfect summer evening at Veterans Field in Chatham to watch the Anglers play host to their divisional foe, the Whitecaps.

The Caps continued to be snakebitten. Once again, the good guys gave up a big inning early as the Anglers scored six runs in the bottom of the second inning. Brewster was never able to recover after that.

The final score was Chatham 13 and the Caps 2. This was the fifth straight loss for Brewster. The only bright spot was a two-run blast by Dumesnil. The most reliable hitter of late has been Dumesnil.

The Brewster Whitecaps are ranked fifth in the CCBL in hitting with a .247 average. Their pitching is tenth out of ten teams. Their team's earned run average is over 5.6 runs per game. That's over one-half run per game more than Harwich, which is ninth in the league. Harwich is now in third place in the East. Brewster is barely ahead of Orleans in fourth. Only the top four teams in each division make the playoffs. Brewster plays host to Orleans in two days.

The pitching has been a season-long problem. The big sluggers that carried the Caps for most of the season have all gone cold over the last week except for Dumesnil. That's a tough predicament if a team is coming down the homestretch of the season scrambling to make the playoffs.

Shevchik had this to say after the loss: "We can't keep giving up a big inning. It's putting us in a hole, and we just can't climb out of it. We keep burying ourselves early. We still have games to play. We're starting to run out of chances, though, if we want to make the playoffs."

For those that have been part of a team, they understand the relationships that are built over the course of a season. Teams, most times, become like extensions of the players' own families.

Saying goodbye at the end of any season can be hard. The bonding that took place within the Whitecaps' family is very strong. Winning and losing games did not have any impact on this.

At the end of the game, one of Brewster's finest and most

Eighth Inning—2024 Cape Cod Baseball League All-Star Game

popular players, Cuvet, left the team to return home for family reasons. The players all lined up with handshakes, hugs, and well-wishes. There is absolutely no question in anyone's mind that Cuvet will be playing baseball for a long time. He is one of the Cape's finest MLB prospects, and he's only nineteen years old.

At this point in the 2024 journey of the Brewster Whitecaps, the author has told the story for the entire organization with barely any references made to himself.

Well, in fact, I too became a part of the Whitecaps family. Shevchik and the entire team of players and coaches have welcomed me for two months with open arms. The friendships that I have built are very real and very strong. In sports, age knows no boundaries.

After traveling, eating, and going through the emotional roller coaster that is baseball for forty games, it's very easy to become immersed with the people you spend ten to twelve hours a day with. Add to that the joking around that takes place. Age had no boundaries with the Brewster Whitecaps in the summer of 2024.

Cuvet shared his feelings on the summer he spent in Brewster when the final out was made. "This was an awesome experience both on and off the field. Meeting new people and creating new relationships with different kinds of people was cool. Getting better as a baseball player but most importantly the people I met here in Brewster and developing so many relationships that will last forever all made this summer special. Some of these guys I'll be seeing again, either playing with them or against them at the next level. I really enjoyed having you with us, Pathfinder. What you are doing here writing CAPE DREAMS is really cool."

You'll hear the name Daniel Cuvet again in the not too far off future.

Whale-Watching Cruise

There is no better way to spend a day off from Cape Cod baseball than with a day on the water. The Cape is known as a great place to bring the family whale-watching. The easiest location to get to if you're staying in the mid-Cape area is Hyannis Whale Watcher Cruises, located at Millway Marina in Hyannis.

The weather was ideal to sign up for a whale-watching excursion. The ocean waves were calm, and there were very few whitecaps to contend with (no pun intended). It only took about thirty minutes to get out far enough on the Atlantic Ocean for the viewing.

The weather and the viewing were spectacular. A group of six humpback whales frolicked and played together for two hours. There were hundreds of dolphins that joined, and even seals were showing off for the visitors from shore.

The narrator at one point became more excited than her guests and shouted out hear ye! The entire trip took three and a half hours. Not one person on the boat became seasick.

The day could not have gone any better. It was the perfect way to enjoy Cape Cod and leave the troubles of the Brewster Whitecaps on shore for a few hours.

Ninth Inning—Orleans Firebirds at Whitecaps

DUMESNIL HAD A SPECIAL GUEST visiting from California. His girlfriend, Maggie Adcock, was in Brewster to show her support. There is not a better guy playing on the Cape than Nick Dumesnil. On top of that, there may not be more than three or four better players playing on the Cape. This gentle giant has a tremendous future ahead of him. With three games left, Dumesnil is one of the league's top hitters at .320.

The pretty brunette with a smile to match attends Cal Baptist along with Dumesnil. She couldn't hold back her pride for her boyfriend. "This is my second trip to Brewster this summer. It's beautiful here. Everything is so green. It's a little more humid than I thought, though. I'm so proud of Nick. He takes everything in stride. He's such a sweetheart. It's such a blessing to be on this journey with him. He's just a great guy. My uncle, Gary Adcock, is the coach at Cal Baptist; that's how we met. We're going out to dinner tonight with his mom, who's also in town."

There will never be one ounce of quit in the 2024 Brewster Whitecaps. Regardless of how much tough luck they have faced and how dire the circumstances may become; this group of Caps will go down swinging until there are no more at-bats for the summer of 2024.

The word "snakebitten" has already been used in this story. The Brewster Whitecaps were bedeviled in their next-to-the-last home game of 2024. When it looked as if the losing streak was at an end, then came the cruelest blow to an already tough-luck summer.

Riding on the stellar pitching of Clemente and Colby Frieda (Troy University), the Caps were on the verge of a four-hit shutout over their rivals the Orleans Firebirds. The Firebirds were down to their last at-bat. Frieda was pitching brilliantly. He was still hitting 91 mph on the radar gun.

Then came the Firebirds. After five straight hits, they took the lead 4–3 going into the bottom of the ninth. Whitecaps Nation looked on in deathly silence. Once again victory was taken from the Caps in the cruelest way imaginable.

What made the loss even more unbearable was that a runner for Brewster was thrown out at third for the last out of the game.

There may be some second-guessing on this one. Frieda was still throwing hard, but he left a couple of pitches too high in the strike zone. Frieda might have been left in one or two batters too long.

With the loss the Caps fell one and a half games behind Orleans for the final playoff spot. The Caps travel to Falmouth for their next game. There are only three games left in the season.

As long as these Caps are breathing, there will always be a way.

Shevchik had this message for his team immediately after the game. "We're not out of it until somebody tells us that we're done. So, if you still have a shot, we must figure out a way to win tomorrow and then the next day, and let it continue to carry on."

Every loss buries morale a little lower, though.

Kelly Nicholson, the longtime manager for the Firebirds, was very kind after the game with his praise for the Whitecaps. This is what Nicholson had to say. "That's a very good club that Shevchik has over there. I've been managing for twenty-three years, and I never remember losing 3–0 with two outs in the ninth and nobody on and coming back to win. That's a sign of a championship team that keeps fighting and won't quit. We were tied for last coming in tonight. Brewster has a great team. Kent, Dumesnil, Faurot, Helfrick, Donay, that's a great team. Anyone can beat anyone on any given day on the Cape. Hopefully the Firebirds are peaking at the right time."

So the never-say-die journey of the 2024 Whitecaps continues.

At least for three more games.

WHITECAPS AT FALMOUTH COMMODORES

Here we go again!

The Brewster Whitecaps' yellow school bus was full of life as it rolled down US Route 6 on the Mid-Cape Highway toward Falmouth. The Caps were all having the time of their lives playing a game called Mafia. Will Ray served as the narrator, and everyone joined in the fun. Mafia is a game that involves two teams, the mafia and the villagers. The game's objective is for the mafia to eliminate the civilians or vice versa. The game has several rounds of elimination. Oh my, what a ride on that school bus! The Whitecaps were full of themselves as the players were slowly being eliminated. Everyone was caught up in the fun except for the bus driver, thank goodness.

As the summer is coming to an end and the Caps keep inventing new ways to lose, the ride to Falmouth proved one thing. The comradery and the friendships that were developed in the summer of 2024 were not impacted by the team's tough losses.

Before the game Shevchik had a brutally honest conversation with the entire ball club. The loss the day before was a tough pill for everyone to take. His message was "Whatever happens over the last three games, we will not just show up and lie down. Last night's loss was tough for all of us. There were some things that I saw after the game that I'm not happy with. Some of our guys were upset, and I can understand that."

Shevchik continued, "Some of our other guys had body language that made me think they were going through the motions and waiting to just go home. We have three games left, and whatever happens, happens. We still have a shot, and I'm not ready to pack it in yet. If we lose, we lose. I can accept that. In no way are we just going to go out there and go through the motions. All we need is to get into the playoffs. We're good enough to knock off anyone in this league. The first round of the playoffs is a single-game elimination. Last night I sat in a chair for four hours when I got home and replayed the entire game. Let's put it behind us and go have some fun."

The game started with renewed optimism. Helfrick got the Caps on the board early with a solo home run to lead off the game. For Helfrick it was his eleventh of the season, which leads the league. He is also the league leader in RBIs. In the bottom of the inning, the Commodores pushed across two runs. The Caps came right back with two of their own in the second to take a 3–2 lead.

The starting pitcher for Brewster, Evan O'Toole (Oklahoma State), was roughed up as he gave up four runs to the Commodores through four innings. It looked like another doom-and-gloom night for Brewster. Through eight frames, Falmouth had a comfortable 7–4 lead.

Then the Caps did the unthinkable and showed Shevchik what they were really made of. They exploded for four runs in the top of the ninth to take an 8–7 lead. Suddenly it looked like the glass slipper was finally going to fit.

The Whitecaps closer Ray was called on to close out the game in the bottom of the ninth. Smiles were back in Whitecaps Nation. Rogers caught the first out on a deep fly to right. Then it happened again.

A SEASON WITH THE BREWSTER WHITECAPS
Ninth Inning—Orleans Firebirds at Whitecaps

Falmouth came right back with a run of their own to tie the score at eight apiece. How this run came across was déjà vu all over again. Trent Caraway doubled for Falmouth. Two errors literally handed the tying run over to Falmouth. The first error was just a sloppy play. After Caraway's double, the relay throw came back into the infield and momentarily kept Caraway at second. The ball then slipped by the infielders, and this allowed Caraway to take third.

The next batter hit a hard grounder to third that took a tough hop, which was ruled an error and allowed Caraway to score the tying run.

The game now was into extra innings. With a playoff berth at stake, Shevchik was not going to settle for a tie. He was managing as if it were for the Cape Cod League championship.

Then the omen struck. The lights in left field went out. You know the rest of the story. After a short delay, play resumed. The Caps were held scoreless in their half of the tenth. In the bottom of the tenth, Ray was as determined as he had been all year.

The extra-inning rule allows a runner to start at second base. Jack Bell laid down a great bunt and moved the runner to third. After Ray induced a ground ball out, Patrick Roche of the Commodores then singled and brought in the winning run.

The final score was the Falmouth Commodores 9 and the Caps 8.

The good news is that the Caps, under the tutelage of Shevchik, will never quit.

The bad news is that the hopes of a playoff berth are dim. The end may be coming very soon. The only hope is that Harwich will lose their last three games, and the Caps must win their final two to get the last berth in the East.

Dumesnil became the all-time base stealer for a single season in Brewster history when he stole third in the top of the eighth.

Shevchik had nothing but praise for his star. "He came to the Cape early, and he's staying until the last game. He turned himself into a possible first-round draft pick. He has all the tools to be a great one."

Tomorrow Yarmouth-Dennis, who have clinched the top spot in the playoffs in the East Division, are back in Brewster for the final home game of the year for the Caps.

After the game, the legendary coach of the Commodores, John Schiffner, was hanging around the Commodores dugout. Schiffner became a Cape Cod Hall of Famer in 2018 from his twenty-five years as the manager of the Chatham Anglers. He was looking back on his career on the Cape when approached for this interview.

"I started playing in the Cape for Harwich while I was a student at Providence College in the mid-1970s. Cape Cod baseball is my life. I've had over 140 Major Leaguers play for me over the years. Over forty have been first rounders. I've been connected to the Cape League in one way or another for over forty years. I'm starting to wear down. I've been in baseball for a very long time, coaching at all levels. I came to Falmouth this year to help my friend Jeff Trundy, who is taking a leave of absence as the manager of Falmouth."

"My teachings were about helping my players grow into successful men. It wasn't about winning at all costs for me. We had a lot of success while I was in Chatham. We were fortunate to win a couple of championships when I was there. I love it when I hear back from one of my former players. Shevchik told me a couple of months ago I was his mentor. That is the greatest compliment I can be given." Schiffner loved every second of talking about his life's passion.

Here's hoping this baseball giant will one day take some time for himself and enjoy another hobby of his, which is fishing.

THE PAUL GALOP COMMISSIONER'S CUP

As the season was coming to an end, the Brewster Whitecaps family was presented with the Cape Cod Baseball League's annual, prestigious Paul Galop Commissioner's Cup. The presentation was made by League Commissioner John Castleberry on the field before the last home game. Receiving the award from Castleberry were President Luke Dillon, General Manager Jon Mecca, Assistant General Manager Jane Sullivan, and Shevchik.

This was the first time in the history of the Brewster franchise that the Whitecaps were selected. Speaking for the entire organization, Dillon had the following words of thanks for the honor. "This is truly a tremendous honor. All the credit has to go to the players, coaches, hosts, interns, volunteers, and our tremendous board of directors."

The formal announcement from the CCBL reads as follows:

"The Paul Galop Commissioner's Cup is presented to the team that demonstrates the highest level of integrity and professionalism on and off the field, ensuring and enhancing the championship caliber of the Cape Cod Baseball League. All aspects of the franchise are taken into consideration in-season and off-season, from staff and players to volunteers and interns, to all activities at the field and in the community. As well, all off-season interactions are assessed in the deliberations."

YARMOUTH-DENNIS RED SOX AT WHITECAPS—
THE MAD CAPS ARE BACK!

Never count out the Brewster Whitecaps. You can step on them, throw rocks at them, even bully them, but they keep coming back for more. Just when the entire baseball world had given the beloved Caps up for dead and buried, their leader Shevchik said, "Hold on, not just yet. Let's just play another day."

So the Whitecaps rolled back onto shore like an angry

northeast blizzard and said, "Take that, Yarmouth-Dennis. We've got our swagger back." The curse of Andrew Fischer (remember "Kid Brett"?) is finally over.

Yarmouth-Dennis pulled their pretty little yellow school bus into Stony Brook Field for Brewster's last home game of the season. They then started parading around knowing they had the best record in the CCBL East Division.

"Not in our house," said Whitecaps Nation.

Before the game the Brewster Whitecaps honored six of their players on the field with their season ending awards. They are:

Ryder Helfrick—2024 Most Valuable Player
Jake Clemente—2024 Outstanding Pitcher of the Year
Will Ray—2024 Relief Pitcher of the Year
Nick Dumesnil—2024 Offensive Player of the Year
Kaeden Kent—2024 Heart of Brewster Award
JD Rogers—2024 Opportunity Award

Brewster jumped all over Y-D starter Ethan Firoved (Pittsburgh) in the first. Rogers and Donay came up with big hits to get things off on the right foot. Firoved didn't help himself by surrendering three walks. By the end of the first inning, the Caps had grabbed a 4–0 lead. This was in stark contrast to the previous few games when the Caps seemed to be always fighting back from early-game deficits.

Marlowe, the comeback kid, was back on the hill for Brewster. Once again, he showed that he has fully recovered from his early season health issues.

In the middle of the second, the annual "Fan of the Year" engraved Brewster Whitecaps bat was presented on the field to Mark "Pathfinder" Epstein. (Who said I was in Brewster only to write a book?) Presenting the award were Dillon, Mecca, and Sullivan.

A SEASON WITH THE BREWSTER WHITECAPS
Ninth Inning—Orleans Firebirds at Whitecaps

In the third Y-D put up three runs in their top of the inning to narrow the lead to 4–3. Marlowe gave Brewster exactly what they needed. He gave them four and two thirds of an inning and allowed only three runs. He left with a 4–3 lead.

Donay had his biggest offensive output of the season. In the sixth he blasted a two-run, 417-foot "tater" to the deepest part of Stony Brook Field to open up a 6–4 lead through six. "Tater" is what former Boston Red Sox great George Scott called his long home runs when he played.

In the seventh, newly acquired designated hitter Michael Iannazzo (Maryland) got into the act when he singled home a run for the Caps to make it 11–5.

Donay wasn't done taking out his revenge for the heartbreaks that his Whitecaps had suffered during the past two weeks. In the eighth Donay added a double to his evening's work. For the game Donay had a single, a home run, and a double with three RBIs.

The message was clearly sent to the entire league. The 13–5 pasting of Y-D let everyone know that Brewster was fighting mad.

The Caps desperately needed a feel-good win. With one game left in the season, a win against Harwich will give them a birth in the playoffs if Orleans also loses to Chatham. If Brewster could somehow win, and if Orleans loses to Chatham, the Caps would be the third seed in the East and would open the playoffs against Chatham on the road. If Brewster loses or Orleans wins, Brewster will finish last in the East and would end up on the outside looking in.

If you can't quite figure out this convoluted scenario, welcome to the club. No one connected to the Brewster Whitecaps could either.

Peter Prodanov, a former Brewster Whitecaps player from 1993 out of Oklahoma State, was back in town to watch his former team win. His daughter, Elise, is currently an intern with the Whitecaps and has kept the family legacy alive. Peter thought it was "cool" to have his daughter following in his footsteps. This is what he had to say about his memories of playing for the Caps. "I had a pretty good year. I remember batting over .300 and making the all-star team. When I went back to school that fall, I became an All-American and got drafted by the Red Sox. Playing on the Cape really helped my baseball career."

"I just want tomorrow's game to be meaningful," Shevchik said before knowing the results of the Harwich and Orleans games that hadn't been played yet. "The last thing I want to do is play a meaningless game on the last day of the season. I don't know if I've ever done that in my career. This win tonight just breathes a little life into these guys right now. They know they can win. Now they just have to put up some numbers."

Donay, the big slugger, was all smiles after the game. He opened up about the topsy-turvy season that is nearing the finish line. The all-star first baseman shared his thoughts, and this is what he said: "Some of those games we lost, I just shake my head and close my eyes and still can't believe it. We sure had some screwy endings to some of our games. I'll always look back and wonder. We as players will never walk away and not look back. As college players none of us have ever experienced anything like this. It is what it is, but it still hurts. We had such a great team here, and add to that the way we lost some games, I'll always remember this entire summer, for sure."

After the game a group of Whitecaps drove to Veterans Field in Chatham. They were there to help cheer on the Anglers in their game against Harwich. The group consisted of Rogers, interns Courtney Faber, Emily Reynolds, Mitch Fink, and Aiden Stepansky. Afterward they celebrated the Chatham win over dinner at the Red Nun Bar and Grill.

Destiny is awaiting the Brewster Whitecaps.

Bottom of the Ninth— Whitecaps at Harwich: Do or Die, One Moment in Time

IN A PERFECT WORLD, THE end of this story would be one where the Brewster Whitecaps Baseball team would be crowned the champions of the 2024 Cape Cod Baseball League.

Well, in fact, this story has an even happier ending. The 2024 Brewster Whitecaps had the greatest season of any baseball team in America when you add up all the new friendships and relationships that have been made.

Winning is great, but developing life-changing friendships is a lot better.

The Whitecaps are champions of life.

Brewster went into the final game of the season versus Harwich knowing they needed a lot of help to get into the playoffs. First, they needed to win. Second, not only did the Caps need to win, but they also needed Chatham to beat Orleans.

Well, neither happened.

For a few innings it looked promising. In the top of the fourth, the Caps got back-to-back home runs from Colby Shelton (Florida) and newly acquired Mike Iannazzo (Maryland). For Shelton, his only home run of the year was a grand slam. This made the score 6–3 in favor of the Caps.

In the bottom of the inning, the old nemesis, pitching, would come back again to haunt Brewster. Detmers gave up nine earned runs that included six walks, and that was it. The Caps couldn't recover. They would go on to lose 15–7.

I want one moment in time,
When I'm more than I thought I could be,
When all of my dreams are a heartbeat away,
And the answers are all up to me.
Give me one moment in time,
When I'm racing with destiny,
Then in that moment in time,
I will feel,
I will feel eternity...
— *"One Moment in Time," lyrics by Whitney Houston*

One of the true heroes of the summer was Bobby Lasbury. Lasbury came to Brewster about three weeks before the season ended. Lasbury, a pitcher from Iona College, injured his shoulder during the past college season. He was only able to pitch six innings throughout the entire 2024 season. His dad, Robert, played for Orleans on the Cape in 1993.

Lasbury was given permission by Shevchik and Mecca to come to Brewster and work out with the rest of the pitchers during pregame workouts. The workout program was being offered to Lasbury with the hopes the program would help rehabilitate his injury. He was given no expectations that he would ever be added to the Brewster roster.

Lasbury came every day and worked very hard. He also developed a great rapport with all the Whitecaps. As the season was coming down to the last couple of games, Brewster found itself shorthanded a couple of pitchers. Three pitchers had gone home, and they had to be replaced.

Lasbury was one of the pitchers added to the roster. His injury had improved, and he would become available in a game if needed. Lasbury is a solid pitcher for Iona and from the Division III school he transferred from before he attended Iona.

Cape Cod baseball is the pinnacle that most college baseball players aspire to someday reach. It is for the elite of the elite. Lasbury was average for the level he performed at throughout his college career. He did not have a receive a Cape Cod invitation to come pitch like everyone else. Lasbury was an emergency addition late in the season.

Shevchik describes the late-season developments. "We decided to activate Bobby right before our last game. Still, I had zero intentions of pitching him. I had a couple of conversations with my coaches about putting him in during the game. I decided to put him in at the end of the game if it was out of reach for us to win."

Shevchik continued, "There were two outs and nobody on in the last inning. We were down eight runs. I walked down to the end of the dugout and asked a couple of our pitchers what their thoughts were of putting Bobby into the game. I took everything into consideration. This became the coolest moment that I had all season. I asked Will Ray, another of our pitchers, if Bobby was a good kid to have around this summer. Without hesitating, Ray said, 'Put him in.' So, I did put him in, but I was scared. This was going to be the height of his career, and I didn't want it to backfire on him. That would have been awful if it didn't work out for him and his dad. I wanted this to be something he could look back on for the rest of his life and smile. I was a nervous wreck. Not about winning the game but about Bobby getting the kid out he was going to face. Bobby struck the kid out for the last out of the game, and our entire dugout exploded. They all came rushing out onto the field to congratulate him," Shevchik said as he relived the special memory.

"We had one really good moment in what was the most dreadful game of our season. Bobby Lasbury did something that he can look back on for the rest of his life with pride.

"STRIKE THREE—YOU'RE OUT…

"Bobby Lasbury got to pitch in the Cape Cod Baseball League," Shevchik said as his voice was cracking.

Finally catching up with Lasbury five days after his memorable "moment in time," he was still on cloud nine. "This has been my dream since I was five years old. I've been coming to Cape games since I was born. My family vacations in Brewster every summer. Since I played T-ball at four years old, I've dreamed of someday standing on a pitcher's mound on the Cape. I still can't believe it happened. Pitching for a Division I program like Iona was something I always wanted to do. This is very different. This is the Cape Cod Baseball League. I had so many emotions. It was the culmination of my entire life in baseball. It was my number-one highlight of my life. I had no idea I would ever get to pitch. Just my getting to wear a Cape League uniform was a huge thrill for my entire family. My dad was beside himself. He played for Orleans in 1993. I never expected to get to pitch. I'm so grateful I was given this opportunity. I was thrilled to just work out with the Caps. All of a sudden, Del Rosso tapped me on the shoulder and told me to start warming up. I thought to myself, this could really happen. My butterflies were all over the place. Even thinking about it now. It's just something different about the experience. The teammates, all of them standing on the top step of the dugout, cheering for me. It was just incredible. When I struck out the last batter of the game and they all poured out of the dugout to congratulate me, that was the coolest thing in the world. For that moment, they put out of their minds that we lost the game. I'll remember that moment forever."

Everyone will remember that moment forever.

Yes, the 2024 Whitecaps led by their leader, Jamie Shevchik, were special.

Regardless of what the results of the Whitecaps game were, the season wasn't going to end the way Whitecaps Nation was hoping it would anyway.

Orleans steamrolled Chatham 7–1, and the Caps' season was officially over.

It took a while after the game for the finality to sink in. The Whitecaps all walked around on the field hugging and shaking the hands of their teammates and new best friends they had spent their last nine weeks going to war with.

Shevchik addressed the players on the field immediately after the game. "The biggest lesson you experienced this summer is learning how to come to the park every single day and battle. You all learned that. That's why I liked this group so much. You were all fighters and wanted to get better.

"What I want you to also learn is that you can't take one day off or an at-bat off. No matter if it's in the beginning or end of the season. Think about how different our season would be if we could just have one game back. Just look back at our season. One play or one at-bat, if we could have it back. Not everything on the Cape can be about winning and losing. You guys were fighters, and I appreciate all of you.

"Just think about this. Forty games in fifty days, and somewhere during this season there could have been a different outcome in just one game. Think of how much different our ending could have been. When you go back to your schools in the fall, regardless of how tired you may be, push yourselves and don't take a day off. You guys were incredible to be around. Good luck to all of you."

Just like that, this was going to be the last time the likable Shevchik would ever speak to this team.

There were no sad faces. There might have been a few tears shed by Sullivan and a few host families.

This was a celebration. Over the course of the summer, over fifty players came and went. Each wore the pride of a Whitecap uniform with a singular purpose: to showcase their incredible baseball skills to the almost one hundred MLB scouts who would attend their games. What ended up happening has been happening on the Cape for over one hundred years.

The players came from every corner of America. Oklahoma, Alabama, Texas, Maryland, South Carolina, Ohio, Florida, North Carolina, Arkansas, Mississippi, Tennessee, Oregon, California, New Jersey, Utah, and many more states across the USA. Their purpose as they set out on their journey was to impress the scouts and move up in the MLB draft.

What they were about to find out was that their experiences would become much more valuable than future riches. Yes, many did increase their potential future wealth. What all gained were valuable life lessons, friendships, and personal growth that will become invaluable as each continues with their life journey.

The new teammates have become lifetime best friends. The relationships with their host families will forever be etched in their memories. The new extended families will always be a part of them. Engagements, weddings, and births of children will be shared by their 2024 hosts. The laughs and the bonds will never fade. When the players move on with their lives and careers, they won't remember the wins and losses. (I take that back: These Caps will in fact remember a few of those crazy losses.)

What they will remember is that Jane Sullivan loved each like her own child. What they will remember is how the town of Brewster, even though it doesn't have a red light, embraced the

A SEASON WITH THE BREWSTER WHITECAPS
Bottom of the Ninth—Whitecaps at Harwich: Do or Die, One Moment in Time

Caps with incredible pride. What they will remember is how much each volunteer gave of themself. What they will remember are the interns, who were also college students, and how they also gained valuable life experiences. What they will remember was what a tremendous guy manager Jamie Shevchik was and how he understood how to balance the entire Cape experience along with winning and losing. What they will remember was the dedication and hard work that the five coaches, Scott Grimes, Brian Del Rosso, Dylan Cooper, Jordan Art, and Rocco DePietro, gave to them. What they will remember are the mafia games played on the back of those uncomfortable yellow school buses that took them to towns on the Cape that they couldn't even pronounce, like Cotuit. What they will remember is shopping for pregame food at Ferretti's Market on Underpass Road. What they will remember are the delicious shrimp burritos at Pico's Taco Shack located directly across the street from Stony Brook Field. What they will remember are the pregame batting practices and infield and outfield workouts before each game when everyone would take turns spitting on the ground because that's what ballplayers do. What they will remember are the morning clinics they helped to conduct and the laughter and smiles the children shared with their heroes. What they will remember are the scores of MLB scouts who sat right behind home plate at Stony Brook Field. What they will remember are the many, many hours of hanging around the dugouts sharing funny stories. Lastly, they will also remember this old author who they all called "Pathfinder" and who wanted to be back in college.

As the summer closes on the Cape Cod Baseball League, the 2024 Brewster Whitecaps will always remain CHAMPIONS!

A final word at the end of the season—A blink of an eye

Alex Valentin

Andrew Fischer

Andrew Koshy

Autograph Table—JD Rogers, Levi Huesman, Ashton Crowther, Grant Conningham, and Blake Binderup

Avery Raimondo, Courtney Faber, and Julianne Shivers

Billy Wagner, Peter Gammons, and Luke Dillon—Two Hall of Famers and a President

Blake Binderup

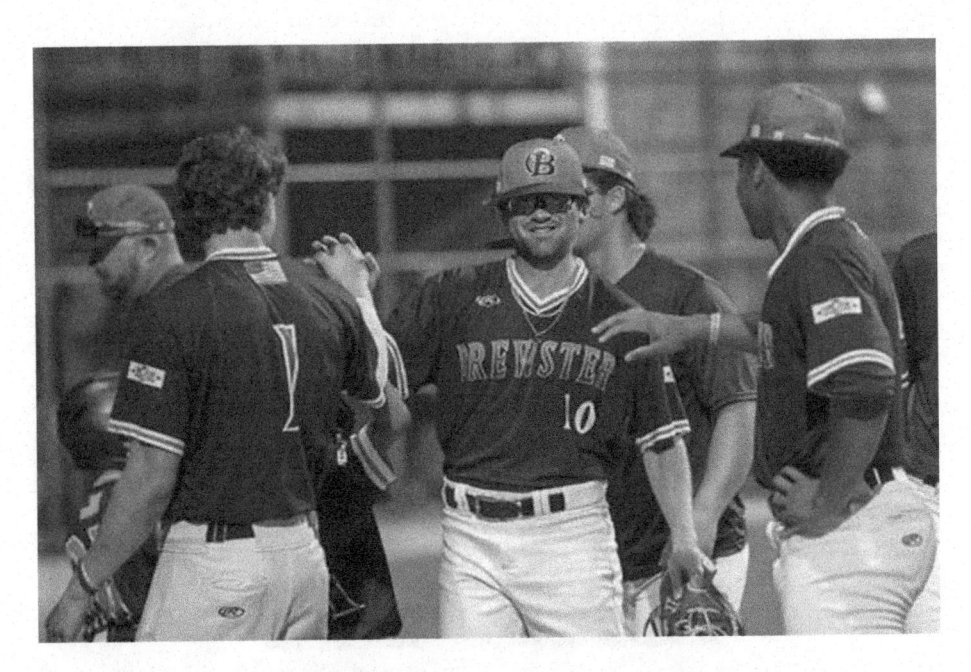

Bobby Lasbury is congratulated by his teammates

Bobby Lasbury—An unforgettable moment in time

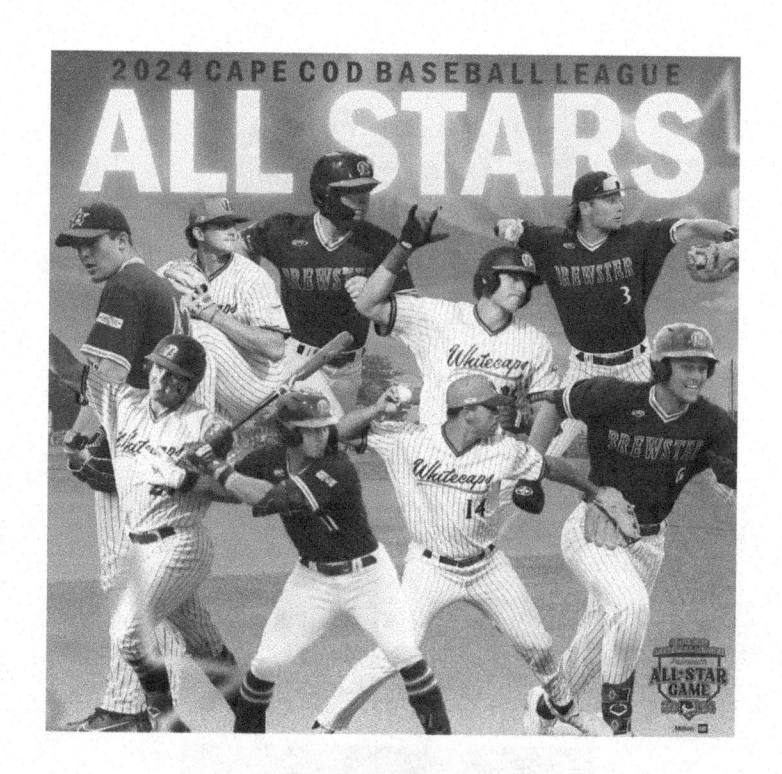

Brewster All-Stars

Brody Donay

Carsten Sabathia

Chase Mora

Chase Mora with the catch of the year

Coach Brian Del Rosso

Coach Dylan Cooper

Coach Jordan Art

Coach Rocco DePietro

Coach Scott Grimes

Colby Shelton, immediately after hitting a grand slam against Harwich

Colby Frieda

Cooper Vest

Dan Cuvet

Darian Smith

DeAmez Ross

DJ Primeaux

Drew Faurot and Dallas Masias

Drew Faurot

Ethan Kagno, Director of Baseball Operations

Evan O'Toole

Gabe Davis

Game day arrival

Gio Cueto

Grace and Raina, two of the finest bat kids in Cape Cod history

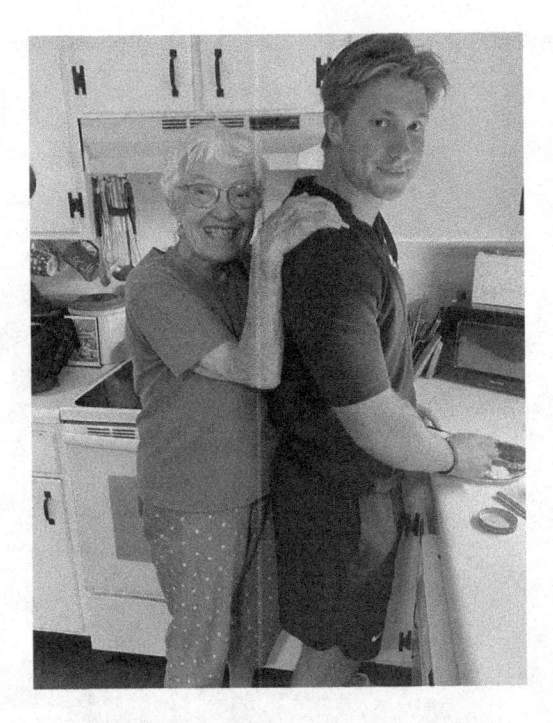

Host Families—JD Rogers preparing his breakfast inside Nancy Sveden's home

In 2012, Major League superstar Aaron Judge played for the Brewster Whitecaps

JD Rogers

Jacob Marlowe

Jake Clemente

James Tibbs and Jane Sullivan

Jayden Hylton

Kaeden Kent

Levi Huesman

Luke Guth

Luke Schmolke

Max Kaufer

Michael Iannazzo

Michael Salina

Ms. Whitecap Jane Sullivan with James Tibbs—Brewster 2023—1st round MLB draft pick San Francisco Giants

Nick Dumesnil

Noah Samol

Onyx Grimes

Parker Detmers

Patrick Forbes

Pregame Snacks at Ferretti's Market

Respect Boston Flannery, Ashton Crowther, Andrew Fischer, Jacob Marlowe, and DeAmez Ross

RJ Johnson JR

Rocco Reid

Ryan Ure

Ryder Helfrick

Seth Tomczak

The Caps at the Brewster Ladies' Library

The Galop Commissioner's Cup received by Jon Mecca,
Jane Sullivan, Luke Dillon, and Jamie Shevchik

The miracle Marlowe

The Shevchik Family—Gigi, Raina, Jamie, Maria and Brielle

Tyler Pettorini

Will Ray and Ryder Helfrick formed a great battery

Will Ray

You're outta here skip!

Zach Johnston

Zach Neto rounding third after his blast clinched the
CCBL Championship for the beloved Caps!

Extra Innings—Just Like That...

THE 101ST EDITION OF THE Cape Cod Baseball League had come to an end. The Harwich Mariners took home the CCBL 2024 Championship. They overcame a seven-game losing streak and a nine-game losing streak in the middle of their season. They finished with an overall record of 15 wins and 25 losses in the regular season. At the end of the summer, the Mariners ignited. This championship came to be partly because Harwich was able to keep their pitching staff together through the playoffs and partly because they were playing their bast ball when it counted most. They beat the Bourne Braves two games to one in the championship series.

The results of the season for the Brewster Whitecaps as well as the other nine teams will be saved forever in the historical archives by the official historian of the CCBL, Mike Richard. Richard has been storing historical data on the Cape League for many years.

But the history in these sacred vaults will never store the real story of the Cape Cod Baseball League.

The real stories are the friendships and the relationships that have been made and cherished for many future generations. Once you attend a game as a fan or a player or a coach, you're hooked for life.

The other stories are the almost two thousand current and former Major Leaguers who showcased their talents on the sandlot fields of Cape Cod and used their summer experiences to go on and play professional baseball.

Cape Cod Baseball grabs onto whoever it is that stops and watches or plays in even one game. It's unlike any sporting tradition left standing in America. When every sport's organization, both professional and amateur (yes, even our youth leagues, which are called travel teams), are getting trampled over by greed and entitlement, the Cape Cod Baseball League is standing strong with the values that were used to build our great nation. For 101 years there has been only one amateur organization that has had the determination to stand strong and say, "Not us. We will not forget our past. Our traditions and our sacred history will forever remain stronger than the ruins of all American sports."

People may ask for several years, "How did one of the strongest rosters that was ever put together in league history struggle the way the Brewster Whitecaps did in the summer of 2024?" Obviously, this is a question that needs to be addressed.

It's complicated. There is no direct, quick answer.

The league has changed a lot in recent years. Players come and go whenever their college coach or a misguided advisor beckons for them. This disgusting reality really gives a beating to team chemistry. It impacts all teams.

Another problem is pitching. It's nearly impossible to put together a complete pitching staff. Whenever a pitcher reaches a relatively small number of innings, their college coach shuts them down. This is not just a Cape problem. It's the way all pitchers are and the way baseball is played at every level in every corner of America.

The Brewster Whitecaps struggled as a team. They won a total of thirteen games. They had the worst record on the Cape.

The Whitecaps pitchers finished last in team ERA (5.89) giving up almost six runs per game. The Caps also finished eighth in the league in batting average with a .247 average. This was supposed to be the team's strong suit, but it just never clicked the way Shevchik and his coaching staff envisioned.

The biggest obstacle they faced was that they were never able to find the on-field chemistry that allowed them to play as a cohesive unit. Off the field, Brewster had phenomenal chemistry. The strength from the bonding as friends and teammates off the field couldn't have been better. It was as good if not better than any other of the nine ball clubs. There was never one situation that occurred where someone got frustrated, blamed, or pointed a finger at someone.

The strength of the team was the amount of home run hitters found up and down the roster. Brewster finished second in the league with forty home runs slugged over the course of the forty-game schedule. Like many teams that rely on the home run ball, Brewster finished second in the league in strikeouts with 376. This is the reason that the team had a hard time sustaining a long offensive rally during the season.

Another problem that impacted several games was sloppy baserunning. The team had a hard time advancing baserunners. This was primarily due to looking for the home run instead of a sacrifice. If the long-ball hitters were not able to hit one of their monster shots, the result many times was a strikeout. To be fair to Brewster, this is the way baseball is played everywhere today. Pitchers are throwing as hard as they can to strike out hitters, and hitters are swinging as hard as they can to hit mammoth home runs. That's what fans want to see, and that's what MLB teams pay the most money for.

The Brewster Whitecaps never quit, and they never held their heads low after one of their many tough losses. They fought tooth and nail to the very last out of the season. They also showed up at Stony Brook Field sometimes six to eight hours before a game and worked through the hot summer sun to improve their skills.

These elite college athletes were as great off the field as they were on the field. Not one single time did any of these future Major Leaguers ever turn down an autograph request or a chance to enjoy a conversation with their large group of followers.

As the season was coming to an end, several took the opportunity to share their feelings and their experiences playing summer baseball in Brewster.

Here are some excerpts from Brewster's very best.

Pitcher Boston Flannery shared his summer highlights: "It was awesome to meet a bunch of new players that I never thought I would get to play with. I'm so thankful I spent my summer in Brewster. This entire summer experience helped me grow as a player and a person."

Max Kaufer explained that he learned "how to use baseball metrics to my advantage" when he catches and is calling a game from behind the plate.

Colby Frieda, the big right-handed pitcher from Troy University, stopped his stretching before a home game to say what he learned in Brewster pitching for the Caps. "I learned a lot from my teammates. Not only were they great teammates, but they also had a great approach to the game."

Darien Smith, the All-American pitcher from Southeastern University in Jacksonville, Florida, has pitched in Brewster for the last two summers. "I love Brewster. The scenery and the atmosphere are beautiful. I love everything about it. I've had two different host families and they've both been great."

Luke Schmolke, the friendly pitcher, was all smiles as he looked back. "It was a great summer with the relationships I've developed with my teammates and the coaches. I love my host family. I had the best one on the Cape. No one wants to lose; of course we want to win. But summer ball is to redefine yourself and to improve."

Parker Detmers from the University of Louisville—probably

the most improved pitcher over the summer months—expressed nothing but a positive experience. "I made a lot of new friends, and I learned a lot about myself."

DJ Primeaux, the left-handed pitcher out of LSU, had a great season pitching in Brewster. "You never meet people like this very often. These are the nicest people I have ever met in my life. I got better as a pitcher, and I learned a lot."

Kaeden Kent, the slick-fielding infielder out of Texas A&M, became a leader for Brewster in the dugout as the season rolled along. This is what the hard-nosed competitor had to say about his summer: "The friendships and the relationships you make here are unlike any other. Baseball is a hard game, and you spend two months in the dugout, and it's up to you if you decide you want to find joy with your teammates. The biggest thing I have gotten out of my two summers of playing on the Cape are the friendships and the incredible relationships I've been able to make."

DeAmez Ross, the popular outfielder from Florida State who announced at the end of the summer he was transferring to the University of Central Florida, couldn't hold back the newfound joy he has discovered toward the game of baseball. "This summer has been unreal. The Whitecaps breathed new life into my baseball career. I have bonded with many of my new teammates unlike anything I could have imagined. Nick Dumesnil and I have become very close. I just love the guy. This whole experience has been awesome. Having hitting and outfield practice every day made me a better player."

Nick Dumesnil is a player who may have improved his draft stock the most this past summer. Watch this kid get ready to explode in the Major Leagues in the next few years. Currently he is rated as the fourteenth best prospect in the 2025 MLB draft. The soft-spoken outfielder out of Cal Baptist lets his play do all the talking. Toward the end of the season, he finally opened up. "My host family was awesome. Every Friday they would take me kayaking with them. I ate my first lobster this summer. This entire summer meant so much to me. Being able to be with my boys and perfecting our craft felt like a dream."

Ryder Helfrick led the entire Cape Cod Baseball League in home runs and RBIs. "This was the best summer of my life. I was able to compete against the best players in America."

JD Rogers looked back at his relationship with Shevchik. "In the beginning of the season, it was tough for me because he called me and challenged me from the start. I didn't like it, but every day when I woke up, I knew I had something to play for. He challenged me as a player. I thought we might have had bad blood between us, but in fact he made me a better player. He started making me believe in the things I'm capable of. In the second half of the season, we bonded. I appreciate what he did for me, but I have to admit it wasn't easy. He had patience with me, and he took a shot with me. I ended up gaining more confidence in my abilities as the summer went along. He fulfilled his promise to me. Once I showed him what I was capable of, I went from a temporary contract to a permanent one and made the all-star team. What he did for me, I see a ton of benefits from. The player I was then to the player I am today is a lot different."

Andrew Fischer, one of the fan favorites of all players that played on the Cape in 2024 shared his feelings of being a Brewster Whitecap. "I developed a bunch of new friendships and relationships from different schools. I enjoyed sharing experiences with other players from different parts of America."

Fischer continued, "Carsten Sabathia was a great guy, and we became great friends while he was on the team before he got hurt. Every day after our pregame workouts, we'd sit in the dugout and have what we called 'story time.' We'd have different players share stories on how they grew up or stories from the schools they played for. Or just funny stories were told. It was really cool to see how everyone got to where they are. If you play on the Cape, you're a serious player and love the game and want to get better."

The affable infielder on his way to Tennessee was just getting started. "The best memories are made during the bus rides and in the dugouts. Developing vulnerable-based trust with your teammates brings about mutual respect. During a season you spend ten to twelve hours each day with your teammates. Playing and practicing takes up only a small part of the time. You must be willing to open up and become vulnerable."

Fischer concluded with "I loved our manager, Jamie. He was always honest with me. He showed me respect, and I gave it right back to him. He was like a secondary father figure to me. Great teams go through tough times. The team was great, but baseball is so hard. That's why the Cape League is the very best summer league in the country."

The conversation got around to the injury that unfortunately sent the future high MLB draft choice home early. "My back is finally feeling better. I had a couple of minor injuries to my back in high school. I'll be ready when the season at Tennessee opens."

"Kid Brett' ended the conversation with the following statement about playing for the Brewster Whitecaps:

"We developed a culture in Brewster that was second to none."

Love That Dirty Water—Acknowledgments

It would be impossible to take on a project such as CAPE DREAMS—A SEASON WITH THE BREWSTER WHITECAPS and share a gem of a story without the help of many. I am truly blessed and indebted. Jane Sullivan told me, two months before I arrived on the Cape, two things. Sullivan said, "Pathfinder, at the end of the summer, you will say the same thing all the players say. That is that the summer of 2024 was the best summer of your life."

Okay Ms. Whitecap, here you go: "The summer of 2024 was the best summer of my life."

The other thing she told me was that "When the season ends and the players leave to go home, you will cry." Right again, Sullivan.

At least, though, when I cried, I was sitting in the Whitecaps' dugout by myself the day after the season ended. I could hear the echoes of the new friends I had made. I could hear funny stories from my buddy Andrew Fischer. I remembered how hard Carsten Sabathia laughed as he recalled his dad CC pitching at crazy Fenway. I could picture standing next to my guy Jamie Shevchik as we watched batting practice day after day. I could still see the endless smile on Cooper Vest's face. I could still see the mammoth home runs hit by Dan Cuvet and the line drives by Nick Dumesnil. I could hear the booming voice of Chris Lynch coming across the speakers. But sadly, I could only really hear the eerie quiet that surrounded Stony Brook Field, located on Underpass Road in Brewster Massachusetts.

I wondered out loud, "How could I have come to Brewster as an author and leave as the luckiest man in the world?" As the tears streamed down my cheeks, all I asked for was that someday, somehow, I wanted to be with everyone one more precious time.

Thank you to my beautiful wife, Barbara, for convincing me I was the right person to tell this story. I sacrificed nothing. Barbara was the one who made the sacrifices. A big thank-you to my niece, Dawn, for giving her uncle a nice place to stay in Brewster for the first two weeks of the season. Thank you to my dear late brother, Bobby "EPPY," and my late sister, Diane, who forever will remain my confidant. You both should never have been taken from me. To Mom and Dad—Sarah and Charlie, I hope I'm making you proud. To my daughters, Brooke and Karli, my sons-in-law, Torrey and Sean, my grandchildren, Sedona (Donut), Aspen Rose (Tornado), Bennett, and Taitum (Tater-Tot)—I love you all, and don't worry, we'll be at another Cape game next summer. Love also to my niece, Faith, and of course to my mini-Aussie Shepherd, Edith Ann, who snuggled by my feet the entire time I authored this story.

To Jamie Shevchik, his wife Maria, and his beautiful children, thanks for bringing me into your Whitecaps family and also into the Shevchik family. We shared the same vision, and your incredible loyalty, "Skip," was the trigger that earned me the players' trust. I was promised total access to everyone and everything, and I received it. Our friendship will never fade. Thank you to the core of the Whitecaps organization—Jane Sullivan, Luke Dillon, Jon Mecca, Ned Monthie, and the entire board of directors—y'all were incredible. I guess I did choose the right organization.

To the 2024 Brewster Whitecaps players, thanks for letting this old author into your Whitecaps family. This entire experience changed my life. I hope I don't leave anyone out. Thank you to

Andrew Fischer, JD Rogers, Cooper Vest, Danny Cuvet, Carsten Sabathia, DeAmez Ross, Will Ray, RJ Johnson, Chase Mora, Dallas Macias, Nick Dumesnil, Ryder Helfrick, Brody Donay, Jake Clemente, Drew Faurot, Darien Smith, Andrew Koshy, Alex Valentin, Parker Detmers, Evan O'Toole, Kellan Oakes, Colby Frieda, Boston Flannery, Zach Johnston, Michael Iannazzo, Blake Binderup, Sonny Fauci, Kyle Percival, Colby Shelton, Ashton Crowther, Rocco Reid, Patrick Forbes, Gabe Davis, Isaac Morton, Gio Cueto, Grant Cunningham, Jayden Hylton, Nolan Schubart, Tyler Pettorini, Jacob Marlowe, Levi Huesman, Luke Schmolke, Max Kaufer, Noah Samol, Ryan Ure, Seth Tomczak, DJ Primeaux, Luke Guth, Kaeden Kent, and Robert Lasbury.

All the coaches were phenomenal as well. Thank you, Brian Del Rosso, Scott Grimes, Dylan Cooper, Rocco DePietro, Jordan Art, and Ethan Kagno.

To Jenny Chandler and her entire staff at Elite Authors Publishing, especially the editors—once again you have all done just a tremendous job. This now makes it three terrific books, thank you.

To the family of Dr. Richard Ulmer, especially the late beautiful Martha of Charleston, SC, I'm eternally grateful for you adopting this wayward Yankee into your family over thirty-six years ago.

To Mr. Hal McCoy, the great Baseball Hall of Fame sportswriter for the past sixty years for the Cincinnati Reds, "You are right!" It was fate the day we sat down next to each other on press row during the three-day 2023 ESPN Charleston Classic. How lucky did I know, Mr. McCoy, that you would become my mentor and close advisor. Your class and inspiration are found on every page in this story, GOD Bless." Also, a huge thank-you to my friend Gene Sapakoff, the former brilliant sportswriter and editor for over thirty years with the Charleston *Post and Courier.*

To the legendary Mr. Peter Gammons, pinch me. How can I

ever thank you for your contributions. To Matt Hyde, I landed in a bucket of honey when Shevchik connected us. I never thought I would say this, but I'll never say a bad word about the Yankees again. (This is going to be really hard.) To J. P. Ricciardi—Worcester love runs deep, friend. Stop being so humble. Your contributions did help to revolutionize baseball.

To Zach Neto, the American League phenom shortstop from the Los Angeles Angels by the way of Brewster, thanks for sharing your Whitecaps memories. Thank you also goes out to the entire Rome family (David, Laurie, Ben, and Sam), who hosted Aaron Judge during the summer of 2012 and shared their memories.

To Jim Collins, I can only hope to duplicate your fine work. Thank you for offering your knowledge and support and for letting me borrow a couple of things from *The Last Best League*. Also, thank you to Tom Bednark, the owner of the Barnstable Bat Company.

Thank you to Mike Richard, the official historian for the Cape Cod Baseball League, for providing me with critical facts, data, and information, always in a timely manner.

Thanks to college interns Mitch Fink and Aiden Stepansky, who both did an excellent job on the day-to-day writing of the online game summaries. Also, thanks to interns Matthew Parry, Austin Barach, and Max Gifford. It won't be long until the three of you are working as the number one broadcast team on ESPN.

Thank you to the college interns—Brielle Shevchik, Julianne Shivers, Courtney Faber, and Avery Raimondo—for the incredible work they did as photographers and for providing the photos found in this book. To Emily Reynolds, your daily greetings and cheerful smiles were a beautiful gift to the entire organization.

The fact-checking in this story was done by using the Google search engine. Also, the baseball websites for many of the players' colleges and universities were used to gather facts, data, and quotes. Also, the official Brewster Whitecaps website was a valuable resource throughout the entire story.

Much love to Bill and Linda Lynds. Thank you for your unwavering support. Prayers go out as you both recover from the rath of Hurricane Helene in your new hometown of Asheville, North Carolina.

Thank you to my homeboys and girls, Bob Kusz, Manny Quintela, Mark Meehan, the late David Meehan, Artie Gazal, Tim Ethier, Lenny Kasprzak, Paul Sullivan, Tom Boland, Jim McGovern, Patti Glennon, Hugh O'Malley, Mary Runyon, Marty O'Malley, Mary Sullivan Police, Kevin McGovern, Brian Hammel, Gina and Jim McCaffrey, and his dad, the late Honorable Judge Francis "Frank Mac" McCaffrey—a great hoop player at St. Michael's and one of the greatest men I have ever known.

Also thanks to my friends with whom I share great memories: Kevin Clark, Tony Jeffreys, Kris Grundberg, Fran Laffin, Coach Jim Girourard, Howie Greenblat, Augie Gwozdz, Eddie Reilly, Doug Safford, Rich Riley, Mike McGovern, Marian McGovern, Dennis Henderson, Bob Berman, Jim and Jill Burke, Mike Murphy, Vinny and Donna DelMonte, Neal "Poink" Portnoy, Erick Ingraham, Vinny Palazzi, Stuart Herman, Ronnie Parker, Mayor Joe Petty, Coach Bill Gibbons Jr., Kevin O'Sullivan, Sopia Barshan, Kathy Fitzpatrick, Billy "Mac" McGreevy who was a terrific ballplayer and who once played for Yarmouth-Dennis on the Cape, and also let's not forget Billy's dad the late Tom McGreevy who was the longtime president of the Ted Williams Little League in Worcester.

Thank you to my favorite Worcester mayor Tim Cooney, and his lovely wife Joyce, Coach Bob Cousy, Dr. Ted Gallagher, Dr. Charles Steinberg, the late Arnie "Butch" and Barbara Ravelson, Lois Berg and her late husband Attorney Uncle Burton Berg, Gail "the Shot" Raney and her late husband the great Jack "the Shot" Foley, Coach George Blaney, Coach Jim Calhoun, Frank and Rose

Foley, Mike and Gail Cosky, Bobby and Linda Eurenius, Donny and Patti Henderson, Chuckie and Gina Robinson, Buddy Beall, Nancy Mayer Bates, Nick Kotsopoulos, Wendy and Linda Rickles, Meg Mulhern, Tim and Kelly Fortugno, Paul Mitchell, Mark and Beth Smiley, Signe Johns, Brendan Clark, Rick Sanford, Sherrie Pompeii, Ginger Reijners, Kevin Bilodeau, Dean and Caroline Delonchamps, Angela May, Sandy Walsh, Elizabeth Freedman, Bill Walsh, Scott Eisberg, AnnMarie Reed, Lynn Reed, and her mom the late Esther Marzilli Fitzgerald, and her dad, Al Fitzgerald, who spent several years working on the board of directors for the Brewster Whitecaps. Also, a shout-out to John and Karen O'Brien Andreoli and Karen's dad, the late Coach Francis O'Brien, who led the Harwich Mariners to the Cape Cod Baseball League Championship in 1990.

I'd like to remember friends of the Epstein family who are not with us any longer. Don Lemenager, Frankie Oftring Jr., Togo Palazzi, George Query, Owen Mahorn, John Murphy, Dr. Joe Lonergan, Mary and Tom McGovern, Danny Trant, Bertha Mann, Candy Bates, Dr. Ken Shelton, Mary Ellen Duffy, Floyd Hiott, Steve Gadaire, Tom Tivnan, Tommy Burns, Coach Buster Sheary, Nick Manzello, Art Andreoli, Coach Dee Rowe, Paul Tivnan, and Coach Ken Coblentz.

Thank you to my Maccabi Coaching Brothers, Ryan Marks, Barry Kleiman, and Howard Fisher.

Thank you to the Charleston County School District and all the skilled professionals I had the chance to work with during my second life.

Finally, to every intern, volunteer, and host family over the past 101 years, your hard work, dedication, passion, and commitment are what have made the Cape Cod Baseball League one of the most important amateur athletic organizations in American sports history.

Major Leaguers from Brewster

(Listed by the year they played for Brewster)

1988 Erik Bennett, J. T. Bruett, Mike Myers, Craig Paquette, F. P. Santangelo, Dave Staton
1989 Rigo Beltran, Damon Buford, Frank Charles, Mike Myers, Eduardo Perez
1990 Garvin Alston, Rigo Beltran, Ricky Greene, Matt Herges, Lyle Moulton
1991 Garvin Alston, Roger Bailey, Chad Mottola, Ken Robinson, Andy Sheets, Mark Thompson
1992 Adam Melhuse, Billy Wagner
1993 Geoff Blum, Brian Buchanan, Jason Rakers, Gary Rath
1994 Sean Casey, Seth Greisinger, Augie Ojeda, Dusty Wathan
1995 Todd Belitz, Seth Greisinger
1996 Jason Grilli, Corey Hart, David Ross, Aaron Rowand
1997 Brandon Duckworth, Aaron Rowand, Terrmel Sledge, Kip Wells
1998 Reed Johnson, Bobby Kielty, Mike Neu, Mike Tonis, Chase Utley
1999 Jason Bay, David DeJesus, Kevin Reese
2000 Rocky Cherry, Mike Rouse
2001 Brian Bannister, Brian Barden, Matt Carson
2002 Mike Avilés, Brad Davis, Chris Dickerson, Tony Gwynn Jr., Justin James, Taylor Tankersley, Sean White

2003   Brian Bixler, Matt Macri, Tommy Manzella
2004   Ryan J. Braun, Cesar Carrillo, Will Rhymes, Gaby Sánchez, Steve Tolleson
2005   Aaron Bates, Brennan Boesch, Danny Dorn, Jon Jay, P. J. Walters
2006   David Adams, David Cooper, Collin Cowgill, Erik Davis, Cole De Vries, Barry Enright, Colt Hynes, Matt LaPorta, Scott Maine, Andrew Romine
2007   Yonder Alonso, Ryan Cook, David Cooper, Erik Davis, Brad Glenn, Blake Tekotte, Adam Warren
2008   Buddy Baumann, Nick Christiani, Caleb Cotham, Mike Freeman, Yasmani Grandal, Ty Kelly, Ryan Wheeler
2009   Scott Alexander, Daniel Butler, Mark Canha, Caleb Cotham, Erik Goeddel, David Goforth, Jedd Gyorko, Bryan Holaday, Jarrett Parker, Tyler Thornburg, Colin Walsh
2010   John Andreoli, Luke Bard, Jake Barrett, Jon Berti, David Buchanan, Andy Burns, Taylor Featherston, Drew Gagnon, Kyle Hendricks, Tommy Kahnle, Colton Murray, Anthony Ranaudo, Chad Smith
2011   Jake Barrett, Jon Berti, Joe Biagini, J. T. Chargois, Taylor Davis, Drew Steckenrider, Andrew Toles, Austin Voth
2012   Ryon Healy, Aaron Judge, Michael Lorenzen, Jeff McNeil, Sam Moll, Adrian Sampson, Tyler Smith, Austin Voth, Luke Weaver
2013   Scott Heineman, Brandon Leibrandt, Ben Meyer
2014   Braden Bishop, Scott Kingery, Cody Ponce, LaMonte Wade Jr.
2015   Tyson Miller, Jacob Robson, Nick Senzel, Jordan Sheffield, Will Smith, Eli White
2016   Ryan Feltner, Zac Lowther, Ryan Noda, Konnor Pilkington, Brent Rooker, Tyler Zuber

2017	Davis Daniel, Jonathan Stiever, Travis Swaggerty, Steele Walker
2018	Dominic Canzone, Reid Detmers, Cam Eden, Michael Massey, Bobby Miller, Chris Murphy, Zack Thompson
2019	Spencer Torkelson
2021	Zach Neto

Whitecaps' Final Hitting and Pitching Statistics

	PLAYER	TEAM	G	AB	R	H	2B	3B
1	Michael Iannazzo DH	BRE	2	6	1	3	1	0
2	Nolan Schubart DH	BRE	9	30	11	9	2	0
3	Daniel Cuvet 3B	BRE	28	102	17	32	3	0
4	Nick Dumesnil CF	BRE	36	135	27	42	12	0
5	Ryder Helfrick C	BRE	36	142	28	37	3	0
6	Andrew Fischer 2B	BRE	19	65	9	15	4	1
7	J.D. Rogers RF	BRE	28	94	18	27	3	0
8	Brody Donay 1B	BRE	28	97	14	22	4	0
9	Drew Faurot SS	BRE	28	99	13	26	6	0
10	Kaeden Kent 2B	BRE	27	105	10	27	5	0
11	Dallas Macias LF	BRE	19	61	13	17	0	0
12	Colby Shelton SS	BRE	14	44	7	9	0	0
13	Chase Mora SS	BRE	8	27	1	7	0	0
14	Max Kaufer C	BRE	14	39	5	8	0	1
15	Jayden Hylton RF	BRE	9	23	4	3	1	0
16	Gio Cueto C	BRE	4	11	0	2	1	0
17	Cooper Vest 1B	BRE	22	64	8	13	2	0
18	Blake Binderup 1B	BRE	11	36	5	6	0	0
19	DeAmez Ross CF	BRE	20	47	2	8	0	0
20	Carsten Sabathia 1B	BRE	4	13	0	2	0	0
21	RJ Johnson CF	BRE	8	25	1	2	0	0
22	Tyler Pettorini 2B	BRE	9	23	2	2	0	0

HR	RBI	BB	SO	SB	CS	AVG	OBP	SLG	OPS
1	2	2	0	0	0	.500	.625	1.167	1.792
3	5	11	16	1	0	.300	.476	.667	1.143
6	20	10	34	1	2	.314	.371	.520	.891
4	15	13	33	26	1	.311	.377	.489	.866
11	37	10	33	8	2	.261	.323	.514	.837
3	14	14	9	2	2	.231	.366	.462	.828
1	4	21	32	12	2	.287	.437	.351	.788
6	13	9	41	3	0	.227	.312	.454	.766
3	16	13	30	4	3	.263	.342	.414	.756
1	13	11	18	2	2	.257	.328	.333	.661
0	10	7	5	1	0	.279	.375	.279	.654
1	6	9	16	2	0	.205	.364	.273	.637
0	5	2	9	1	0	.259	.364	.259	.623
0	3	4	12	1	0	.205	.277	.256	.533
0	1	5	11	2	1	.130	.355	.174	.529
0	1	1	5	0	0	.182	.250	.273	.523
0	2	4	25	0	1	.203	.282	.234	.516
0	1	5	18	0	0	.167	.268	.167	.435
0	3	6	12	1	1	.170	.264	.170	.434
0	0	0	4	0	0	.154	.154	.154	.308
0	1	2	8	2	0	.080	.207	.080	.287
0	2	3	5	2	0	.087	.192	.087	.279

	PLAYER		TEAM	W	L	ERA	G	GS	CG	SHO
1	Robert Lasbury	P	BRE	0	0	0.00	1	0	0	0
2	Alex Valentin	P	BRE	0	0	0.00	2	0	0	0
3	Isaac Morton	P	BRE	0	0	2.25	1	0	0	0
4	Ryan Ure	P	BRE	0	0	2.89	4	3	0	0
5	Jacob Marlowe	P	BRE	1	0	2.95	8	2	0	0
6	Jake Clemente	P	BRE	1	2	3.00	6	6	0	0
7	Patrick Forbes	OF	BRE	0	0	3.29	4	4	0	0
8	Micheal Salina	P	BRE	1	0	3.60	1	1	0	0
9	D.J. Primeaux	P	BRE	2	3	4.88	12	1	0	0
10	Colby Frieda	P	BRE	0	1	4.91	4	0	0	0
11	Will Ray	P	BRE	0	2	4.91	14	1	0	0
12	Seth Tomczak	P	BRE	1	1	4.96	5	3	0	0
13	Ashton Crowther	P	BRE	0	2	5.73	4	2	0	0
14	Sonny Fauci	P	BRE	0	0	6.00	2	0	0	0
15	Luke Schmolke	P	BRE	1	0	6.32	7	1	0	0
16	Luke Guth	P	BRE	1	1	6.56	8	5	0	0
17	Darien Smith	P	BRE	1	2	6.60	5	3	0	0
18	Boston Flannery	P	BRE	0	1	6.75	7	1	0	0
19	Noah Samol	P	BRE	0	1	6.75	1	1	0	0
20	Kellan Oakes	P	BRE	1	0	6.94	8	0	0	0
21	Zach Johnston	P	BRE	1	0	7.20	8	0	0	0
22	Parker Detmers	P	BRE	0	1	7.48	10	1	0	0
23	Levi Huesman	P	BRE	2	0	7.66	9	1	0	0
24	Evan O'Toole	P	BRE	0	1	8.00	3	2	0	0
25	Gabe Davis	P	BRE	0	0	8.10	2	0	0	0

SV	SVO	IP	H	R	ER	HR	HB	BB	SO	WHIP	AVG
0	0	0.1	0	0	0	0	0	0	1	0.00	.000
0	0	2.2	0	0	0	0	0	1	2	0.38	.000
0	0	4.0	2	1	1	1	1	0	3	0.50	.154
0	0	9.1	5	3	3	0	0	7	8	1.29	.156
0	0	18.1	21	6	6	1	0	2	14	1.25	.288
0	0	27.0	16	13	9	0	2	11	29	1.00	.165
0	0	13.2	9	5	5	1	2	6	22	1.10	.188
0	0	5.0	5	2	2	0	0	3	3	1.60	.278
0	1	24.0	20	14	13	0	3	12	26	1.33	.233
0	1	11.0	15	6	6	0	1	3	16	1.64	.300
2	4	22.0	24	14	12	3	6	2	23	1.18	.276
1	1	16.1	22	9	9	3	0	0	15	1.35	.319
0	1	11.0	12	8	7	1	2	5	10	1.55	.273
1	1	3.0	2	3	2	0	1	4	4	2.00	.182
0	0	15.2	21	17	11	4	1	8	12	1.85	.323
0	0	23.1	27	18	17	2	5	11	22	1.63	.297
0	0	15.0	20	14	11	1	0	10	17	2.00	.308
0	0	12.0	18	14	9	0	3	13	4	2.58	.340
0	0	2.2	2	2	2	0	0	5	6	2.63	.200
0	0	11.2	11	9	9	2	3	8	15	1.63	.250
1	1	15.0	18	13	12	1	1	9	12	1.80	.305
1	1	21.2	21	19	18	0	2	16	22	1.71	.256
0	2	22.1	33	21	19	1	3	11	27	1.97	.330
0	0	9.0	9	8	8	1	2	4	6	1.44	.265
0	0	3.1	4	3	3	0	0	1	9	1.50	.308

Standings

[Division ⌄]   [Standard | Expanded]

CCBL EAST	W	L	TIES	PTS	PCT
Y-D #	24	12	4	52	.667
CHA @	20	20	0	40	.500
HAR @	16	24	0	32	.400
ORL @	15	25	0	30	.375
BRE	13	25	2	28	.342

CCBL WEST	W	L	TIES	PTS	PCT
HYA #	24	14	2	50	.632
COT @	22	17	1	45	.564
WAR @	22	17	1	45	.564
BOU @	21	16	3	45	.568
FAL	16	23	1	33	.410

Postgame Announcements—Testimonials

Praise for *Cape Dreams: A Season with the Brewster Whitecaps*

"The life that these kids live here on the Cape is a major step in their careers in professional baseball. This Cape League is so important. Every baseball fan should read this book. This league is critical toward the future success of Major League Baseball."
—Mr. Peter Gammons, National Baseball Hall of Fame, 2004, considered the most authoritative voice for the sport of baseball.

"One of my favorite summers of my life was 1994 when I got a chance to play for the Brewster Whitecaps. The people in Brewster and the town of Brewster were such a welcoming and comforting place. I will always cherish the memories and the people that I met there. I'm thrilled I will get to relive those wonderful times in Mark Epstein's excellent book *CAPE DREAMS*."
—Sean Casey, Cincinnati Reds Hall of Famer and three-time NL All-Star, Brewster Whitecaps' 1994

"As a writer myself for more than a half century, I feel I know great writing when I see it. And it is easy to see that Mark Epstein is in that class. Prepare yourself to read not only great writing but entertaining and informative work from my great personal friend who dedicates himself to the writing profession. From near obscurity,

Mark has arrived as one of the best of the best and is fast gaining that recognition and reputation."

—Hal McCoy, National Baseball Hall of Fame, 2002. For over fifty years Mr. McCoy has covered the Cincinnati Reds for the *Dayton Daily News.*

"This is my dream: to watch my son Carsten play for the Brewster Whitecaps in the Cape Cod League against the best competition in America. I can't wait for this story *CAPE DREAMS* to come out. It will be spectacular."

—CC Sabathia, Major League pitching legend, future Baseball Hall of Famer

"Mark Epstein has hit a home run with his book *CAPE DREAMS: A Season with the Brewster Whitecaps.* He shares his unique perspective about the day-to-day life of college players as they compete in the best wooden-bat summer showcase league in America. A must-read for fans of all ages."

—J. P. Ricciardi, general manager of the Toronto Blue Jays and longtime VP of the Oakland A's, New York Mets, and San Francisco Giants

"This Cape Cod baseball book, *CAPE DRESAMS: A Season with the Brewster Whitecaps,* by my friend Mark Epstein has brought back some of the greatest baseball memories I have in my life. I remember my teammates and experiences fondly from the three seasons I pitched in Falmouth of the Cape Cod Baseball League. I haven't seen my teammates since I left the Cape in 1971. Back then we were the Yankees of the Cape. We were hated because we would win every year. I feared our manager Bill Livesey back then. He was tough to play for, but he brought the best out in all of us. I stayed with the same host family all three seasons. I even became the godfather to one of their children. I really appreciate this opportunity to look back at my Cape Cod career. Thank you, Mark, for writing this book and including me."

—Paul Mitchell, CCBL Hall of Famer, owner of the greatest pitching career in the history of the Cape Cod Baseball League, Falmouth Commodores 1969–1971. Still the record holder for many of the Cape Cod career pitching records. Former Major League pitcher: Orioles, A's, Mariners, Brewers.

"FANTASTIC!! This book is going to be amazing. There is such joy in the essence of our game, and the spirit of the Cape Cod Baseball League makes all of us connected to it young and believing. Thank you, Pathfinder, for telling the story of an American treasure. And thank you for becoming my friend in the process."

—Matt Hyde, New York Yankees scout, ranked as one of the most influential people in the sport of baseball

"The Cape is so special, and the tradition of the league is so important. Brewster is a part of my heart now. It was a very special time for me."

—Zach Neto, Los Angeles Angels shortstop and Brewster Whitecaps legend